Social History of Africa

CHIEFS KNOW THEIR BOUNDARIES

Recent Titles in
Social History of Africa Series
Series Editors: Allen Isaacman and Jean Allman

CHIEFS KNOW THEIR BOUNDARIES

ESSAYS ON PROPERTY, POWER, AND THE PAST IN ASANTE, 1896–1996

Sara S. Berry

HEINEMANN
Portsmouth, NH

JAMES CURREY
Oxford

DAVID PHILIP
Cape Town

Heinemann
A division of Reed Elsevier Inc.
361 Hanover Street
Portsmouth, NH 03801-3912
USA
www.heinemann.com

James Currey Ltd.
73 Botley Road
Oxford OX2 0BS
United Kingdom

David Philip Publishers (Pty) Ltd.
208 Werdmuller Centre
Claremont 7708
Cape Town, South Africa

Offices and agents throughout the world

ISBN 0–325–07003–2 (Heinemann cloth)
ISBN 0–325–07002–4 (Heinemann paper)
ISBN 0–85255–694–2 (James Currey cloth)
ISBN 0–85255–644–6 (James Currey paper)

British Library Cataloguing in Publication Data

Berry, Sara
   Chiefs know their boundaries : essays on property, power and the past in Asante,
   1896–1996.—(Social history of Africa)
   1. Ashanti (African people)—Kings and rulers 2. Chiefdoms—Ghana 3. Land tenure—
   Ghana—History 4. Kumasi (Ghana)—Politics and government—20th century 5. Kumasi
   (Ghana)—Social life and customs—20th century
   I. Title
   966.7'03
   ISBN 0–85255–694–2 (James Currey cloth)
   ISBN 0–85255–644–6 (James Currey paper)

Library of Congress Cataloging-in-Publication Data

Berry, Sara S.
   Chiefs know their boundaries : essays on property, power, and the past in Asante,
   1896–1996 / Sara S. Berry.
      p. cm.—(Social history of Africa, ISSN 1099–8098)
   Includes bibliographical references and index.
   ISBN 0–325–07003–2 (alk. paper)—ISBN 0–325–07002–4 (pbk. : alk. paper)
   1. Ashanti (African people)—Kings and rulers. 2. Ashanti (African people)—Politics and
   government. 3. Ashanti (African people)—Land tenure. 4. Chiefdoms—Ghana—History.
   5. Land tenure—Ghana—History. 6. Kumasi (Ghana)—Politics and government.
   7. Kumasi (Ghana)—Social life and customs. I. Title. II. Series

   DT507.B47 2001
   966.7—dc21   00–035036

Paperback cover photo: Organizing a ceremony, Kumawu, December 1993. Photo courtesy of author.

Printed in the United States of America on acid-free paper.

04 03 02 01 00 SB 1 2 3 4 5 6 7 8 9

Copyright Acknowledgment

The author and publisher gratefully acknowledge permission to reprint chapter 2, "Unsettled Accounts: Stool Debts, Chieftaincy Disputes, and the Question of Asante Constitutionalism," which originally appeared in *Journal of African History* 39 (1998): 39–62 under the same title. Reprinted with the permission of Cambridge University Press.

CONTENTS

ILLUSTRATIONS

MAPS

TABLE

ACKNOWLEDGMENTS

Research for this study was carried out in Ghana in 1993–1994, with the support of a Fulbright Senior Scholar award. I am grateful to the Fulbright program and to the staff at the U.S. Information Service office in Accra, especially Sarpei Nunoo, for welcoming me to Ghana and providing much appreciated assistance with immigration formalities and other logistical arrangements. The Institute of African Studies at the University of Ghana kindly accorded me research affiliate status for the duration of my stay in Ghana. I am grateful to Professor Kwame Arhin, then Director of the institute, for his hospitality, for his help with introductions to friends and colleagues in Kumase, and for stimulating discussions of mutual research interests. Staff members at the institute went out of their way to be helpful and welcoming whenever I turned up in Accra, offering companionship as well as advice, administrative assistance, and, often, accommodation at the institute's guest chalets.

I am also grateful to the archivists and staff at Balme Library and the Institute of African Studies in Legon, the Manhyia Record Office in Kumase, the National Archives of Ghana in Kumase and Accra, the Land Administration Research Center and the Department of Planning at the University of Science and Technology in Kumase, and Rhodes House in Oxford for granting me access to their collections, and for unfailingly courteous assistance in locating and accessing research materials. While working on the material I collected in Ghana, I benefited on many occasions from the expert assistance and friendly reception of the librarians and staff of the Herskovits Africana Library at Northwestern University. Final preparation of the manuscript was carried out during a sabbatical year at the Center for Advanced

Study in the Behavioral Sciences in Stanford, California, where Deanna
Knickerbocker provided invaluable assistance in producing the maps.

Throughout my work on this study, I have been stimulated and instructed
by innumerable discussions with students and colleagues at Legon, Kumase,
Johns Hopkins, and Northwestern, and by opportunities to present work in
progress to Africanists and other colleagues at Berkeley, Boston University,
Columbia, Chicago, Michigan, Pennsylvania, Roskilde, the Christian
Michelson Institute in Bergen, CODESRIA, and the Universities of Zimba-
bwe and the Witwatersrand. It is not possible to acknowledge individually
everyone who contributed to my thinking during this process, but I owe
special thanks for insights, encouragement, and spirited debate to Kojo
Amanor, Kwame Arhin, Herman Bennett, Donald Carter, Gillian Feeley-
Harnik, Jane Guyer, Gillian Hart, Christian Lund, Takyiwaa Manuh, Achille
Mbembe, William Munro, William Rowe, Michel-Rolph Trouillot, Chris
Udry, and Larry Yarak. None of them is in any way responsible for the use
I have made of their insights, or the contents and conclusions of this book.

My greatest debt is to the many, many people in Ghana who kindly and
patiently shared their knowledge and experiences with me, challenged my
ideas, instructed me in Ghanaian ways, and offered me hospitality and friendship. Officers and colleagues at the Lands Commission, the Forestry Department, and the Kumase High Court were unfailingly generous with their
time and knowledge. I am especially grateful to Justices Owusu Sekyere
and Rose Owusu, for permission to attend sessions in their rooms at the
high court; to Mr. Yeboah for his patient efforts to teach me a bit of Twi; to
Francis Balfour, Julia Falconer, Jane Gronow, Daniel Mensah, and Robin
Milton of the Forestry Department for their collegiality and friendship; and
to the many neighbors in Kumase and Kumawu whose friendly reception
helped to make my time there enjoyable as well as educational.

Above all, I want to thank the chiefs and citizens of Amakom, Asokore-
Mampong, Kenyase Kwabre, and Kumawu for welcoming me to their communities and going out of their way to facilitate my research and advance
my education. All those whose individual stories and insights are acknowledged in the following chapters, and many who are not, contributed graciously and generously to my comfort as well as my quest for information
and understanding, and I am deeply appreciative of their interest and their
efforts. I was especially fortunate to work closely with three research assistants—Michael Adu Gyamfi, Yaw Badu, and Agnes Obiri Yeboah—who accompanied me on numerous visits to informants and assisted ably and tact-
fully in our discussions. Their knowledge and insights informed and guided
my inquiries, and their patience, good humor, and companionship enriched
my work and my experience in Ghana at every turn. I am also warmly
grateful to Allan Cole for sharing his immense knowledge of land matters

and local history in Kumawu; to Madam Alice Aduana Norris for her hospitality; and to Mr. B. A. Mensah who graciously provided me with accommodation during my two-month stay in Kumawu in 1994. Without the knowledge, friendship, and hospitality of all these people, this book would not exist. I hope they will enjoy reading it.

Finally, I want to thank my son Jonathan, who accompanied me for the first two months in Ghana, my daughter Rachel, who put up with my long absences, and my sisters, Caroline and Cornelia Sweezy, whose willingness to shoulder extra family responsibilities made my research trips possible. As always, their support, humor, and understanding make everything worthwhile.

ABBREVIATIONS

ACC	Ashanti Confederacy Council
CCA	Chief Commissioner, Ashanti
CCK	Chief Commissioner, Kumasi
CS	Chief Secretary
CDR	Committee for the Defence of the Revolution
CEP	Commissioner, Eastern Province
CPP	Convention People's Party
CWP	Commissioner, Western Province
DC	District Commissioner
GBC	Ghana Broadcasting Corporation
GLRD	Ghana Law Reports Digest
GNTC	Ghana National Trading Corporation
IAS	Institute for African Studies (Legon)
KHC	Kumase High Court
KPHB	Kumase Public Health Board
MRO	Manhyia Record Office
NAGA	National Archives of Ghana, Accra
NAGK	National Archives of Ghana, Kumase
NDC	National Democratic Congress
NGO	Nongovernmental Organization
NLM	National Liberation Movement
NPP	New Patriotic Party

PC   Provincial Commissioner
PM   Police Magistrate
PNDC   Provisional National Defence Council
SLBSC   Stool Lands Boundaries Settlement Commission
SSC   Secretary of State for the Colonies
TKSS   Tweneboa Kodia Secondary School
UST   University of Science and Technology (Kumase)

INTRODUCTION

H. C. Belfield, a colonial official dispatched to Kumase in 1912 to compile a report on customary rules of land alienation, was told by his informants in Asante that land is held by the chiefs "in trust for the people."[1] Chiefs could allocate land to both subjects and strangers and collect tribute from the latter, but they could not alienate land itself. If chiefs could not buy or sell land, Belfield wondered, wouldn't they try to take it from one another, leading to disputes and disturbances? Chief Frimpon, the Adontenhene, thought it unlikely. "Chiefs generally know their boundaries," he explained; if one stool tried to encroach on another's territory, everyone would know it.[2]

In 1993, I spent several months in Kumase working on a study of changes in the way Asantes have made and exercised claims on land since the end of the nineteenth century.[3] Stools still control much of the land in Asante, but the process of allocating it has become thoroughly commercialized and formalized. Chiefs sell fifty- or ninety-nine-year leaseholds to individuals or firms; plots are carefully surveyed; and records are kept at the Lands Commission to avoid mistakes or fraudulent transactions. Despite numerous inquiries, however, I was unable to locate a map showing the location and extent of stool lands, or the boundaries between them. How are stools' claims verified, I wondered, in cases of dispute? No problem, the head of the Lands Commission assured me: "Chiefs know their boundaries. . . . "[4]

What do chiefs know, and how do they know it? What kinds of knowledge serve to define and legitimate claims on property in Asante? How has access to land changed over the course of the twentieth century? If stools retain significant authority over land today, does this mean that Asante is an exception to the widely held perception that land rights in Africa are becoming increasingly individualized and exclusive?[5] Has "custom" provided a stable, consistent framework of precedents and prerogatives, as colonial officials hoped, or does the rhetorical continuity of "chiefs know their boundaries" mask significant change? Given the substantial amount that has been written in recent years about land tenure and development in Africa, is there more to be learned from a detailed study of the Asante case?

In exploring these questions, this book both draws on and departs from my own previous research on agrarian change in Africa.[6] Unlike my last book, *No Condition Is Permanent*—a comparative study of farmers' access to and uses of land and labor in four local agrarian societies—in this one, I examine processes of making and exercising claims on land in just one region, Asante, but I look at urban as well as rural areas. Rather than focus on relations between resource access and resource use in agriculture, I take claims on land in general as a point of entry into broader debates over the nature of property in Africa, its relationship to the mobilization and exercise of authority, and the place of property in the political and economic transformations of the twentieth century.

I set out in this study to place contemporary land tenure issues in historical perspective by tracing changes in the way people have made and exercised claims on land over the course of the twentieth century. As I began to explore the archives and talk with people in Asante, however, I soon discovered that I was not the only one interested in history. One can hardly open a file or begin a conversation about land matters in Asante without encountering the past. Whether defending land claims in court or discussing them in casual conversation, Asantes refer continually to history—recounting not only recent events and transactions but also incidents dating from the founding of the Asante state (ca. 1700) or before. What began as an inquiry into the history of land claims in the twentieth cenury soon expanded into a study not only of land acquisitions and disputes but also of the way that competing interpretations of the past figure in contemporary struggles over property and power. Like contemporary land claims themselves, my approach to Asante history in the twentieth century is framed by representations of the more distant past, drawn from popular as well as scholarly discourse.

Venturing into the richly documented terrain of Asante history is a daunting prospect, and I do not pretend to have gone very far with it. This book is not a history of land tenure in Asante: I simply do not know enough to attempt a systematic reconstruction of land claims, methods of access, and the distribution of land holdings throughout the Ashanti Region over the course of the last century. Instead, what follows is a series of essays about the way land claims have been negotiated and contested at particular times and places within that spatial and temporal domain. In Ghana, I drew on archival sources, oral accounts, and courtroom observations for examples of land claims by individuals, families, firms, stools, and communities, at different locations and points in time. In the chapters that follow, I use these microhistories to illustrate local processes of land acquisition, transfer, and dispute and, I hope, to illuminate some of the ways in which wealth and power have been generated and transformed in Asante during the course of the twentieth century.

PROPERTY AND POWER

Land has been a key focus of economic and political struggle in Africa throughout the twentieth century and shows no signs of diminishing in importance or contentiousness at the beginning of the twenty-first.[7] The pressures of population growth and economic expansion on fixed supplies of land are only part of the story: even today, farmers in many parts of the continent are as likely to complain of labor shortages as of scarcity of land, and those who can afford them can find building plots on the outskirts of Africa's rapidly expanding cities without much difficulty. Struggles over land have been as much about power and the control of people as about access to land as a factor of production. In South Africa, Kenya, and Zimbabwe, for example, large-scale appropriation of land by European settlers followed the imposition of European rule, while in areas of earlier white settlement, such as the Zambezi valley or coastal enclaves along the Atlantic seaboard, conflict between Africans and Europeans had more to do with control of trade and people than of land. Further, in the settler colonies where land did become a central focus of anticolonial (or antiapartheid) movements in the twentieth century, the issue was not simply a struggle over access to an increasingly scarce productive resource. European settlers took far more land than they could use, and they were fundamentally dependent on African labor to make it produce anything at all. The value of land to the settlers lay in their ability to exercise power over African labor and African societies by controlling people's access to it.

Control over land also served as a fulcrum of authority in African societies that never experienced significant inflows of European settlers under colonial rule. Much has been written, in West Africa and elsewhere, about historically created divisions of ritual and practical authority between "owners of the land" and "owners of the people."[8] The latter are often cast as descendants of immigrants who acquired political power through conquest or negotiation, but whose success remains contingent on the spiritual and material power of the land and its "original" inhabitants. Long before the era of European conquest, the allocation and transfer of authority over land served as an important avenue of political competition and control, both in centralized states such as Asante and in relatively decentralized African polities. Under indirect rule, colonial strategies of administration reinforced this tendency, even as officials struggled to harness it to their own ends. After independence, African states continued to treat land policy and administration as a vehicle for consolidating power as well as for seeking rent, and citizens invested in land, individually or in groups, as a source of social and political leverage as well as income. Rising land prices should not distract us from recognizing that land has social and political as well as economic value, and that "perfecting" land markets will not do away with conflict.

Both scholarly and official debates over land and property rights in Africa have been deeply influenced by paradigms of political economy that take the history of western capitalism as a benchmark and assume that exclusive ownership is a necessary condition for accumulation and the creation of wealth. Colonial officials regarded "traditional" land tenure arrangements in Africa as fundamentally different from European forms of freehold ownership, and African political economies as far removed from agrarian and industrial capitalism. They often disagreed about Africans' capacities to develop on their own, and they debated whether to preserve customary arrangements as a source of social stability or transform them to accelerate commercial development, but they rarely questioned the underlying premise that property arrangements had the power to shape the course of economic and social history.

At the time of independence, many African regimes nationalized land, believing that ownership would give them the means to promote economic growth as well as to assert national sovereignty. Statutory change did not give rise to sustained development, however, or to political stability. State-sponsored development schemes frequently bogged down in inexperience or mismanagement, and land soon became a focus of discontent as Africans accused politicians and bureaucrats of turning "national" land into personal estates. Following the severe economic crises of the 1970s, pressure from Africa's international creditors reactivated colonial-era debates over whether and how to rewrite the rules governing ownership and transfers of rights to land. Advocates of market liberalization insisted that "well defined property rights" were a necessary condition for sustained and sustainable development.[9] Some argued that individualized rights are evolving naturally under pressure of population growth and commercialization, while others urged African governments to expedite the process by registering land holdings and issuing titles.[10] Critics of the liberal paradigm pointed out that free markets do not benefit everyone, and that "reforms" that replace flexible local tenure arrangements with uniform rules and fixed boundaries can lead to conflict without enhancing productivity.[11] But many would agree that property rights in Africa are becoming more individualized and exclusive over time, even in the absence of formal registration and titling.

In part, the history of land claims in Asante bears these arguments out. Since the early years of colonial rule, transactions in land rights have become increasingly formalized and thoroughly commercial: long-term leaseholds are registered, bought, and sold; properties are mortgaged; and rights of cultivation, residence, extraction, or transit are formally documented and exchanged.[12] The emergence of a modern land market has not detached land claims from the social and cultural context in which they are made. In Asante, the legal formalization of various claims on land—titles, leaseholds, mortgages, and so on—has occurred in a context of ongoing debate over what constitutes evidence of a legitimate claim and what land claims mean for access to wealth and power. To understand the significance of these developments for the changing character of the Asante political economy, however, it is important to look not only at the growing volume and variety of commercial transactions in rights to land but also at the way those rights have been defined, exercised, and contested.

In the following chapters, I will argue that property in Asante is negotiable—socially and conceptually as well as commercially. Claims on land are routinely exchanged for money, but land itself is subject to multiple, overlapping claims and ongoing debate over these claims' legitimacy and their implications for land use and the distribution of revenues. Rather than induce or impose consensus on rules and boundaries, the formalization of land administration and processes of adjudication have added new layers of interpretation and debate, complicating rather than hardening the lines of authority and exclusion. Property is powerful in Asante not only as a source of wealth but also as an arena of contest and negotiation over access, authority, and accountability. To assess the significance of commercial transactions in land, we need to understand what is being negotiated, and how processes of negotiation shape not only the allocation of scarce resources among alternative uses but also the constitution of wealth and power.

CONCEPTUAL ISSUES AND DEBATES

"Free markets," the World Bank tells us, "cannot be expected to produce efficient and sustainable results when property rights are not clearly defined, complete, enforced and transferable."[13] Officials of the Gold Coast Colony would have agreed. Government, wrote one, should create a register of land holdings, "conferring absolute title, guaranteed by the State. . . . [I]t is absurd that each owner should not know and that others should not know what precisely is his holding. . . . "[14] That was in 1928. If the case for well-defined property rights has been self-evident for so long, why is the Bank still exhorting African governments to get on with it?

Advocates of liberal property rights reform argue that clear titles to land and other valuable assets give titleholders both the opportunity and the incentive to use resources productively and preserve their value over time. By empowering individual or corporate agents to exclude others from access to resources, well-defined property rights allow right holders to capture the benefits of resource use and/or realize the present value of assets by transferring them to others. Since property holders have a vested interest in maintaining or increasing the value of their property, well-defined property rights are also said to encourage investment and guard against resource depletion. In cases where resources are used in ways that benefit the owners but impose costs on others, registration of title is said to facilitate regulation by making it easier to hold property owners accountable for the consequences of their actions.[15]

These arguments rest on a series of assumptions—about relations between power and wealth, between individual agency and social process, and between historical events and representations of them—which are called into question by ethnographic and historical evidence from Africa. In reexamining those assumptions, I do not mean to suggest that Asante is an exception to the mainstream of human experience, understandable only in its own terms. Rather, I will argue, the historical specificities of economic and political transformations in twentieth-century Asante help to illuminate the limitations of arguments that conceptualize property as a set of rules and enforcement mechanisms. By viewing property as a social process rather than a set of initial conditions, we may be better able to address both the general reality that property rights (like markets) are never "complete" and the particular reality of Asante where, in order to exercise claims on land, people have to keep making them.

Wealth and Power

In recent literature on property and development, property is generally understood not as "a thing, but a network of social relations that governs the conduct of people with respect to the use and disposition of things."[16] This does not mean that individuals must resort to coercion to translate their rights into effective control. On the contrary, it is usually assumed that property holders' powers of exclusion are both conferred and guaranteed by a governing body, such as the state, whose powers are constituted and exercised independently of the production and circulation of wealth. Wealth derived from the use of property may be used to acquire more property, but it should not be used to influence the definition and enforcement of property rights themselves, nor should agents of the state use their power to appropriate wealth. In other words, the power to exclude others from particular resources is presumed to be conferred and guaranteed prior to, and independently of, the production and circulation of wealth.

The concept of property as a relation of power that defines the conditions under which wealth is produced and accumulated is central to both Marxist and neoclassical political economy. Indeed, the basic disagreement between Marxist and neoclassical theories over the possibility of building a just and equitable society on the basis of private ownership reflects a consensus that property has the power to shape the way wealth is created and distributed. Following the neoclassical approach, critics of Africa's "failed states" regularly attack the inability or unwillingness of postcolonial regimes to separate the production and appropriation of wealth from the pursuit and exercise of power,[17] while critics of colonial and "neocolonial" capitalism attribute growing disparities between rich and poor to the concentration of property and power in the hands of ruling elites.[18] Both arguments have been made with respect to Asante and/or Ghana. Scholars such as Allman, Arhin, Austin, and Rathbone argue, for example, that commercialization and economic growth fostered class formation in the long run.[19] Others have blamed the decline of Ghana's economy in the 1960s and 1970s on corruption, neopatrimonialism, and economic mismanagement by the state, and they have celebrated the role of budget cuts and deregulation in bringing about economic recovery since the mid-1980s.[20]

On one level, both interpretations are correct. In Asante, and in Ghana as a whole, political power has been used to appropriate wealth, and vice versa, throughout the twentieth century, and the state has played an active role in safeguarding the interests of the accumulating classes. Although colonial officials complained about the "sale" of stools and misuse of chiefly office for personal gain, their insistence that land was vested in the stools virtually guaranteed that rising land values would commercialize the pursuit of chiefly office as well.[21] Although their prerogatives were greatly diminished after independence, chiefs continue to wield influence over the way claims on land are defined and contested. Nkrumah launched a major assault on chiefly authority in Asante, and complaints about official and chiefly corruption have remained a staple of both popular and scholarly political discourse in postcolonial Ghana.[22] Chiefly authority has continued to flourish during the economic recovery of the late 1980s and 1990s, suggesting that Ghana's political and economic restructuring has been shaped by internally generated processes as well as the dictates of the world market or the World Bank.[23]

Such debates raise questions about the widely held assumption that it is both possible and desirable to separate the pursuit of wealth and power—in theory and in practice. Neoclassical economists are particularly insistent on this point, treating power in the marketplace as an "imperfection" that "distorts" the allocation of resources. Yet the logic of self-interest, on which their analysis is predicated, would suggest that property holders have as much reason to trade material goods for influence as for other material goods, and that office holders are no more indifferent to economic opportunity than anyone else.[24] "Open" markets are volatile and uncertain, and economic agents routinely seek to protect themselves by gaining some measure of control over the conditions of exchange. Neoclassical economists certainly recognize this point, but they prefer to treat it as an accounting problem—one of calculating the costs and benefits of coping with incomplete information—rather than a political question.[25]

However carefully defined, property rights will shape social action only if they are enforced.[26] But agencies of enforcement do not float, like heads of hydroponic lettuce, rootless and disconnected from their social context. Whether rules and mechanisms of enforcement are agreed upon between the governing and the governed or imposed by the former on the latter, the process by which they come into being is likely to affect the way they are exercised. In either case, it is unlikely that a system of property rights, once established, will be immutable: agreements are always subject to (re)negotiation, and impositions are likely to be contested. In thinking about the role of property in economic and social change, it is important to ask what is being negotiated, by whom, and how ongoing processes of negotiation shape the way influence is acquired and brought to bear on the production and distribution of wealth.

Agency and Identity

Arguments for well-defined property rights as a condition for economic progress tend to assume that social outcomes are the sum of individual decisions, and that the quality of outcomes depends on people's ability to make rational choices and act on them. By giving individual agents the power to exclude others from material resources, it is argued, well-defined property rights allow people to detach decisions about resource use from social obligations and relationships that might "distort" market signals. Exclusion "frees" property holders from having to take other people's interests into account in deciding how to use the things they own—and analysts from having to think about the wider social context in which property rights are transacted. In a "complete" market system, where conditions of access are precisely specified and paid for and contracts consistently and impartially enforced, property holders' decisions are presumed to be unencumbered by personal or other social pressures and obligations. Freed from personal and social entanglements, owners make decisions about resource allocation in economically rational ways, and the economic and social consequences of property rights are not dependent on who exercises them or who feels their effects.

The argument that property rights are (or ought to be) increasingly individualized is part of a broader paradigm of modernity in which persons are constructed as autonomous individuals, their actions driven by self-interest rather than molded by social position or group identity, and social processes are determined by individual action. Self-realization is both a means and an end of social progress. By empowering individuals to exclude others from access to particular things, "well-defined" property rights release them from social entanglements and obligations that might inhibit their ability to use resources in their own interest, as measured by market conditions. Whether these conditions are, or ought to be, met in contemporary Africa is the subject of much popular as well as academic discussion. Scholars who analyze social processes through the lens of methodological individualism find a ready counterpart in popular discourse about the virtues of self-help and the declining importance of kinship and community.

At the same time, there is plenty of academic and popular discussion that leans the other way—questioning whether the disentangled individual of post-enlightenment modernity has completely taken over African social practices and understandings.[27] For example, the literature on wealth-in-people raises questions about how African understandings of personhood and the value of people compare with western concepts of individualism, and whether culturally specific understandings of personal capacity shape social practices in distinctive ways.[28] African cosmologies are not particularly fatalistic: individuals have agency and can exercise it in both helpful and harmful ways.[29] Beliefs in witchcraft, for example, assign considerable power to individuals' ability to influence the fortunes of others—and reports of the continued salience of witchcraft in contemporary Africa, as a practice and a system of explanation, abound in both popular media and ethnographic literature.[30] But the philosophy of witchcraft also makes it clear that individual agency alone does not *determine* social outcomes. People act, with good or evil intent, but the social effectivity of their actions depends not only on their own capacities but also on their access to sources of power that lie outside the individual and beyond his or her control.

Asante is a case in point. In a recent article, Akyeampong and Obeng argue suggestively that in Akan understandings of the world, access to spiritual power is not only crucial to the social effectivity of individual action but may also place limits on the hegemonic power of the state:

Onyame (the Supreme Being) . . . created a universe impregnated with his power . . . and individuals and groups that successfully tapped into this power source translated this access into authority. . . . Authority . . . could be monopolized, but access to power (Twi: *tumi:*, "the ability to bring about change") was available to anyone who knew how to make use of Onyame's powerful universe for good or evil.[31]

Their argument parallels Bledsoe's illuminating discussion of child fostering and education in Sierra Leone, where children are taught that there is "no success without struggle."[32] No matter how talented children may be, or how hard they study, Sierra Leoneans believe that they will not succeed unless they also earn "blessings," by demonstrating proper respect for divinity and their social superiors. However laudable or culpable a person's actions may be in their own right, their effectivity depends on earning the support of others.

In the case of property, such arguments suggest that making and enforcing rules to guide individual transactions is only part of the story. To make and exercise claims on property effectively, it is important to develop and sustain relations with other people, and with the gods.[33] Like persons, social and spiritual relationships are made as well as born. An individual may be born into a descent group, a religious order, a community, or an occupation, but his/her position and influence within any particular social group are not fixed but negotiable. An individual's status and influence may vary over time depending, in part, on the skill and resources s/he "invests" in cultivating them. Carefully cultivated, social relationships may enhance people's access to wealth and knowledge. Even if they fail—because of conflict or a decline in other people's fortunes—the presumption of efficacy remains: if one relationship fails, people are more likely to seek new or alternative social ties than attempt to go it alone.[34]

In recognizing that people's access to resources and opportunities are often mediated through social relationships and vice versa, I do not mean to imply either that access is somehow assured by membership in particular social groups, or that communities manage resources more effectively or harmoniously than individuals do. Like wealth and power, social identities are neither stable over time nor fully controlled by their "owners." People may be identified in ways they do not intend or accept, or rejected by those with whom they seek to identify. Status, like money, may be intentionally acquired, but it can also "visit" or desert people in unexpected ways.[35] Identity, like property, is negotiated and contested—shaped and reshaped over time by multiple, sometimes conflicting forces. In Asante, as we shall see, debates over the legitimacy of land claims often revolve around debates over claims to kinship or community membership. All three are subject to negotiation and reinterpretation. Who "belongs" depends on whom one asks, and on the context in which the question is posed.[36]

History

In most societies, claims on land and other forms of property rest, in part, on historical precedents. Whether recorded in a written lease or title deed or stored in the memories of transactors and witnesses, acts of negotiation, exchange, and appropriation carry forward in time, helping to define or legitimate claims in the future. The process of making and exercising claims on property involves the production of history, as well as the exchange of money or goods and the exercise of influence in the present.[37] My point is not that people routinely fabricate historical precedents to support their claims in the present (although sometimes they do). Deliberate falsehoods are likely to be challenged, and historical precedents carry more weight if they refer to well-known events and personalities. Rather, I want to draw attention to the way that, in making claims on property and power, Asantes both invoke the past and debate its significance for ordering people's affairs in the present.[38] In almost any discussion of land claims, from casual conversations to formal testimony in the courts, people continually make reference not only to relatively recent events—transactions recorded in allocation papers, mortgages, wills, and so on, or attested to by living witnesses—but also to episodes that date to the founding of the Asante state, in the late seventeenth century, or before. Such references include specific events that may be located chronologically ("in the time of" Osei Tutu, Opoku Ware I, or others) and invocations of timeless custom—social arrangements or practices said to date "from time immemorial." They are not simply fanciful: Ghanaian statutes endorse the continued legitimacy of customary claims to land and office, and accounts of "traditional history" are admissible as evidence in the courts.[39] Nor are they limited to relatively localized domains, such as family land or rural areas. In several cases pending before the courts in the 1990s, disputes over the Asantehene's land rights in metropolitan Kumase turned on conflicting interpretations of the conquests of Osei Tutu.[40]

Historical narratives have not merely survived in the context of contemporary struggles over land and office: they have flourished. The transmission and interpretation of history is not the exclusive province of a few specialists, schooled in esoteric "tradition" or university classrooms, but a living process in which many people take part, bringing new perspectives and skills as well as information to bear on understanding the past and interpreting its significance for the present. Over the course of the twentieth century, the corpus of salient historical sources has grown, as people have carried out new transactions and debated the meaning of old ones. Claims may be based, of course, on written deeds, wills, and/or witnesses' recollections, but people also draw on archives, scholarly publications, and the testimony of men and women well versed in "traditional history." Among patrons of the National Archives in Kumase, academic researchers are regularly outnumbered by litigants. Scholars may find their publications quoted in court or set aside in favor of the wisdom of elders.

The proliferation of historical accounts may be traced, in part, to colonial strategies of indirect rule, which, in trying to order the changing present according to a supposedly stable body of custom, provoked ongoing debates, among colonial officials and Asantes as well as between them, over what constituted "custom" and who had the authority to decide.[41] Together with the simultaneous introduction of statutory law and the use of British common law as precedents in colonial courts, these debates fostered a system of legal pluralism that has outlasted colonial rule. Following independence, Ghanaian governments commuted chiefs' judicial and administrative roles to ceremonial ones and took steps to limit the legal force of customary rules and practices as well.[42] Yet neither the codification of statutory and customary law nor the accumulation of written evidence on land claims and transactions has produced consensus on either the interpretation of Asante history or its relevance to contemporary claims on property and power. Far from converging toward a single hegemonic narrative, both written and oral accounts of Asante history have proliferated—stimulating rather than stifling debate, and promoting rather than silencing the reinterpretation of tradition.

In the following pages, I will argue that the continued salience of custom and proliferation of historical accounts and interpretations has led not so much to a regime of property rights encumbered by an increasingly anachronistic and unwieldy body of rules and precedents, or mired in confusion, but rather to a process in which the transmission and interpretation of historical knowledge are predicated on social engagement. Asantes' representations of the past are performed rather than simply reproduced,[43] in a variety of social arenas. For many Asantes, some of the most venerated sites of historical performance are the *adae*—recurrent ceremonies in which chiefs, family heads, or other representatives of the living visit the ancestors, seeking their protection and blessings through prayer, libations, and offerings. On these and other ceremonial occasions, each ancestor is represented by a stool that s/he used while alive and that has been carefully blackened and preserved, as both a memorial and a material representative of the ancestor's continued membership in—and responsibilities toward—the community of his or her descendants.[44] During the *adae,* the blackened stools are washed, fed, smeared with sheep's blood, and supplicated on behalf of the community as a whole. In the process, the stools take on multiple meanings, serving

as both tangible manifestations of historical truth and sites for the rene-
gotiation of social ties and obligations. In making regular offerings and
appeals to the ancestors on behalf of their kin and compatriots, chiefs
and elders reaffirm both the plasticity of social boundaries, which en-
compass the dead as well as the living, and the permanence of social ties
and responsibilities, which cannot be broken, even by death.[45]

Prayers and offerings to the blackened stools of the ancestors are conducted in secret—inside the stool house, where the stools are kept, or at
a sacred location under cover of night—with only the chief, elders, and
a few attendants present. But the whole community knows when they
are offered—at prescribed times during the six-week cycle that marks a
basic unit of the Akan calendar—and expects the chiefs to fulfill their
responsibilities for protecting the general welfare by performing the appropriate rites. The secrecy of the rites themselves underscores their so-
lemnity and the reverence due to the ancestors: it enhances the power of
the past in the present, and it dramatizes the chiefs' and the ancestors'
responsibility for the well-being of the community. Similarly, in the course
of negotiations or disputes over land, Asantes invoke the past to authen-
ticate their claims by appealing to knowledge that is shared, and respected,
by their contemporaries. On a number of occasions during my fieldwork,
I heard people refer to history as "a secret," implying that it was not for
public consumption. In some cases, assertions of secrecy proved to be
purely rhetorical, being followed by detailed recitals of historical information to me and anyone else who happened to be present. At other
times, people kept their secrets, professing ignorance, changing the subject, or simply failing to show up for an appointment or respond to a
summons to testify in court. At first, I found such "silences" frustrating,
especially when they occurred in the midst of a case I was trying to
follow! But gradually I realized that assertions of secrecy were themselves a kind of performance, serving less to suppress historical information than to remind listeners of the "speaker's" power.

By claiming the power to silence the past, whether or not they choose to
exercise it, speakers make the production of history into a social process, in
which the audience is integral to the historian's effect. "Secrets" told are
presented as a kind of gift: they lay claim to the auditors' goodwill and
imply an obligation to reciprocate. Even when people keep their secrets—
by repeatedly failing to appear in court, for example—their reticence amounts
to a public demonstration not only of their power to withhold historical
knowledge but also of their relationship with the (frustrated) audience. In
such situations, silence is a performative tactic rather than a sign of the
unthinkable: it establishes a relationship between "speaker" and would-be
audience, acknowledging that the former's power depends, in part, on the

presence of the latter. Secrets have little power if no one knows they are being kept.

Frequently, then, Asantes' invocations of the past not only reaffirm or reconstruct relations of authority and obligation in the present but do so in a way that promotes rather than prohibits participation. In the context of contemporary claims on property and power, the proliferation of historical sources and performative reaffirmations of their importance work against the convergence of multiple claims into individualized and exclusive forms of ownership. Access to land and the revenues derived from it are often very unequal but, in practice, as long as debates continue over historical precedents and their import for present claims on property and power, people are not completely precluded from taking part in the discussion. Since no one has "all" the facts, history is continually revised and reinterpreted. In the process, land claims are contested and redefined, and wealth and power are recreated and redeployed. The roles of claimant and historian overlap, sometimes merge, and the conversations continue.[46]

NEGOTIABLE PROPERTY

In the following chapters, I elaborate and illustrate these arguments, using evidence from Asante on processes of land acquisition and dispute and their place in struggles over authority and wealth during and after the colonial period. Experiences in Asante suggest that property is more than a set of rules, a bundle of rights, or an established pattern of relationships between people in respect of things. Viewed in historical perspective, property appears as a multidimensional social process in which people debate and negotiate the constitution of authority, the distribution of wealth, and the relationships between them. On a general level, this is true in all societies: the mobility and ambiguity of property relations is, however, especially visible in cases such as Asante and other African societies, where access to wealth and authority are undergoing rapid change or are subject to intense contestation. For conceptual debates over the role of property in economic and political transformations, the story of Asante is significant not so much as an "exception" to the historical mainstream but rather as a spotlight on dynamic complexities that may be obscured in less turbulent or precarious contexts.

In stressing the dynamism and multivocality of ongoing negotiations over property, I do not mean to imply that the many who participate in debates over property and authority do so on equal terms. To the extent that ongoing negotiation works to subvert the possibility of decisive or irreversible action, it tempers exclusion—if only by postponing it. At the same time, however, those who participate in open debate in one social context may be effectively excluded from, or vulnerable to, the deployment of wealth and power in others. The cases examined in the following chapters suggest that while wealth and power were unequally distributed in Asante, both under colonial rule and after independence, many people participated in debates over their provenance, and those in positions of authority were frequently called upon to account for the way they used it.

How far demands for accountability carry—and who listens—remains an open question, however. In the era of structural adjustment, the Ghanaian government has frequently exercised its statutory authority to acquire land "for public purposes" to override stool and/or family claims for the benefit of foreign investors. Concessions for mining, timber exploitation, and agribusiness have been issued to international firms, whose access to global capital and commodity markets *together with* their exemption from local political pressures and obligations set them apart from potential Ghanaian competitors, and give them the potential to marginalize local debates in a way that neither the colonial administration nor successive Ghanaian regimes have been able or willing to do.[47] While the majority of Asantes continue to debate the merits of competing claims to land and authority with one another, recent changes in Ghana's articulation with the global economy may be fundamentally altering the context and effect of those debates.

In the chapters that follow, I use microhistories of claims on land and related struggles over office, rent, and precedent, to illustrate the processes of negotiation that have prevailed in Asante for much of the past century. To bring the immediacy of people's experience to bear in analyzing social process, I describe the actions and utterances of particular individuals in specific settings: communities, neighborhoods, offices, courts, and the courtyards of homes and chiefly palaces. To use such localized cases to shed light on the history of a region, however, it is necessary to place them in context—to show how they represent broader commonalities or particularities in the history of a larger social setting. Since I had never worked in Ghana before undertaking this study, getting a handle on the wider context was the biggest challenge I faced—and one I have only partly succeeded in addressing. To avoid cutting off significant avenues of enquiry before I discovered them, I deliberately pursued an exploratory style of research and the evidence I collected is decidedly, perhaps unfortunately, fragmentary and eclectic. While reasonably confident that these essays demonstrate some of the ways in which local debates engaged or refracted the projects of the colonial and postcolonial states, I do not claim to have adequately explored their salience in the face of globalization.

Though smaller, in territory and population, than their precolonial predecessor, both the colonial protectorate and the Ashanti Region of contemporary Ghana are far too large and extensively documented to study comprehensively in nine months. In order to get a feel for the region as a whole, I began my research in Kumase, reading as widely as I could in archival collections from the colonial period,[48] as well as secondary sources. At intervals throughout my research, I also consulted scholars at the Universities of Ghana (Legon) and of Science and Technology (Kumase); officials at the Lands Commission, the Forestry Department, the Asantehene's Secretariat, the Town and Country Planning Division, and the Department of Land and Surveys in Kumase; and judges and officials at the High Court in Kumase. Drawing on their advice and my ongoing reading in the archives, I selected one neighborhood in Kumase and two villages on its outskirts, and I spent several weeks interviewing residents, chiefs, and local entrepreneurs about the history of the area or community and their own experiences in making claims on land.[49] I also selected a few current land dispute cases and attempted to learn as much about them as I could, attending sessions of the high court when the cases were called, and interviewing litigants, witnesses, and lawyers. To compare histories of land claims in and around the city with those of a rural area, I also selected a rural town, Kumawu, located about 50 km east of Kumase in the ecological transition zone between forest and savannah. In addition to assembling whatever relevant material I could find in libraries and archives, I lived in Kumawu for two months in mid-1994, collecting microhistories of settlement, land claims, social relations, and chieftaincy affairs in Kumawu and some of its satellite villages.[50]

The following chapters draw on these materials to illustrate processes of making and exercising claims on land at particular times and places, and to explore the relationships between land claims, authority, and economic change in colonial and postcolonial Asante. Chapter 1, "Elusive Boundaries," describes the way in which territorial boundaries were challenged and renegotiated among individuals, families, and stools; traces efforts by the colonial government to correlate territorial with social and administrative boundaries; and discusses these boundaries' implications for debates over "citizenship" and chiefly jurisdiction. In chapter 2, "Unsettled Accounts," I use a case study of political turmoil in Kumawu from 1915 to 1925 to explore connections between the perennially contentious issues of stool debts and chieftaincy disputes and broader struggles to define the structure of authority and the relationship between wealth and power under indirect rule.

Chapters 3 and 4 take up the history of land claims in and around metropolitan Kumase, using local examples to trace the connections between urban growth, local and national politics, economic fluctuations, and property in the period since 1935.[51] Chapter 3, "Who Owns Kumase?" focuses on land claims and chieftaincy politics in Kumase; chapter 4, "On the Suburban Frontier," examines land allocation and community development in two villages on the outskirts of the metropolitan area. In chapters 5 and 6, I use evidence from Kumawu to examine relationships between land claims, chieftaincy politics, and economic crisis and recovery since the 1970s. Chapter 5, "Migrants, Tomatoes, and History," discusses changes in farming practices and land claims in Kumawu in the 1980s and 1990s and explores the interrelated dynamics of property, family, and community in a rural town. Chapter 6, "Battles for the Afram Plains," examines recent struggles over stool lands and rent-seeking opportunities in Kumawu in long-term historical perspective. In the conclusion, I offer some reflections on the significance of the Asante story for broader debates over the sociality of wealth and power in recent African history.

NOTES

1. This study is set in the Ashanti Region of Ghana. The modern administrative region lies at the center of Asante, a state that controlled most of present-day Ghana for much of the eighteenth and nineteenth centuries. Following modern scholarly practice, I have used the spelling Asante except when quoting or citing sources that use Ashanti. The stool is the symbol of chiefly office in Asante, and the term is commonly used to refer both to a chief's office and to the land and people under his/her jurisdiction. Stools control other kinds of property besides land, and the relationship between the property of the stool and that of the chief has long been a bone of contention. See ch. 2.

2. National Archives of Ghana, Accra (NAGA) ADM 5/3/13, H. C. Belfield, Report on legislation governing the alienation of native lands in the Gold Coast Colony and Ashanti, Cd 6278, 1912. Having been educated at the coast during the late nineteenth century, the Adontenhene was one of the few senior Asante chiefs who could communicate with colonial officials in their own language. See chs. 1 and 3.

3. With the support of a Fulbright Senior Research Award, I carried out archival and field research in Ghana for eight months in 1993 and 1994 and gathered additional information during a return visit in July 1996.

4. Interview with Mr. Sarpong, Senior Lands Officer, Kumase, 9/23/93. I heard the same words from the Asantehene's Lands Officer, Mr. Agyen, at Manhyia, Kumase, 9/8/93. Sarpong had been with the Lands Commission since the early 1970s, and Agyen had held the post of Asantehene's lands officer since 1947.

5. See, e.g., S. Migot-Adholla et al., "Indigenous land rights systems in sub-Saharan Africa," *World Bank Economic Review* 5, no. 1 (1991): 155–75; J. Bruce and S. Migot-Adholla, eds., *Searching for land tenure security in Africa* (Dubuque, IA: Kendall/Hunt, 1994).

6. S. Berry, *No condition is permanent: The social dynamics of agrarian change in sub-Saharan Africa.* (Madison: University of Wisconsin Press, 1993). The four locali-

ties are the cocoa-growing regions of southwestern Nigeria and south central Ghana; the former African reserves in Central Province, Kenya; and Northern Province, Zambia—until recently, an area of limited agricultural commercialization and substantial labor outmigration.

7. Contestation over land in the late twentieth century has drawn increasing attention from scholars. See, *inter alia*, C. Lund, *Law, power and politics in Niger: Land struggles and the Rural Code* (Hamburg: LIT Verlag, 1998); K. Izumi, "Economic liberalisation and land question in Tanzania" (Ph.D. diss., Roskilde University, Roskilde, Denmark, 1998); A. Adams and J. So, *A claim to land by the river: A household in Senegal, 1720–1994* (Oxford: Oxford University Press, 1996); F. Mackenzie, *Land, ecology and resistance in Kenya, 1880–1952* (Edinburgh: Edinburgh University Press, 1998); L. Rose, *The politics of harmony: Land dispute strategies in Swaziland* (Cambridge: Cambridge University Press, 1992); R. Levin, *When the sleeping grass awakens* (Johannesburg: University of Witwatersrand Press, 1997); K. Katinga, "The land question in Kenya: Struggles, accumulation and changing politics" (Ph.D. diss., Roskilde University, Roskilde, Denmark, 1998); D. Hughes, "Frontier dynamics: Struggles for land and clients on the Zimbabwe-Mozambique border" (Ph.D. diss., University of California, Berkeley, 1999); P. Nyambara, "A history of land acquisition in Gokwe, northwestern Zimbabwe, 1945–1990s" (Ph.D. diss., Northwestern University, 1999); B. K. Fred-Mensah, "Changes, ambiguities and conflicts in Buem, eastern Ghana" (Ph.D. diss., Johns Hopkins University, 1996).

8. See, e.g., D. Biebuyck, ed., *African agrarian systems* (London: Oxford University Press, 1963); T. Bassett and D. Crummey, eds., *Land in African agrarian systems* (Madison: University of Wisconsin Press, 1993).

9. The literature on this point is voluminous. For a recent restatement, see World Bank, *Towards environmentally sustainable development in sub-Saharan Africa. A World Bank agenda* (Washington, DC: World Bank, 1996).

10. See n. 6.

11. See, e.g., T. Bassett, "Cartography, ideology and power: The World Bank in northern Côte d'Ivoire," *Passages* 5 (1993): 8–9; P. Peters, *Dividing the commons: Politics and culture in Botswana.* (Charlottesville: University of Virginia Press, 1994).

12. There was also an active market in land in Asante in the eighteenth and nineteenth centuries, but it appears to have been organized differently from the markets in land rights that developed during and after the colonial period. See ch. 1.

13. World Bank, *Towards sustainable development*, 19.

14. NAGA ADM 11/1/1000, Secretary for Native Affairs, Memo on proposed reforms, 4/26/28.

15. The power of exclusion, which lies at the heart of this conception of property and its role in history, may be deployed in many ways. The right to exclude other people may refer to specific uses of a thing rather than the thing itself: a person may, for example, own the right to cultivate a piece of land and exclude others from doing so but may not be entitled to use it in other ways—gathering fruit from naturally occurring trees, for example. In western property law, ownership of an asset usually conveys the right to alienate it, while in many parts of Africa this is not the case, particularly with respect to land. Ownership, or the power to exclude others, may be vested in groups rather than individuals, in which case resource use depends, in part, on the internal organization or governance of the collectivity in ques-

tion. If people get along, they may manage resources more effectively together than they would individually. The "tragedy of the commons" is by no means an inevitable consequence of collective ownership. See, e.g., D. Bromley, "Property relations and economic development: The other land reform," *World Development* 17, no. 6 (1989): 867–77; T. Bassett, "Land use conflicts in pastoral development in northern Côte d'Ivoire," in Bassett and Crummey, eds., *Land*; B. McCay and J. M. Acheson, *The question of the commons: The culture and ecology of common resources* (Tuscon: University of Arizona Press, 1987); E. Ostrom, *Governing the commons: The evolution of institutions for collective action* (Cambridge: Cambridge University Press, 1990); J. Galaty, "Rangeland tenure and pastoralism in Africa." Session on policy, politics, and the crisis of pastoral property, *Proceedings of the International Congress on Anthropological and Ethnological Science* (Mexico City, 1993).

16. E. Hoebel, *Anthropology: The study of man* (New York: McGraw Hill, 1966), p. 424. Quoted in C. M. Hann, ed., *Property relations: Reviewing the anthropological tradition* (Cambridge: Cambridge University Press, 1998).

17. R. Bates, *Markets and states in tropical Africa* (Berkeley and Los Angeles: University of California Press, 1981); Bates, *Beyond the miracle of the market: The political economy of agrarian development in Kenya* (Cambridge: Cambridge University Press, 1989); R. Sandbrook, "State and economic stagnation in tropical Africa," *World Development* 14, no. 3 (1986): 319–32; M. Bratton and N. van der Walle, "Neopatrimonial regimes and political transitions in Africa," *World Politics*, 46, no. 4 (1994): 453–89; K. Cleaver and G. Schreiber, *Reversing the spiral: The population, agriculture, and environment nexus in sub-Saharan Africa* (Washington, DC: World Bank, 1994).

18. This is a large literature, but see, e.g., R. E. Downs and S. P. Reyna, eds., *Land and society in contemporary Africa* (Durham, NH: University Press of New England, 1988); I. G. Shivji, *Class struggle in Tanzania* (Dar es Salaam: Tanzania Publishing House, 1975); H.W.O. Okoth-Ogendo, "Land ownership and land distribution in Kenya's large-farm areas," in T. Killick, ed., *Papers on the Kenyan economy: Performance, problems and policies* (Nairobi: Heinemann, 1981); I. Markovitz, ed., *Studies in class and power in Africa* (New York: Oxford University Press, 1987); Bassett and Crummey, eds., *Land*.

19. J. Allman, *Quills of the porcupine: Asante nationalism in an emergent Ghana, 1954–1957* (Madison: University of Wisconsin Press, 1993); K. Arhin, "Peasants in 19th-century Asante," *Current Anthropology* 24, no. 4 (1983): 475; G. Austin, "The emergence of capitalist relations in south Asante cocoa-farming, c.1916–1933," *Journal of African History* 28 (1987): 259–79; Austin, "Capitalists and chiefs in the cocoa hold-ups in south Asante, 1927–1938," *International Journal of African Historical Studies* 21, no. 1 (1988): 63–95; B. Grier, "Contradictions, crises, and class conflict: The state and capitalist development in Ghana prior to 1948," in I. Markovitz, ed., *Studies*; A. Phillips, *The enigma of colonialism: British policy in West Africa* (London: James Currey, 1989); R. Rathbone, "Parties' socio-economic bases and regional differentiation in the rate of change in Ghana," in P. Lyon and J. Manor, eds., *Transfer and transformation: Political institutions in the new Commonwealth* (Leicester, England: Leicester University Press, 1983). Others have traced class formation in Asante to the nineteenth century. I. Wilks, *Forests of gold: Essays on the Akan and the kingdom of Asante* (Athens,

OH: University of Ohio Press, 1993); G. Austin, "'No elders were present': Commoners and private ownership in Asante, 1807–1896," *Journal of African History* 37 (1996): 1–30.

20. J. Herbst, *The politics of reform in Ghana, 1982–1991* (Berkeley and Los Angeles: University of California Press, 1993). Compare the balanced assessment in E. Hutchful, "Ghana," in P. Engeborg-Pedersen et al., *The limits of structural adjustment in Africa: The effects of economic liberalization, 1986–1994* (Copenhagen: Centre for Development Research, 1997).

21. See ch. 2.

22. See, e.g., M. Oquaye, *Politics in Ghana, 1972–1979* (Accra: Tornado, 1980); K. Ninsin and F. Drah, eds., *Political parties and democracy in Ghana's Fourth Republic* (Accra: Woeli, 1993); K. Yankah, *Woes of a Kwatriot: No big English* (Accra: Anansesem Publications, 1990).

23. See, e.g., E. Gyimah-Boadi, ed., *Ghana under PNDC rule* (Dakar: CODESRIA, 1993); Herbst, *Politics of reform*; P. Nugent, *Big men, small boys and politics in Ghana: Power, ideology and the burden of history, 1982–1994* (London and New York: Pinter, 1995); Hutchful, "Ghana"; K. Donkor, *Structural adjustment and mass poverty in Ghana* (Aldershot, England: Ashgate, 1997), 233.

24. As Bates, Sandbrook, and others have argued for Africa. See n. 17.

25. Modeling the economic implications of incomplete information—a fact of life in every real economy—has been a central concern of neoclassical economics for the last thirty years.

26. World Bank, *Towards environmentally sustainable development*.

27. P. Riesman, "The person and the life cycle in African social life and thought," *African Studies Review* 29, no. 2 (1986): 71–198; M. Jackson and I. Karp, eds., *Personhood and agency: The experience of self and other in African cultures* (Uppsala: Almqvist and Wicksell, 1990); K. Gyekye, *Tradition and modernity: Philosophical reflections on the African experience* (New York and Oxford: Oxford University Press, 1997).

28. The idea of "wealth-in-people" as a distinctive feature of African economic cultures has featured prominently in the literature on African slavery, and it has been taken up by students of postemancipation economies as well. See, e.g., S. Miers and I. Kopytoff, *Slavery in Africa* (Madison: University of Wisconsin Press, 1977), "Introduction"; C. Bledsoe, *Women and marriage in Kpelle society* (Stanford, CA: Stanford University Press, 1980); J. Guyer, "Wealth in people and self-realization in equatorial Africa," *Man* (NS) 28 (1993): 243–65; K. Barber, "Money, self-realization and the person in Yoruba texts," in J. Guyer, ed., *Money matters: Instability, value and social payments in the modern history of West Africa* (Portsmouth, NH: Heinemann); B. Cooper, "Women's worth and wedding gift exchange in 19th and 20th century Maradi, Niger," *Journal of African History* 36 (1995): 121–40.

29. See, e.g., W. Arens and I. Karp, eds., *Creativity of power: Cosmology and action in African societies* (Washington, DC: Smithsonian Institution, 1989); Gyekye, *Tradition and modernity*.

30. P. Geschiere, "Kinship, witchcraft and the market: Hybrid patterns in Cameroonian societies," in R. Dilley, ed., *Contesting markets: Analyses of ideology, discourse and practice* (Edinburgh: Edinburgh University Press, 1992); P. Geschiere with C. Fisiy, "Domesticating personal violence: Witchcraft, courts and confessions in Cameroon,"

Africa 64, no. 3 (1994): 323–41; K. Crehan, *The fractured community: Landscapes of power and gender in rural Zambia* (Berkeley and Los Angeles: University of California Press, 1997); J. and J. Comaroff, eds., *Modernity and its malcontents: Ritual and power in postcolonial Africa* (Chicago: University of Chicago Press, 1993).

31. E. Akyeampong and P. Obeng, "Spirituality, gender, and power in Asante history," *International Journal of African Historical Studies* 28, no. 3 (1995): 483. See also K. Gyekye, *An essay on African philosophical thought: The Akan conceptual scheme* (Cambridge: Cambridge University Press, 1987), esp. 119ff; K. Wiredu, *Cultural universals and particulars: An African perspective* (Bloomington: Indiana University Press, 1996); T. C. McCaskie, *State and society in precolonial Asante* (Cambridge: Cambridge University Press, 1995).

32. C. Bledsoe, "'No success without struggle': Social mobility and hardship for foster children in Sierra Leone," *Man* (NS) 25, no. 1 (1990): 70–88.

33. For a similar argument about the sociality and efficacy of prayer in Yoruba religious practice, see K. Barber, "How man makes god in West Africa: Yoruba attitudes towards the *orisa*," *Africa* 51, no. 5 (1981): 217–37.

34. This observation is not peculiar to Asante. See, e.g., Berry, *Fathers work for their sons: Accumulation, mobility and class in an extended Yoruba community* (Berkeley and Los Angeles: University of California Press, 1985).

35. Compare T. Falola, "Money and informal credit institutions in colonial western Nigeria," in Guyer, ed., *Money matters*.

36. Compare P. Burnham, *The politics of cultural difference in northern Cameroon* (Edinburgh: Edinburgh University Press, 1996).

37. See, e.g., Bassett, "Cartography and power"; Peters, *Dividing the commons.*

38. Throughout these essays, I am writing only of the twentieth century: I will try to elucidate some of the ways in which narratives of precolonial Asante have figured in social practices of the colonial and postcolonial periods, but am not competent to comment on the way history was produced and interpreted in Asante in earlier times.

39. See ch. 6, 174–75.

40. See ch. 3.

41. The government's decision, in 1935, to reinstate the office of Asantehene under the aegis of colonial authority was motivated, in part, by the hope that holders of that office would serve as definitive arbiters of customary knowledge. In practice, the restoration did little to stem the production of varied and conflicting interpretations of history. See ch. 2. Compare the colonial official who observed, in 1947, that "[land] disputes involve, not unnaturally, questions of historical fact. . . . rather than Court decisions on legal principles. . . . For this reason it has not proved possible to abstract from the material used . . . any general principles of Akan land tenure." Quoted in A.A.Y. Kyerematen, *Inter-state boundary litigation in Ashanti*, African Social Research Documents No. 4, (Cambridge: African Studies Centre, University of Cambridge, 1971), p 36. See also I. Sutton, "Law, chieftaincy and conflict in colonial Ghana: The Ada case," *African Affairs* 83, no. 330 (1984): 41–62; R. Crook, "Decolonization, the colonial state, and chieftaincy in the Gold Coast," *African Affairs* 85, no. 1 (1986): 75–105; K. Mann and R. Roberts, eds., *Law in colonial Africa* (London and Portsmouth, NH: James Currey & Heinemann, 1991); R. Gocking, "Indirect rule in the Gold Coast: Competition for office and the invention of tradition," *Canadian Journal of African Studies* 28, no. 3 (1994): 421–46; S.

Berry, "Hegemony on a shoestring: indirect rule and access to agricultural land," *Africa* 62, no. 3 (1992): 327–55.

42. In 1966, an observer concluded optimistically that by "divorc[ing] the chief from the land" Ghanaian law had "struck directly to the heart of the institution of chieftaincy itself," adding that "[i]t is thus difficult to see how the chiefs can long remain a significant factor in the social, political or governmental life of the country." W. B. Harvey, *Law and social change in Ghana* (Princeton, NJ: Princeton University Press, 1966), pp. 121–22.

43. This is not to say that Asantes do not avail themselves of new technologies of reproduction. Photocopies of historical documents are, for example, used frequently in negotiations or disputes over land—and their meaning is just as subject to contestation and debate as any other form of historical representation.

44. Not every dead person is venerated as an ancestor. Only those whose lives have been worthy of emulation and respect are honored by having their stools blackened, preserved, and attended by subsequent generations. See, e.g., P. K. Sarpong, *The sacred stools of the Akan* (Accra-Tema: Ghana Publishing Corp., 1971); K. A. Opoku, *West African traditional religion* (Accra: FEP International, 1978); McCaskie, *State and society*; Wilks, *Forests of gold*.

45. History is produced and reinterpreted in a number of different social arenas. In addition to *adae*, funerals—perhaps the most common and conspicuous social ritual in Asante today—are another important arena in which history is continually brought to bear on the negotiation of contemporary relations of authority, obligation, and allegiance. See, *inter alia*, K. Arhin, "The economic implications of transformations in Akan funeral rites," *Africa* 64, no. 3 (1994): 307–22; M. Gilbert, "The sudden death of a millionaire: conversion and consensus in a Ghanaian kingdom," *Africa* 58, no. 3 (1988): 281–305; R. S. Rattray, *Ashanti* (Oxford: Clarendon Press, 1923), ch. 11; R. Rathbone, *Murder and politics in colonial Ghana* (New Haven, CT: Yale University Press, 1993); T. C. McCaskie, "Death and the Asantehene: A historical meditation," *Journal of African History* 30 (1989): 417–44; G. S. Dei, "The economics of death and funeral celebration in a Ghanaian Akan Community," *Culture* 9, no. 1 (1989): 49–62, and ch. 5 below.

46. See ch. 5; also Berry, "Tomatoes, land and hearsay: Property and history in Asante in the time of structural adjustment," *World Development* 25, no. 8 (1997): 1225–41.

47. This possibility is forcefully articulated in a recent study of land concessions and foreign investment in forestry and agribusiness in southern Ghana. K. S. Amanor, *Global restructuring and land rights in Ghana: Forest food chains, timber and rural livelihoods,*. Research Report No. 108 (Uppsala: Nordiska Afrikainstitutet, 1999).

48. The principal repositories of records from the colonial period are the National Archives in Kumase, and the archive located at the Asantehene's palace at Manhyia and managed by the Institute of African Studies at the University of Ghana in Legon. Some colonial records pertaining to Asante are housed in the headquarters of the National Archives in Accra.

49. I conducted fieldwork in Amakom, one of the oldest stools in Kumase and now a sprawling neighborhood of residential, commercial, and industrial structures; Asokore Mampong, a village on the suburban fringe of the metropolitan area; and Kenyase Kwabre, a village about 5 km east of Kumase that is rapidly becoming a kind of low-income bedroom community, many of whose inhabitants work or trade in the city. I also

collected some information about land dispute cases in Duase, Kwamo, Kaase, Aputuogya, and metropolitan Kumase itself.

50. My fieldwork in Kumawu would not have been possible without the invaluable help and guidance of Nana Osei Bediako Firaw and my research assistant, Michael Adu Gyamfi. Further details concerning sources and informants, in Kumawu, Kumase, and other locations, are given in the following chapters.

51. In 1935, the colonial administration reversed its previous policy, of dividing up the precolonial Asante state in order to secure its own power, and "restored" the traditional monarchy. The significance of this moment as a watershed in contemporary Asante history has been debated ever since, as we shall see.

1

ELUSIVE BOUNDARIES: RENT-SEEKING, LAND, AND CITIZENSHIP IN EARLY COLONIAL ASANTE

Two recent articles, one by Gareth Austin, the other by Emmanuel Akyeampong and Pashington Obeng, have reopened debate over the sources and distribution of power in Asante in the 19th century.[1] Austin reexamines Wilks' argument that the political struggles that shook Asante in the 1870s and 1880s amounted to an attack on the monarchy by a small group of wealthy state traders who wanted to break away from the state to become an independent bourgeoisie. He argues that both opposition to the monarchy and participation in trade and production for the market were more broadly based: neither the state nor a small class of state functionaries-turned-capitalists controlled trade or production for the market, and the dissidents included commoners (*nkwankwaa* or "free citizens without office")[2] of modest as well as substantial means. Akyeampong and Obeng take up T. C. McCaskie's thesis that the power of the state was rooted in Asante cosmology. While agreeing with McCaskie that for Asantes, power transcends human agency, they maintain that for this very reason, the state's power to render dissent unthinkable was more circumscribed than he suggests. "[D]iffuse by nature and immanent in the Asante cosmos," power, they argue, "was accessible to all."[3]

If state power was less concentrated and all-encompassing in precolonial Asante than previous scholarship has suggested, how was it affected by the imposition of colonial rule? The British occupation of Kumase in 1896 followed a period in which the state appeared to be recovering from the civil wars of the 1880s. Elected to the Golden Stool in 1888 after a five-year interregnum, Asantehene Agyeman Prempeh I set out to reunite the kingdom and reassert the authority of the central state. His efforts were hampered, however, by the Gold Coast colonial government, which refused to repatriate refugees from the Asante civil wars, placed several neighboring states under British "protection," and pressured Asante to follow their example. Prempeh and his advisers were eager to gain access to coastal markets and British resources, but not at the price of Asante's independence, and the Colonial Office was averse to forcible conquest.[4] After several years of inconclusive negotiation, officials in the Gold Coast Colony took matters into their own hands. In January 1896, Governor Maxwell arrested the Asantehene, together with senior members of his family and government, and presented the Colonial Office with a *fait accompli*. Prempeh and his supporters were exiled, first to Elmina and later to Sierra Leone; separate treaties were signed with a number of Asante *amanhene* (provincial chiefs); and a committee of chiefs was appointed to handle the daily administration of Kumase under the watchful eye of a British Resident.[5] In 1900, provoked by British demands for higher taxes and possession of the Golden Stool, Kumase-based forces attacked British troops on the outskirts of the capital and laid siege to the Kumase Fort. When the siege was broken after four months, the British took full control. Asante was made a Crown Colony, separate from the Gold Coast but answerable to the same governor, and the end of the old order was sealed by shipping Prempeh and his retinue to the Seychelles.[6]

British officials and merchants had long been interested in securing unhindered access to resources and markets in Asante, and they moved quickly to turn *de jure* rule to economic advantage. Their efforts were welcomed by Asante merchants engaged in the lucrative rubber trade and other commercial ventures, and by chiefs who anticipated gains from mining and timber concessions. Asantes were generally opposed however, to any resumption of the estate taxes and other prestations imposed by the precolonial regime, and the new colonial administration was loath to provoke unrest by levying direct taxes of its own.[7] Since duties on external trade were collected at the coast, the Ashanti administration depended on grants from Accra, which fell chronically short of what they considered to be their region's fair share of total receipts.[8] To cut costs and augment their meager revenues, officials turned to the chiefs.

From the outset, the administration's efforts to incorporate traditional officeholders into the apparatus of colonial rule were complicated both by the history of colonial occupation and by the process of conflict and reorganization within Asante that preceded colonial rule. By dismantling the monarchy, the British left Kumase in confusion: cut off from its head, the hierarchy of chiefly authority was thrown open to contestation, as senior officeholders scrambled to pro-

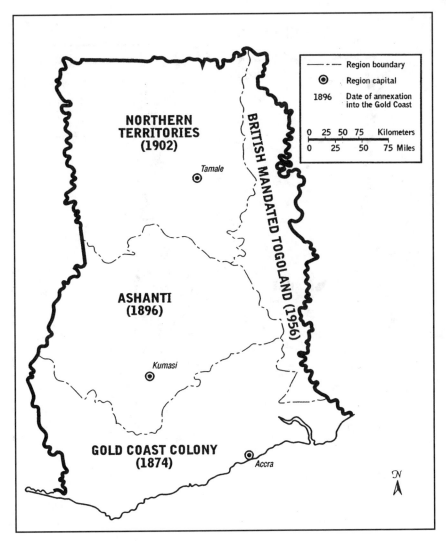

Map 1.1 The Gold Coast.
Source: Adapted from W.E.F. Ward, *A History of Ghana*. London: Allen & Unwin, 1958, 24.

tect or advance their positions within the new order. Moreover, the repercussions of chiefly competition spread far beyond the precincts of the capital. Under the precolonial state, officeholders exercised authority separately over land and people. Individuals who resided in a single town or village might owe allegiance to several different chiefs and occupy land that belonged to still others. Many officeholders in the capital controlled land and/or subjects that

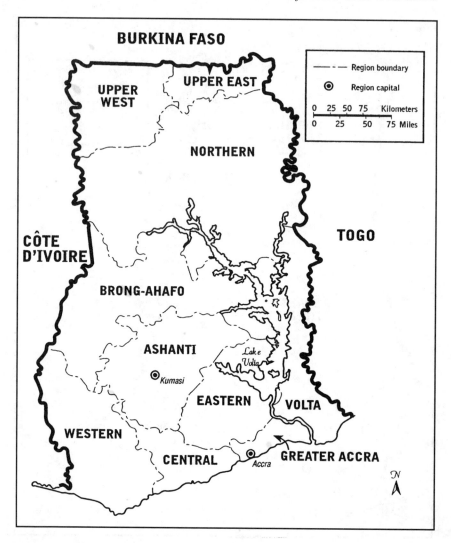

Map 1.2 Ghana, 1994.

Source: Adapted from L. Berry, *Ghana: A Country Study.* Washington, DC: Federal Research Division, Library of Congress, 1995.

were scattered over a wide area, interspersed with the lands and subjects of provincial as well as other Kumase chiefs.[9] To complicate matters further, in negotiating her son's election to the Golden Stool in 1888, Asantehemaa Yaa Kyaa had promised his supporters that "any property that had been seized by Prempeh's predecessors should revert to the original owners" following his accession[10]—touching off a complex process of restitution that was still underway at the time of Prempeh's arrest. Inserted into a dynamic field of political contestation, the colonial administration's efforts to govern according to "custom" added fuel to the fires of chiefly ambition and dispute.

In addition to ongoing political struggles among Asante officeholders, the early years of British rule in Asante were marked by accelerated commercial and economic growth. Stimulated by the rubber boom of the 1890s and the advent of British concession seekers, trade expanded rapidly in the late 1890s and early 1900s. As European and African traders moved into Kumase to take advantage of new market opportunities in the region, rising demand for building plots helped to create a market in urban land. In the next two decades, cocoa cultivation spread into Asante from the Gold Coast Colony,[11] leading to further increases in demand for land, labor, and commodities (both local and imported), which intensified both the commercialization of the regional economy and competition over control of its resources. Both established residents and newcomers from the coast or savannah communities to the north of Asante invested money, time, energy, and imagination not only in trade and in agricultural and resource extraction but also in gaining control over the means of production and establishing claims on income streams arising from increased production and trade. Land proved valuable on both counts: landholders could profit by putting land to use for agricultural production, resource extraction, or building, or they could collect rent from others who planned to do so. Rent could also be derived from offices whose occupants were in a position to mediate access to the colonial state. As in most colonial societies, Africans employed by the colonial regime—as clerks, messengers, policemen, inspectors, and so forth—derived more than wages from their positions, however marginal, as agents of the state. In Asante, chiefs were in an even more favorable position—not only because of the administrative and judicial prerogatives assigned to them by the colonial state but also as a result of colonial officials' reading of Asante custom with respect to land.[12]

Some scholars have argued that colonial land policy in Ghana was designed to protect the interests of European merchants and investors by preventing the emergence of an African bourgeoisie,[13] but in Asante, problems of security and administrative viability seem to have predominated in the early years of colonial rule. With the siege of 1900 fresh in their minds, administrators in Asante claimed land surrounding the Kumase Fort for the Crown, but otherwise refrained from provoking their new subjects by appropriating their land.[14] Instead, they turned their attention to matters of land administration and the adjudication of land disputes. Worried that unrestrained commercialization would foster litigation and weaken the fabric of customary authority, the administration decided to forestall the emergence of a land market in Asante by upholding traditional practice. Accord-

ing to custom, they declared, ownership of land in Asante was vested in the
stools, but "ownership" did not include the right of alienation. Chiefs could
allocate rights to use land in perpetuity, if they wished, but land

> cannot be alienated from the stool. . . . The natural possessor of land
> holds it from the stool by family right, enjoys the fruits thereof and can-
> not be dispossessed; yet, nor can he transfer ownership which he does
> not possess. . . . [S]ale . . . cannot be recognized. Possession may pass a
> hundred times, ownership never.[15]

Although set forth as a tenet of time-honored custom, the prohibition on
land sales appears to have been a departure from precolonial practice.[16] In
the eighteenth century, rulers of the Asante state extended their domains by
conquest and consolidated their power through the confiscation and redistribution of office, land, and subjects.[17] Offenses against the state and its
laws were punished by fines, payable in gold, or by sentences of execution
from which the condemned could purchase reprieve, also with gold. Trans-
gressors who lacked the wherewithal to make these payments could raise it
by selling their authority over land and/or people.[18] A good deal of the
wealth that the state acquired through adjudication was redistributed as gifts
to loyal clients and potential allies. Authority over land and people changed
hands frequently, for cash or credit, in what McCaskie has aptly termed "a
marketplace of power."[19]

Whether Asante's new colonial rulers were ignorant of these practices,
or chose to ignore them, they were firm in insisting that land alienation was
contrary to "native customary law," and they structured colonial policy accordingly. Moreover, although they acknowledged that rights in land had
previously been held and transacted separately from rights over people, the
colonial rulers worked to consolidate chiefly jurisdictions in order to sim-
plify the task of administering them. An Asante chief put the matter suc-
cinctly. Before the British came, he declared, land rent did not exist; now, it
"shows [the] allegiance" of subordinate office holders to their Head Chiefs.[20]
Confirmed in their rights over land and subjects but prevented from selling
them, chiefs were obliged to realize the value of land and labor by exploiting them, and set about doing so with enthusiasm.

In effect, then, colonial rule not only ended the practice of chiefs "selling" subjects to defray their debts but touched off a lengthy series of debates over who owed allegiance to whom. Debate was not confined to chiefs:
faced with new, sometimes onerous, chiefly demands for tribute and services, commoners often "voted with their feet." In 1906, an official inspec-
tion of eastern Asante found that "Chiefs were all quarrelling among themselves—some subjects openly defied their Chiefs, while others sought the

protection of other Headchiefs, thus giving a pretext for undue interference (eagerly taken advantage of) which might at any time lead to serious complications."[21] Although anxious to establish a stable hierarchy of allegiances, in which every Asante subject was assigned a place and competing or overlapping allegiances were minimized, administrators were reluctant to force people to remain under the authority of a chief whom they disliked. Thus, relocations continued, giving rise to frequent complaints about subjects who had "run away" or been "stolen" by rival chiefs and further complicating the process of sorting out jurisdictional claims.

By vesting land in the chiefs or the Crown, colonial administrators ensured that access to land and claims on rent would be mediated through competition over access to the state. They also placed themselves in the position of adjudicating competing interpretations of traditional rules and precedents. Committed to resolving questions of jurisdiction and chiefly prestations in accordance with "custom," colonial officials found themselves obliged to learn what custom was. Not surprisingly, their inquiries elicited multiple, often conflicting interpretations from Asantes eager to advance their own interests within the colonial order. In practice, officials' attempts to govern through tradition were as likely to prolong disputes as end them, and their search for knowledge of customary rules and historical precedents produced debate rather than consensus about the past.[22]

To cope with the flood of conflicting stories elicited by their efforts at governance and adjudication, colonial officials tried both to clarify custom and to codify it. They conducted periodic inquiries into "native custom" and Asante history,[23] issued numerous rulings both in and out of court,[24] and carefully recorded their findings and decisions, hoping to create a stable, comprehensive record of precedents and precepts that would "settle" disputed claims once and for all. In the resulting archive of administrative decision and discovery, records of boundaries occupy a prominent place. Colonial administrators devoted considerable time and attention to demarcating boundaries—administrative boundaries to define their own jurisdictions; territorial boundaries to resolve competing claims to land and office; and social boundaries to define arenas of authority and obligation for chiefs and commoners alike. Like written compilations of custom, colonially demarcated boundaries were influential in subsequent struggles over wealth and influence—not as fixed or binding constraints on social action, but as focal points for further debate. In the course of these debates, knowledge of custom and claims to historical expertise proliferated: rules and boundaries remained open to challenge and reinterpretation, no matter how clearly they were drawn or how authoritatively they were sanctioned. If, in precolonial Asante, power derived from material and spiritual sources that defied concentration, under colonial rule it came also to rest on the production of

history—a process that proved equally difficult to contain. Like the historical precedents on which they were based, colonial boundaries were as elusive as they were ubiquitous.

In their efforts to ensure social and administrative stability in Asante,
officials barred lawyers as well as land sales from the region. Many of the
cases brought before the commissioners' courts were linked, directly or in-
directly, to the economic growth that accompanied the imposition of colonial rule. Colonial officials welcomed the increase in income and trade but
worried that "unsophisticated natives" would become corrupt and unruly if
they were exposed too quickly to the pressures and temptations of commerce and "civilization." Lawyers, they believed, were an unscrupulous
lot, eager to line their own pockets by taking advantage of their illiterate
countrymen. In contrast to the Gold Coast Colony, no independent judiciary was established in Asante until the 1930s. Lawyers, like land sales,
were proscribed, and British commissioners, most of whom had no legal
training, held court—in self-conscious imitation of the precolonial monarchy[25]—where they took evidence directly from litigants and witnesses and
issued rulings based on their own interpretations of both "customary" and
colonial law.[26]

PROPERTY RIGHTS AND THE PRODUCTION OF HISTORY: SOME PRELIMINARY CONSIDERATIONS

In the disputes over land that flooded the commissioners' courts in the
early years of the twentieth century, claims were frequently couched in
terms of historical precedent. These were not limited to recent occurrences:
many litigants traced their claims from events connected to or preceding
the founding of the Asante state in about 1700. In 1906, to take just one
example, Edwesohene Yaw Awuah claimed a tract of land known as Ahiresu,
on the grounds that his ancestor had killed its erstwhile overlord, Kwatchi
Depoah, during the reign of Opoku Ware I (ca. 1720–50).[27] His claim was
challenged by the headman of Nyamieni, a subordinate of a prominent
Kumase chief, Kwesi Nuama. Appearing before the district commissioner
on behalf of his subordinate, Chief Nuama contradicted Chief Awuah's testimony. Kwatchi Depoah, he explained, was killed by one Aponsim of
Nyamieni (whose nephew was the father of Osei Tutu) in the time of Chief
Obiri Yeboah (who died in the early 1680s).[28] He added that the
Edwesohene's ancestor, a son of the chief of Nyamieni, had come to the
disputed land with the latter's permission, and that chiefs of Edweso had
subsequently sent tribute to the chief of Nyamieni. The case went before
the Kumase Council of Chiefs, who ruled in favor of Nyamieni, and the
Edwesohene appealed to the chief commissioner. Fuller's judgment is not

recorded, but subsequent records suggest that, whatever it was, it did not settle the dispute. In 1927, the district commissioner noted that this land "has [been], and still is, the subject of prolonged and bitter litigation . . . ,"[29] and it was contested again, at length, before the Asantehene's court in the 1950s.[30]

Frequent and protracted disputes over the ownership of land did not necessarily impede its exploitation.[31] Permission to use a portion of stool (or family) land was usually acknowledged by a small gift, known as *aseda*, or "thanks," presented to the stoolholder or family head in the presence of witnesses, whose recollections served as a record of the transaction in subsequent disputes. When a stranger requested permission to farm or settle on stool land, s/he presented the chief with "drinks" to solemnize the agreement. As land values rose, "drinks" were frequently accompanied or replaced by monetary payments equivalent to the going market price for land. Even before the introduction of cocoa, some Asante chiefs received sizable cash payments for granting timber and mineral concessions to foreign firms and demanded tribute, in cash or in kind, from rubber tappers and other collectors of marketable forest produce.[32] Cocoa increased these revenues manyfold and redefined relations between holders and users of land. In explaining how they came to occupy a particular site, Asantes often tell stories of migration, describing their forebears' movements from place to place in search of suitable land for their families and followers "to feed on."[33] In the past, it is implied, land was valued primarily as a means to attract followers, rather than as an asset in its own right; with the advent of cocoa, however, the priorities were reversed. Chiefs began to demand substantial amounts of tribute from farmers who were growing cocoa on their land. Farmers protested, especially when the sums demanded were large, and chiefs and headmen quarreled with one another over the right to collect them.

In addition to seeking rent through customary claims to "homage" and "tribute," chiefs experimented with new instruments of surplus appropriation introduced by their colonial rulers. In Kumase, the use of long-term leases soon spread from Crown Land to that of the stools. In 1905, it was still possible for the Wesleyan Mission to protest a government plan to build a hospital on the Kintampo Road, claiming that Chief Obuabasa had allocated the land to them, by verbal agreement, in 1896. The director of the mission admitted that he could not document the chief's gift, but pointed out that Captain Stewart had confirmed the arrangement and the mission had assumed, as a matter of course, that "the word of a British officer . . . would be duly ratified."[34] As land values rose, however, chiefs as well as officials began to place land allocations on a more formal basis. Led by the redoubtable Chief Kwame Frimpon—

a wealthy and educated businessman, who owed his stool to the British—chiefs in Kumase began to issue formal leases on their stool lands and demanded compensation for plots the government had appropriated for public use.[35]

Formal leases and other documents did not, however, replace oral history as sources of evidence concerning claims on land; instead, both were adduced and debated, in and out of court. In effect, the adjudication of land disputes in colonial Asante turned on simultaneous and contradictory processes of codification and proliferation of narratives about the past. The resulting tensions produced neither a master narrative of invented tradition nor a coherent counterhegemonic discourse, but an ongoing process of historiographical debate, which defied contemporary efforts at administrative rationalization. Codification was never complete: each revision, when incorporated into colonial law or applied to the adjudication of land and chieftaincy disputes, produced competing narratives and further debate. This was just as true of farm and stool boundaries as it was of leaseholds on building plots.

"FULLER BOUNDARIES":
MAPPING CLAIMS TO LAND AND SUBJECTS

When Francis Fuller arrived, in 1905, to take up his appointment as chief commissioner, he found Kumase divided and confusing. "I could not get a grip on Coomassie affairs. They eluded me. Each chief came and told me the story he wished me to believe. . . . "[36] Fuller's solution was to give the chiefs a stake in the new colonial order by creating a Kumase Council of Chiefs to advise him on town affairs and local customs. The results were gratifying: within a year he felt able to report that membership on the council had become "an honor" and gave "the Chief Commissioner a strong weapon over the lucky holders of office."[37]

Fuller lost no time in deploying his new weapon in the line of duty. "Nothing opens up the country, nothing admits more light, than goods [*sic*] Roads," he wrote enthusiastically to the governor in January 1906, adding hopefully that better roads would help to "strike the doom of native hostility and resistance" by stimulating trade.[38] But funds for road construction were few and far between. Fuller was obliged to wait eight months for a reply to his letter, and then he received only £1000 for road construction, instead of the £8000 he had requested.[39] Strapped for cash, the chief commissioner turned to custom. Noting that chiefs were "traditionally" entitled to services from their subjects, he demanded that they provide labor for road work. Chiefs whose subjects proved recalcitrant or unavailable could, he thought, use part of their "rents" to get the job done for hire.[40]

The government's demands for road labor placed chiefs in an awkward position. Subjects were apt to desert chiefs whose demands they found onerous, and the government provided little help in getting them back. In 1907 and 1908, Edwesohene Yaw Awuah lodged several complaints with the district commissioner concerning subjects and/or subchiefs who wanted to transfer their allegiance to other stools.[41] When a group of disaffected residents threatened to decamp from the village of Ayenasu, the chief appealed to the district commissioner to stop them: otherwise, his letter warned, "the village will be left in ruins and the Government roads between Odomose and Kyekyewere will have no any cleaners."[42] Faced with government demands for labor, some chiefs temporized, while others sought to make subjects responsible for hiring their own replacements as laborers. In 1926, for example, the Kumasehene's court ruled that a farmer, who claimed to have spent £70 on road work for the Tafohene, could not credit the amount towards his seven years' arrears of tribute to the chief.[43] Noting that service to chiefs was given "grudgingly and only because it is compelled by the government," the commissioner of the Western Province observed that chiefs knew better than to press the point. For example, he added, the Berekumhene refuses to post signs indicating which villages are responsible for cleaning sections of the road.[44] Other chiefs found, however, that accepting responsibility for clearing the roads could be used to advance their claims to land. In 1926, a farmer was excused from paying tribute to the Tafohene when his uncle agreed to accept responsibility for clearing the road.[45]

Tension over chiefly jurisdictions was widespread. At the beginning of 1906, the chief commissioner complained that chiefs in the eastern districts "were all quarrelling among themselves—some subjects openly defied their Chiefs, while others sought the protection of other Headchiefs. . . . "[46] Subchiefs, as well as subjects, frequently challenged their superiors or defected to preferred patrons.[47] While divisions among the chiefs tended to strengthen the hand of the colonial state, land disputes were time-consuming and their political advantages waned as the colonial regime consolidated its power. Hoping to forestall future disputes as well as resolve current ones, officials worked to demarcate boundaries between the disputants. Chief Commissioner Fuller, who was trained as a surveyor, took up the task with enthusiasm. He visited many disputed sites in person to inspect the terrain, interview local witnesses, and survey and map boundaries between the litigants' lands. During his administration, entries in the chief commissioner's Boundary Book[48] began to include exact coordinates as well as physical descriptions of the boundaries between stool lands, and "Fuller boundaries" are still adduced as evidence in land litigation at all levels of the Ghanaian judicial system.[49]

In addition to "fixing" boundaries between rival stools, the colonial regime also demarcated boundaries around its own administrative jurisdictions. One of the government's first projects after the annexation of Asante was to demarcate an official boundary between Asante and the Colony. Fearful of losing land by administrative fiat, chiefs on both sides of the proposed colonial boundary protested, and their pleas were taken up by some of the Colony's most prominent citizens. In 1905, John Mensah Sarbah warned the Legislative Council that "it is one thing to fix the boundaries of tribal lands and another to define the jurisdictions of districts."[50] Government agreed, in principle: in surveying the proposed boundary between Ashanti and the Gold Coast Colony, Guggisberg explained, he had made every effort to follow "the tribal boundaries between the Ashanti Akyems and the Okwawos."[51] But it was not always practicable to do this. Noting that the colonial boundary would pass through land under dispute between Kwahu and Bompata, Guggisberg advised against waiting until the dispute was settled. It could drag on for years and "besides, the Boundary being one for administrative purposes chiefly, it would not be a matter of very serious importance if, should the area in question be eventually decided as belonging to the Okwawos, it lay within the Ashanti limits." After all, he reasoned, there was nothing to prevent a person from owning land "in another country."[52]

Once gazetted, however, administrative boundaries proved irresistably convenient. Pointing out that Guggisberg's boundary offered "an excellent opportunity to end, once and for all, these more or less airy claims . . . ,"[53] Fuller invoked it in 1907, to settle a dispute between the Asante stool of Kumawu and the chiefs of Kwahu in the Colony. A year later, he peremptorily dismissed a Gold Coast official's appeal on behalf of the Kwahus, noting that it would be "most unwise to allow natives of one administration to walk over the frontier and hold lands in another."[54] By 1910, the secretary for native affairs doubted there ever *was* a definite boundary between the two stools and noted with approval that Guggisberg had been careful to follow natural features of the landscape "to the exclusion of considerations of shadowy ancestral rights."[55]

The relationship between colonial and "customary" jurisdictions remained contentious, however. In 1912, the secretary for native affairs complained that administrators in Asante insisted on "accept[ing] the administrative boundary as marking rigidly the tribal boundary."[56] Chiefs continued to ignore or defy the former: in 1913, Fuller reprimanded the Juabenhene for writing directly to a chief in the Colony whose subjects were farming in Juaben, instead of referring the matter to him.[57] By 1920, the surveyor general was optimistic that firm administrative boundaries would soon bring about a more stable social and political order:

> When the boundaries are definitely fixed on the topographical map the stool lands will become, I believe, definite entities in a way they have probably not been before. . . . A paramount chief will have definite authority as to who is under him and who is not, and Provincial Commissioners will be able to fix responsibility as to overlordship in the case of every village and portion of ground.[58]

However precisely they were drawn on paper, boundaries could be remarkably elusive in practice. In 1917, the chief of Tredeh appealed a boundary that Fuller had drawn, five years earlier, between his lands and those of the neighboring stool of Pekyi. Arguing that they understood Fuller's line to indicate the boundary between the Central and Southern Provinces, not the "long existing native land boundary between Pekki and Tredeh," the elders of Tredeh complained that the latter interpretation would deprive Tredeh of its land and subjects.[59] Several years later, a surveyor sent to review the boundary was confronted by the chief and an angry crowd, who insisted that the "land (i.e., tribal) boundaries have never been fixed at all."[60] Stool boundaries were no more fixed in the city. In 1914, the town surveyor produced a map that indicated the boundaries of the principal stool lands in Kumase (map 1.3); in 1920, the surveyor general wrote as if no such map had ever existed.[61] Administrators reacted to such vagaries with a mixture of exasperation and resignation. In 1928, the secretary for native affairs declared briskly that government should proceed at once to create a register of land holdings, "conferring absolute title, guaranteed by the State. . . . [I]t is absurd that each owner should not know and that others should not know what precisely is his holding."[62] But a provincial commissioner in Asante pointed out that such a scheme was impracticable. "To legislate regarding land tenure will be a ticklish problem and I feel sure will meet with opposition . . . from the people."[63] The register was never created.[64]

Colonial boundaries were often arbitrarily drawn, and they have been criticized for ossifying historically flexible patterns of access to land and eroding the rights of socially marginal or powerless people.[65] In Asante, gains from rising land values *were* unequally distributed, but this was not a straightforward result of colonially imposed rigidities in hitherto flexible systems of property rights. By inviting multiple "readings" of Asante history, indirect rule continually subverted its own agents' efforts to produce decisive sets of rules and precedents.[66] Fuller no doubt envisioned his bound-

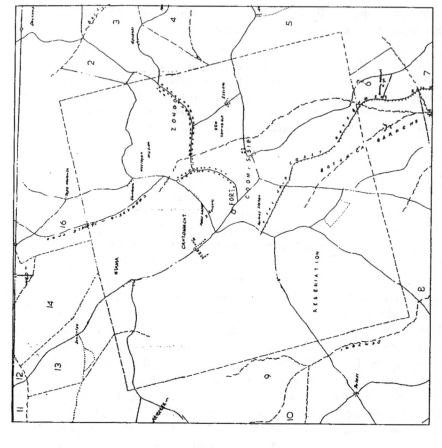

Map 1.3 Stool lands, Kumase, 1914.
Source: NAGK.

aries as final solutions to troublesome and time-wasting disputes, but their influence on subsequent struggles over property and power was neither definitive nor hegemonic. Land disputes typically dragged on for years, even decades.[67] Far from inscribing onto the Asante landscape a master narrative of exclusionary rigidity, "Fuller boundaries" tended to fade in and out of subsequent debates over land and office like the Cheshire cat, with more persistence than predictability.

WHO IS A "STRANGER"?

In addition to disputes over stool boundaries, the spread of cocoa growing in Asante provoked lengthy debates over how to divide the proceeds of this unprecedentedly lucrative crop. As chiefs and commoners confronted each other over who was obliged to pay, how much, and to whom, their debates raised questions about the scope and meaning of chiefly jurisdiction over people as well as land. Under the combined influence of indirect rule and the colonial policy of treating land as the inalienable property of Asante stools, debate over the rights and obligations of tenants became entangled with discussion of the meaning of citizenship. Like disputes over territorial boundaries, these debates turned on questions of historical precedent as well as customary precept.

As in the case of stool boundary disputes, debates over cocoa tribute posed something of a dilemma for the administration. In the interests of social and fiscal stability, officials considered it essential to uphold chiefs' authority over their subjects and ensure that their revenues were adequate to their responsibilities as agents of the colonial state. But the stability and solvency of the colonial order also depended on the effort and cooperation of the mass of agricultural producers. While officials generally supported chiefs' demands for tribute, they also worried that excessive demands would backfire. "[M]en work hard to make a cocoa farm," argued one, "and it is not right that they should be taxed . . . for cocoa which they themselves have grown. . . . [C]ocoa is different from rubber which grows wild."[68] A stranger, he thought, could be asked to pay "rent," but the amount should be fixed in advance, rather than calibrated to the amount of cocoa the farmer produced.

Faced with a growing volume of complaints from chiefs and commoners alike, officials pondered the merits of codification as opposed to ad hoc solutions. In 1913, Fuller "laid down the rule in the Central Province that strangers should pay tribute of 1/10 of the cocoa—either in cash or in kind" and advised the commissioners of other provinces to follow his lead.[69] Fuller's "tithe" did not, however, impress Asante chiefs—who had heard that their counterparts in the Colony were get-

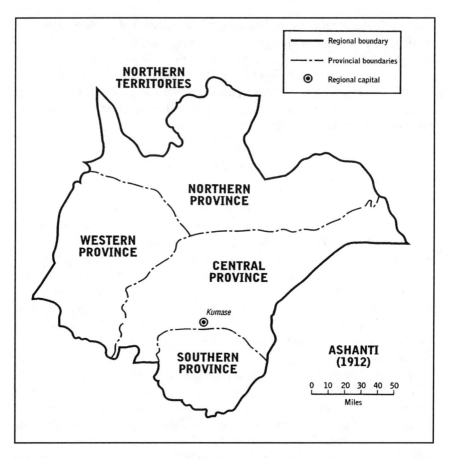

Map 1.4 Ashanti, 1912.
Source: Colonial Reports, Ashanti, 1912.

ting as much as a third of the crop from stranger cocoa farmers. Their efforts to collect tribute at the same rate in Asante evoked vehement protests, from cocoa growers and sympathetic commissioners alike, and tempers rose on all sides.[70]

At this potentially delicate juncture, it was the police magistrate who hit on a solution. Having learned from the director of agriculture that at the prevailing price of 5d/lb of cocoa beans, farmers realized about 15d on average from a mature cocoa tree, and might get 20d if they took "better care" of their farms, he proposed that chiefs "be permitted to charge 1d per tree per annum" as tribute. At 5 percent of the value of the crop, he argued, this would not impose an undue burden on farmers, and it might provide an incentive for better husbandry.[71] The police magistrate's proposal was unanimously endorsed by the Kumase Council of Chiefs, and Fuller wrote enthusiastically to the governor's secretary that he too supported the plan and "hoped there would be no objections." The governor was disinclined to hurry. "Pending the outcome" of the West African Lands Committee's investigations into "customary native tenure," he replied, there was nothing to be done. Inaction was soon overtaken by events. A few months later, Fuller informed his superior that the chiefs "have taken up 1d per tree" on their own.[72]

Indeed, "1d per tree" quickly attained the status of custom. Barely two months after the idea was first proposed, Fuller ruled in a dispute between Patriensa and Dwansa that subjects of either stool who had planted cocoa on land belonging to the other could continue on their farms, free of charge, for three years, but "must pay the usual tribute of 1d per tree to the owners of the land"[73] thereafter. In 1924, the district commissioners of the Eastern Province recommended that government recognize 1d per tree as the legal standard for cocoa tribute in Asante. Such an arrangement, they argued, was not "repugnant to the English sense of justice" and "closely resembles the native customary method of collecting tribute on indigenous crops."[74] One provincial commissioner went further: by helping stools get out of debt, he suggested, such a measure would "stabilitate [*sic*] their finances and consequently their administration."[75] Once again, the governor counselled caution: since 1d per tree "cannot be regarded as part of native customary law . . . ," chiefs would be better advised to place existing practice on a sound statutory footing by enacting by-laws.[76]

On the face of it, the governor's suggestion was an attractive one—not only would it expedite adjudication but, by encouraging Asante chiefs to engage in acts of formal legislation, would nudge them towards administrative modernity. On reflection, however, both chiefs and commissioners began to have doubts. If cocoa tribute were made a statutory requirement, it would become indistinguishable from a tax: government would become responsible for enforcing payment, rather than negotiating ad hoc compromises when disputes happened to break out, and the revenue collected would go into the stool's treasury rather than the chief's pocket. Moreover, forcing the issue of by-laws might reopen or inaugurate disputes over stool boundaries. In principle, all tribute collected on a given stool's land belonged to the occupant of the stool but, as one official pointed out, land is "actually divided up into parcels and held by Chiefs, Sub-chiefs and Headmen," and many chiefs received tribute from other chiefs' subjects. If by-laws were passed, all such arrangements would "be declared null and void—which is impossible."[77]

Two years after the issue was broached, the chief commissioner warned against precipitous action: the question of cocoa by-laws, he wrote, is "so intimately connected with the constitution of Native Treasuries . . . that until there is a decision arrived at regarding these, I have not pressed the amanhin to pass the[m]."[78] Eventually, the governor's office ratified prevarication: "His Excellency notes that you propose to postpone the passing of any Cocoa Tribute Bye-laws in Ashanti until the finances of the Stools are in order."[79] In fact, most stools never passed cocoa by-laws, and those that did rarely enforced them.

In addition to debating appropriate rates of cocoa tribute, chiefs and commoners argued over who was obliged to pay. Like their counterparts in the Colony, commissioners in Asante adopted the general rule that chiefs could demand tribute from strangers who were farming on their stool lands. But who was a "stranger"?

In the eighteenth and nineteenth centuries, the Asante state ruled over subjects of varied provenance. Formed through confederation and conquest, the precolonial polity included subjects of allied, conquered, and tributary chiefs, immigrants from other West African societies, and large numbers of captives and purchased slaves. Most Asantes belonged to one of several dispersed Akan matriclans, but the number and origin of these clans have been subject to debate, and it is not clear that they constituted the only criterion for membership in the Asante polity.[80] Rattray speculated that the clans evolved gradually from smaller "family" units and argued that membership in them was based on "belief in a common descent from some ancestress. . . ."[81] In contrast to Rattray's "evolutionary approach," Wilks has proposed a "'big bang' theory of Akan history"[82]—suggesting that the Akan matriclan was not a product of evolution but an organizational solution, developed in the fifteenth and sixteenth centuries, to the problem of mobilizing sufficient labor to clear densely forested land for farming. To facilitate labor recruitment, he adds, the clans were relatively open to outsiders, and both servile and nonservile strangers were readily assimilated.[83] With the consolidation of state power in the late seventeenth and early eighteenth centuries, separate clans and chieftaincies were merged into a unified polity, and "the descendants of free settlers became ɔmanmufoɔ, citizens."[84]

McCaskie argues that assimilation became more difficult over time, and that people of non-Asante origin were increasingly stigmatized as slaves. The state "not only preserved but also sedulously reinforced" the principle that jural status or citizenship was "exclusively vested in and defined by membership of an *abusua* and, more broadly, an *abusua kesee*"[85]; hence, slaves of non-Asante origin (*nnonkɔfoɔ*) "did not exist—fully and legally— as . . . person[s]" unless they could assimilate to an Asante lineage.[86] Arhin paints a different picture. Citing Rattray, he argues that slaves had clear, if limited, legal rights—to own property, marry, claim adultery fees, testify in court, and even litigate against their owners—and that "the effect of the enjoyment of these rights was to naturalise them as Asante citizens without guaranteeing their positive acceptance as members of the slave-owning lineages; they became inferior citizens."[87] But they agree that slave descent carried a lasting stigma, and that people of non-Asante origin were commonly presumed to be slaves or, at best, potential subversives.[88] Like allegations of slave ancestry, public reference to a person's non-Asante origins could be considered an actionable offense.[89]

The association between "citizenship" and descent had not lost its force when Britain annexed Asante at the end of the nineteenth century, and it continued to play a role in official thinking for some time afterwards. "Originally," wrote one administrator in the 1920s, the term "stranger" referred to people "from the Colony or the Northern Territories."[90] By the late nineteenth century, the balance of power in Asante had shifted from the central state towards the provincial *aman*, a trend that the British were eager to reinforce. As cocoa increased the returns on cultivated land, chiefs throughout Asante pressed for a broader definition. Not content to collect tribute from the relatively small population of non-Asante cocoa farmers,[91] they insisted that "strangers" included everyone farming on their stool lands who were not actually their subjects. The administration took the point. In 1913, Fuller proclaimed that, in connection with cocoa tribute, "'stranger'. . . means anyone Ashanti or non-Ashanti, not belonging to the particular Division or Clan, on whose territory he has made himself a Plantation."[92]

Fuller's ruling quickly became part of the lexicon of contestation over both tribute and citizenship. In 1917, for example, a group of farmers at Oyoko in Dadease denied that they were in arrears to Chief Yao Boaten for £600 cocoa tribute. Declaring that they had lived in Oyoko and Dadease and served Yao Boaten for a long time—even testifying on his behalf in land disputes with neighboring stools—the farmers complained that the chief was "cheat[ing] us out of our rights as citizens of the place by trying to claim tribute today."[93]

In the early 1920s, Fuller's successor (and erstwhile critic)[94] C. H. Harper attempted to revive the earlier meaning of Asante citizenship. Hoping to end a long-standing land dispute between the stools of Doyina and Esienmpon, Harper rejected Doyina's claim for tribute from subjects of Esienmpon who happened to be farming on Doyina's land. Not only were farmers entitled to the fruits of their labor, he argued, but as Asantes, the Esienmpons were no "strangers" in Doyina. If government ruled otherwise, Asante would soon become divided into a small number of large landlords and an extensive rent-paying population of small farmers. Such an outcome would be undesirable not because it was unjust—Harper was no socialist—but because it would "negate the principle of communal ownership which has hitherto been the basis of the social and tribal system of the Colony of Ashanti."[95]

There is little evidence to suggest that Harper's ruling interfered appreciably with the flow of cocoa tribute to Asante chiefs, or that it ended debate over the meaning of Asante citizenship. In 1924, the district commissioners of Asante collectively reaffirmed Fuller's rule that a "stranger" is "a native who is living or working on land belonging to a division whose Head Chief he does not serve."[96] Rather than being frozen, stabilized, or even clarified by colonial rule-making, "citizenship" could be redefined at the stroke of an administrator's pen. In 1915, hoping to end persistent friction between the chiefs of Juaben and Asokore, Fuller transferred Asokore and its discontents to Mampon. An immediate, perhaps unanticipated, consequence of the transfer was that an ongoing series of land disputes between Asokore and the neighboring stool of Efiduase were "resolved" by administrative fiat. To the dismay of both chiefs, their respective subjects—newly defined as "brothers" in allegiance to the Mamponhene—were declared exempt from all obligations to pay tribute to the other stool.[97] The new arrangement did little to alleviate tension or stabilize jurisdictional boundaries: Asokore's relations with Efiduase soured, and the chief got on no better with his new paramount than he had with the old one. The conflict "fizzled out when the Ashanti Confederacy was restored [in 1935] and Asokori broke away from Mampong,"[98] but debate continued over the broader question of who was a stranger. In the late 1930s, when the Ashanti Confederacy Council proposed to eliminate all but nominal tribute for Asantes farming on another stool's land, it was the Assistant Chief Commissioner who considered the proposal "customary" but impracticable![99]

PROPERTY AND PRECEDENCE:
THE CAREER OF ADONTENHENE JOHN KWAME FRIMPON

Collectively, as we have seen, Asante chiefs were well positioned to reap substantial rents from the expanding colonial economy, and they did. But no individual chief was guaranteed either a lifetime seat on the stool or unquestioned access to a stable flow of "customary" revenues. Accumulating wealth and influence required continual vigilance—to guard against rival claims to office, land, and subjects, as well as keep abreast of commercial opportunities—and ongoing participation in the interpretation of custom. The most successful rentiers were active in chiefly politics as well as commerce and the courts, and they often proved as resourceful at deploying historical precedents to defend or advance their interests as they were

at spotting commercial opportunities and calculating returns. The career of
Chief John Kwame Frimpon is a case in point.

Originally from Baaman, a village northeast of Kumase near Edweso,
Frimpon spent the closing years of the nineteenth century at the coast,
where he attended school and developed ties with both the British and
the "expatriate" community of Asante *asikafoɔ*—well-to-do traders who
had fled to the Colony to escape the escalating predations of the Asante
state.[100] It is not clear just when Frimpon returned to Kumase, but he
was on hand when the governor arrived, in March 1901, to consolidate
Britain's defeat of Yaa Asantewa by destooling her supporters and replacing them with "loyalists." Frimpon was made Adontenhene of
Kumase[101] and promptly embarked on an energetic and successful career in business and politics. "Monies [he] initially raised from stool
lands, traditional prerogatives and court fines were judiciously invested
in the modern sector—cocoa, timber, transportation, light-engineering
works and urban development."[102] He was deeply involved in the emerging land market in Kumase, as landlord, tenant, and intermediary—competing with foreign investors for prime commercial sites on Crown Land,
and leasing out portions of stool land to European firms and missions.[103]
He also negotiated leases on behalf of other chiefs and, "inspired by the
sense of what he considered a due return for services rendered," demanded a share of their rents.[104] For example, on New Year's Day in
1915, he and Amakomhene Kweku Atta co-signed a lease to the English
Society for the Propagation of the Gospel, for a parcel of land on the
Edweso Road. In 1929, when the city acquired the site to enlarge the
grounds of St. Augustine College, Chief Frimpon bargained for £72,
instead of the £60 initially agreed upon as compensation to the stool,
and pocketed a third of the proceeds.[105]

As a senior Kumase chief who was literate in English, Chief Frimpon
was well placed to mediate between Asantes and their colonial rulers, and
he took full advantage of his position to wield influence over both. Playing
adroitly on officials' expectations, he set out to maximize the advantages of
his dual role as chief and cultural broker.[106] In 1915, Atipinhene Kweku
Dua contested Chief Frimpon's claim to Ahwia, a village on the Ejura Road,
agruing that his (Frimpon's) ancestor had sold his authority over the people
at Ahwia and three other villages in the area to the then Asantehene, who
gave them in turn to the Atipin stool. The provincial commissioner was
prepared to assume that the land went with them but changed his mind
when he learned that residents of one village had already paid tribute to
Chief Frimpon—an act that suggested the chief's ancestor had "sold" the
people, but not the land. Kweku Dua took his case to the chief commissioner, but his appeal was dismissed, in part because "the plaintiff clears

the road."[107] In effect, Chief Frimpon won the case by outdoing his opponent in what the government expected of a chief.

He also combined business and politics in dealing with his colleagues on the Kumase Council, with results that impressed the administration. Together with his "forceful personality and aptitude for business," wrote one official, the "special recognition accorded to him by Government" had enabled Chief Frimpon not only to prosper but also to gain considerable "ascendancy" over other chiefs—negotiating their business transactions with Europeans, supporting them in litigation, and representing their interests to government.[108] In 1926, the governor described him as "a strong man, advanced, educated, a trader and wealthy," and added that "[h]e lends money; in fact practically all the Chiefs are indebted to him."[109]

Their indebtedness could be turned to political as well as financial advantage. For years, Chief Frimpon waged a vigorous campaign to parlay his position as head of the Adonten *fekuo* into claims on the income and property of his fellow chiefs. Appealing to the administration's investment in chiefly hierarchy, he insisted that the other Adonten chiefs were his subordinates, owing him homage, allegiance, and a share of their "customary" revenues from oath fees and fines. In 1906, he tried to persuade the chief commissioner to remove Amakomhene Eninbaja from the Kumase Council of Chiefs, observing pointedly that the Amakomhene had not only failed on many occasions to render customary homage and tribute to him, the Adontenhene, but was also in arrears to the government.[110] Fuller ignored the advice, but Chief Frimpon was not discouraged. After Eninbaja's death, he overrode staunch opposition to gain the Amakom stool for Kweku Atta who, according to the district commissioner, "has been obliged ever since to lean upon Chief Frimpon's support to appease his own subjects and to satisfy his creditors."[111] In 1920, he paid the fine to get another Adonten chief, Antoa Mensah, released from jail (where he had been confined for his role in the Yaa Asantewa rebellion) and reinstated as Antoahene in Kumase.

Both Fuller and his successor, C. H. Harper, treated Chief Frimpon as a key informant. In 1912, he was invited to give evidence in the first official enquiry into Asante land tenure, and his views were frequently cited in official memoranda.[112] Not long afterwards, when a complaint was lodged against Chief Frimpon by another Kumase chief, an official dismissed it as the work of men who feared being left behind "by the go-ahead section of the community."[113] In the book that Fuller published after he left Asante, Chiefs Frimpon and Nuama were featured prominently—a distinction much resented by the other chiefs on the Kumase Council, who complained to Fuller's successor that the "Ashanti nation [had been] falsely degraded by unreasonable people who knew nothing of its history" and demanded that the book be banned.[114]

Harper declined to censor his predecessor; in fact, he actively courted the Adontenhene. In 1920, he issued a judicial decision that supported Chief Frimpon's claims to ascendancy over the other senior Adonten chiefs.[115] He also appointed Frimpon to the Kumasi Public Health Board—a quasi-official body, composed primarily of Europeans, which functioned in the 1920s as a *de facto* municipal council—and even helped some of the chief's relatives find jobs in Accra.[116] Others in Kumase's European community were less enthusiastic. After a lengthy enquiry into the turbulent affairs of the Adonten *fekuo*, District Commissioner Furness-Smith discounted much of Chief Frimpon's testimony and repudiated Harper's earlier judgment. For the most part, he concluded, Chief Frimpon's claims to the subservience and property of the other Adonten chiefs were self-acquired rather than "traditional."[117] In 1926, when Chief Frimpon petitioned to recover a plot in Kumase, which government had appropriated but never used, the president of the Public Health Board gave grudging assent to his petition. Noting sourly that "Chief Frimpon [had acted] with his usual disregard for correct procedure and . . . complete lack of manners,"[118] he warned his colleagues to expect further petitions from the chief, "as his greed will be entirely unappeased by this."[119]

The other chiefs of the Adonten *fekuo* were equally sceptical of Chief Frimpon's claims. During Furness-Smith's enquiry,[120] Chief Frimpon, Amakomhene Kweku Atta, and Antoahene Antoa Mensah all testified at length, as did Chief Kwesi Nuama and several senior members of the Kumase Council. Much of the testimony centered on competing narratives of Asante history. Arguing that his stool had presided over the Adonten *fekuo* since the time of Osei Tutu, Chief Frimpon complained that Amakomhene and Antoahene had repeatedly contravened custom, by slighting their obligations to render him deference or homage on ceremonial occasions. They had also failed to turn over his rightful share of their oath fees (which they received for hearing disputes) and of the "drinks" and tribute from their stool lands. The other Adonten chiefs countered that Chief Frimpon's claims were opportunistic rather than traditional. They admitted that he had helped them negotiate leases, but denied that he was customarily entitled to a share of the proceeds. "[W]e received [payment] through him because he understands English and arranged the sale." Undaunted, Chief Frimpon continued to play to official ambivalence—admitting that many of his claims were based on government promises rather than tradition, while declining to answer inconvenient questions on the grounds that "it is against our custom to explain all these things to the British."[121]

The polyvalence of Chief Frimpon's politics were nowhere more apparent than in his complex relationship with the Prempehs. Within a
decade of Prempeh I's removal to the Seychelles, members of his family and the Kumase Council of Chiefs began to petition the government
to repatriate him. At first these appeals were firmly rejected, and they
were suspended during the war in Europe. By the early 1920s, however,
support for Prempeh's return had spread beyond Asante: the issue was
raised in the Legislative Council of the Gold Coast by leading members
of the Aborigines Rights Protection Society and some members of the
administration.[122] In December 1924, after a year of intense negotiations
over the conditions of his return, "Mr. Edward Prempeh" travelled to
Kumase at government expense, to take up residence as a private citizen.[123] As one of the most senior chiefs in Kumase, Frimpon took care
to associate himself publicly with these appeals. In 1912, he attempted
to establish a dynastic link with the royal clan by marrying Amba Kyaa,
a niece of the exiled Asantehene. However, the marriage soured and,
although Chief Frimpon wrote to Prempeh in the Seychelles, asking him
to arrange a reconciliation, Prempeh declined to do so. Soon afterwards,
the Adontenhene was accused of inciting a group of "youngmen" in
Kumase to defy the authority of the chiefs, on the grounds that "Prempe
will not come."[124]

Though Chief Frimpon continued to endorse petitions for Prempeh's repatriation, officials were well aware that he harbored mixed feelings towards the exiled Asantehene. During Furness-Smith's enquiry into the affairs of the Adonten division, Chief Frimpon went out of his way to portray
the Asantehene's office as an anachronism—arguing, for example, that since
the British had abolished the office of Asantehene, the old system of state
confiscation of personal wealth through death duties (*awunnyadeɛ*) had become unthinkable.[125] As the likelihood of Prempeh's return increased, Chief
Frimpon positioned himself on both sides of the "ex-king's" interests. A
few months before Prempeh's scheduled arrival, he warned the chief commissioner that the "youngmen" of the Kotoko Society were poised to demand his reinstatement as Asantehene and urged that the chiefs be made to
sign a bond, guaranteeing to keep the peace and hold Prempeh to his status
as private citizen.[126] A few weeks after the "ex-king" arrived in Kumase,
however, Frimpon joined a group of chiefs to request that Prempeh be allowed to build his house at Manhyia, instead of at the government's proposed site at Bantama. Bantama, they complained, was so far from Kumase
that it "will almost cut him off from his people."[127]

In the following months, the Adontenhene intrigued with the Kotoko
Society against the Kumase Council of Chiefs and vice versa, in the
apparent hope that divisions of any sort among Kumase's political elite

would weaken Prempeh's position.[128] He also tried to discredit Prempeh in the eyes of the administration. In March, the government was disconcerted to learn that Prempeh had sent a message of thanks to the chief of Yendi for helping to effect his return from the Seychelles. When Duncan Johnstone objected that Yendi had been independent of Asante rule since 1880 and hence took no part in Asante affairs, Prempeh countered that "Chief Frimpon has misled me."[129] In 1926, after unsuccessfully opposing Prempeh's elevation to the newly created office of Kumasehene, Chief Frimpon led the other Kumase chiefs in publicly expressing their gratitude for his promotion. And when Prempeh I died, in 1931, the Adontenhene both lobbied against replacing him—since "Nana Prempeh during his six and a half years administration did not do anything good for the Division"[130]—and tried to influence the government's choice of a successor.

Despite, or perhaps because of, his repeated attempts to thwart their return to power, both Prempeh I and his successor, Prempeh II, endeavored to coopt Chief Frimpon rather than openly oppose him. During Prempeh I's tenure as "Kumasehene," Chief Frimpon not only retained his seat on the Kumase Council of Chiefs but was also made head of one of the seven "clan courts," created in 1928 to help handle the large volume of litigation pending before the Kumase Native Tribunal.[131] As Adontenhene, he occupied a senior position on the "restored" Asante Confederacy Council after 1935 and was later appointed to its executive council. He also played an increasingly prominent role as a native court judge, presiding over some of the most important land and chieftaincy cases to come before the Asantehene's court in the late 1930s and 1940s. When colonial authorities "re-graded" a number of Asante stools in 1947, his was the only senior stool in Kumase to be accorded paramount status, placing it on an equal footing with those of the most senior chiefs of the realm.[132]

Throughout his long and active career, Chief Frimpon amassed a diversified portfolio of commercial assets and political connections, and he shifted resources among them in a tireless campaign to expand his wealth and power. As chief, judge, government confidant, and municipal appointee, he used his position to acquire claims on land and capital, and his capital to assert claims and exercise influence over both chiefs and colonial officials. He allied himself with most of the principal factions among Kumase's elite, playing government, chiefs, youngmen, and royals against one another with energy and insouciance. Sought as a key informant by the colonial administration, Chief Frimpon proved as adept at manipulating the contradictions of indirect rule as he was at playing the markets of Kumase. His career not only attests to the personal agility and persistence with which he negotiated the social landscape of colonial Asante but also illustrates how determined participation in the production and reproduction of custom helped to constitute the terrain of contest over wealth and power.

CONCLUSION

In their quest for historical precedents to legitimate claims over property and people, Asantes directed their energies and imaginations not toward cornering the market in historical knowledge—an impossible task—but to vigorous and continued participation in reproducing and interpreting it. Although "traditional history" repeatedly defied their efforts at codification and synthesis, colonial officials had little choice but to keep trying. In the process, they seesawed between determined efforts to compile and record definitive rules and boundaries, and pragmatic admissions that this was probably not possible. Representations of Asante history were never final: maps, charts, even judicial decisions, as well as oral narratives, remained subject to reinterpretation. Accumulation of wealth and power was predicated, *inter alia*, on the production of history, and history in turn was continually contested and reproduced in the course of struggles over land and office.

Struggles over wealth and power did not, of course, originate in the colonial period. From the early eighteenth until the late nineteenth century, the Asante state presided over a "marketplace of power" in which the monarchy maneuvered to appropriate or channel the resources and ambitions of its wealthy and powerful subjects and extend its control over the services and allegiance of lesser folk. Historians have debated how far the state realized its quest for hegemony: Wilks and McCaskie have focused on the state's efforts to control the wealth and energies of its subjects, while Austin, Akyeampong, and Obeng suggest that the divisibility of wealth and the universality of spiritual power made it difficult for anyone to monopolize either.

What changed under colonial rule was neither the interdependence of wealth, power, and belief nor the complexity of contestation, but the cast of contestants and the terms in which they framed and negotiated claims. Rather than confiscate and redistribute subjects' wealth, in the manner of its precedessor, the colonial state sought to define and regulate the terms on which office and resources were acquired or exchanged. Their efforts drew officials into debate, with and among their "subjects," over the relative merits of competing claims and the historical precedents on which they were often based. Incorporated into the apparatus of colonial administration, chiefs enjoyed multiple opportunities to appropriate surplus *if* they could successfully argue their claims to land and subjects, but the price of success was continued engagement in the process of negotiation and debate. In this context, it appears, rent-seeking did not simply divert surplus wealth from productive investment to conspicuous consumption, although that certainly happened; it also entailed a process of making and debating claims on people, land, and history, in which the proliferation of possible precedents and connections tended to subvert official efforts to demarcate stable boundaries between land holdings and chiefly jurisdictions. Access to wealth and power depended less on codifying boundaries or the terms of surplus extraction than on continued participation in debates over their interpretation.

NOTES

1. Austin, "No elders"; Akyeampong and Obeng, "Spirituality."
2. Austin, "No elders," 24.
3. Akyeampong and Obeng, "Spirituality," 506–7.
4. W. Tordoff, *Ashanti under the Prempehs, 1888–1935* (London: Oxford University Press, 1965), 43ff; T. J. Lewin, *Asante before the British: The Prempean years, 1875–1900* (Lawrence: Regents Press of Kansas, 1978), 161–62.
5. Tordoff, *Ashanti*, 82ff; Wilks, "On which foot was the boot?" in C. Lentz and P. Nugent, eds., *Ethnicity in Ghana* (New York: St. Martins, 1999).
6. Wilks discusses in detail the problems that resulted from the bifurcated colonial administration in Asante and the Gold Coast Colony. Wilks, "On which foot?"
7. Dissatisfaction with death duties and other levies had contributed to the conflicts which engulfed Asante in the 1880s, and traders were vocal in their opposition to any resumption of such levies under colonial rule. K. Arhin, "Some Asante views on colonial rule: As seen in the controversy relating to death duties," *Transactions of the Historical Society of Ghana* 15, no. 1 (1974): 63–84. See also I. Wilks, *Asante in the nineteenth century: The structure and evolution of a political order* (Cambridge: Cambridge University Press, 1975); McCaskie, *State and society*; Lewin, *Asante*; and ch. 2.
8. See, for example, NAGA ADM 12/5/114, CCA to CS, 3/3/23, and governor's memorandum on that letter.
9. T. J. Lewin and D. Fitzsimons, "The political organization of space in Asante, Parts I–III," *Asante Seminar*, nos. 4–6 (1976).
10. Evidence given before the Kyidom Clan Tribunal in Kumase, 1928, quoted in T. C. McCaskie, "*Ahyiamu*—a 'place of meeting': An essay on process and event in the history of the Asante state," *Journal of African History* 25, 2 (1984): 182.
11. The history of cocoa growing in southern Asante has been analyzed in detail by Gareth Austin. See, e.g., Austin, "Emergence" and "Capitalists and chiefs."
12. Chiefs could collect license and court fees and raise levies to meet stool expenses, and they received a portion of the fines that they imposed as penalties in the courts. Jurisdiction in civil cases was limited to small amounts, however, and colonial officials consistently refused to grant chiefs the power to collect taxes—a prerogative reserved for the state. For further discussion of debates over what constituted "taxation," and its relevance for struggles over land and chiefly office, see ch. 2 below.
13. Grier, "Contradictions"; Phillips, *The enigma of colonialism*. Both Grier and Phillips argue, persuasively, that restrictions on land sales served the interests of the

colonial regime, but they draw opposite conclusions—Grier maintains that the policy succeeded in stunting the growth of African capitalism, while Phillips argued that African farmers and traders became capitalists in spite of it. Neither study explores the tensions generated by the contradictions of colonial policy or their implications for the process (as opposed to the rate) of accumulation.

14. A decade later, officials were lamenting that more land had not been claimed when the Crown "was in a position to dictate terms." NAGA ADM 5/3/13, Belfield Report, 1912.

15. National Archives of Ghana, Kumase (NAGK) 316, CEP to CCA, 10/2/28. See also Berry, "Hegemony," and Berry, *No condition is permanent*, ch. 5.

16. The idea that land was traditionally inalienable in Africa derived, in part, from arguments advanced by the Aborigines Rights Protection Society and others to prevent the British from appropriating "unused" land in the name of the Crown. See Berry, "Hegemony" and *No condition is permanent*.

17. See, *inter alia*, Arhin, "Some Asante views"; Arhin, "Rank and class among the Asante and Fante," *Africa* 53, no. 1 (1974): 2–22; Arhin, "Trade, accumulation and the state in Asante in the nineteenth century," *Africa* 60 (1990): 524–37; and Arhin, "Monetization and the Asante state," in Guyer, ed. *Money matters*; McCaskie, "State and society, marriage and adultery: Some considerations towards a social history of precolonial Asante," *Journal of African History* 22 (1981): 477–94; McCaskie, "*Ahyiamu*"; McCaskie, *State and society*; Wilks, *Asante* and Wilks, *Forests of gold*.

18. Transactions in allegiance or authority over subjects are not to be confused with the buying and selling of slaves, which was also a common practice in precolonial Asante. See, e.g., Wilks, *Forests of gold*; McCaskie, *State and society*; A. N. Klein, "Inequality in Asante: A study of the forms and meanings of slavery and social servitude in pre- and early colonial Akan-Asante society and culture" (Ph.D. diss., University of Michigan, 1981).

19. McCaskie, "*Ahyiamu*," 176.

20. NAGA ADM 11/1/1338, Organization and constitution of Kumase stools, 1924. The speaker, Adontenhene John Kwame Frimpon, is discussed in detail below.

21. NAGK 6, Chief Commissioner, Kumasi, to Colonial Secretary, Accra, 1/4/06, Reorganization of Ashanti, 1906, 1930.

22. As I have argued elsewhere. Berry, "Hegemony" and ch. 2 of *No condition is permanent*. See also R. Gocking, "Competing systems of inheritance before the British courts of the Gold Coast Colony," *International Journal of African Historical Studies* 23, no. 4 (1990): 601–18; and Gocking, "British justice and the native tribunals of the southern Gold Coast Colony," *Journal of African History* 34, no. 1 (1993): 93–113.

23. In 1921, the Ashanti administration created its own Anthropology Department, under the direction of Capt. R. S. Rattray. Published in three volumes, Rattray's studies remain classic works of reference on Asante history and ethnography. Rattray, *Ashanti*; *Religion and art in Ashanti* (Oxford: Oxford University Press, 1927); and *Ashanti law and constitution* (London: Oxford University Press, 1969; first published in 1929).

24. In addition to recording their judgments in particular disputes, commissioners issued general rules to be followed in judging future cases. Some of these colonial dicta came to be looked upon as "custom": in 1928, for example, one district commissioner observed that "the 'Fuller' scale of adultery fee has become Native custom all

over Ashanti. . . . " NAGK 318, DC Mampon to CEP, 6/15/28. The case of cocoa tribute is discussed below.

25. McCaskie, "*Ahyiamu*," 176; and McCaskie, *State and society*, 87, 227ff.

26. Lawyers were barred from practicing in Asante until 1933. Tordoff, *Ashanti*, 115ff., 309.

27. NAGK 721, Land dispute between Kumase and Ojesu. Doyina-Ejisu Boundary, 1907, 1927. In another claim against Nyamieni, the Chief of Kwaaso testified that land his ancestors had purchased from Nyamieni was taken away by Asantehene Kwaku Dua but given back by Prempeh I, in return for Kwaaso's support—the kind of exchange referred to in the oath at Ahyiamu. See also NAGK 538, Traditional histories of divisions, 1929.

28. Wilks, *Forests of gold*, 245.

29. NAGK 721, Land dispute between Kumase and Ojesu.

30. NAGK SCT 211/4/694 and 6/696.

31. A counterinterpretation is offered, with respect to some localities in the Colony, by K. Firmin-Sellers, *Transformations of property rights in the Gold Coast* (Cambridge: Cambridge University Press, 1996).

32. According to Fuller, Asantes paid only token amounts of tribute for access to land and natural resources "until we taught them the value of rubber." NAGA ADM 5/3/13, Belfield Report, 1912, 14.

33. Rattray, *Ashanti law*, 354–55. Rattray bases his interpretation on conversations with the head chief of Kumawu. I encountered the same expression during numerous conversations, in Kumawu and elsewhere, in 1993–94.

34. NAGK 577, Bartrop to CCA, 1/25/05.

35. For a discussion of Chief Frimpon's long and multifaceted career in business and Asante politics, see below.

36. NAGA ADM 11/1/1313, CCA to CS, 8/28/16.

37. Ibid.

38. NAGK 6, CCA to CS, 1/4/06.

39. Ibid., CS to CCA, 8/27/06.

40. NAGA ADM 5/3/13, Belfield Report, 1912, 87. How often this was done is not clear. It is likely, however, that such outlays were an early and nagging source of dispute over the difference between chiefs' private income and the revenues of their stools. This issue is discussed more fully in ch. 2.

41. NAGK 713, Refusal of Kodwo Tawiah to remain under Ejisu, 1907; NAGK 736, Respecting some 100 subjects of Chief Yaw Awuah . . . , 1908; NAGK 746, Chief of Biposu—re his intention to take his land of Biposu and serve with it under the Chief of Kokofu, 1911, 1923.

42. NAGK 736, Respecting some 100 subjects of Chief Yaw Awuah, 1908.

43. Manhyia Record Office (hereafter MRO), Kumasehene's Native Tribunal Record Book, 1926.

44. NAGK 316, PC Sunyani to CCA, 9/18/28.

45. MRO, Kumasehene's Native Tribunal Record Book, 1926. A decade earlier, the chief commissioner awarded a disputed tract of land on the Ejura Road to the "plaintiff [who] clears the road." NAGK 875, Chief J. Q. [*sic*] Frimpon v. Chiefs Kweku Dua and Kwamin Adabor, 1915.

46. NAGK 6, CCA to CS, 1/4/06.

47. In 1907, Edwesohene Yaw Awua charged that a village headman, Kodwo Tawia, had flouted his authority by refusing to build a house at the Edwesohene's court, bringing a "fetish" to his village without informing the Edwesohene, and failing to pay his share of the fee for a liquor license for Edweso. NAGK 713, Refusal of Kodjo Tawia to remain under Ejissu, 1907.

48. NAGK SCT 30/5 and 30/6. Boundary Book, Chief Commissioner, Ashanti.

49. The National Archives of Ghana serve today as a major repository of historical material deemed relevant to contemporary disputes over property and power. Over a period of eight months in 1993 and 1994, when I visited the archives in Kumase two or three times a week, I never encountered another academic researcher in the Search Room. All the other patrons were searching for evidence to use in cases then under litigation.

50. NAGA ADM 11/1160, Legis. Co. Min., 10/16/05.

51. Ibid., Guggisberg to CS, 6/30/06.

52. Ibid.

53. NAGK 684, CCA to CS, 7/18/07.

54. Ibid., 8/12/08.

55. NAGA ADM 11/242, SNA to CEP, 5/18/10.

56. Ibid., SNA Minute, 10/23/12.

57. NAGK 797, CCA to CEP, Colony, 7/17/13.

58. NAGA ADM 11/1/1371, Surveyor-General's Memorandum, 10/1920.

59. NAGK 850, K. Ashanti to PC, 3/17/17 and 4/10/17.

60. Ibid., DC's Report, 10/21/24.

61. NAGA ADM 11/1/1371, Surveyor General's Memorandum, Oct. 1920.

62. NAGA ADM 11/1/1000, Memorandum, 4/26/28.

63. NAGK 316, CWP to CCA, 9/18/28.

64. In 1993, the Ghanaian government undertook a pilot project to register land holdings in one or two neighborhoods of Accra and announced plans for a similar experiment in Kumase. Queried about the likely progress of this exercise, the head of the Lands Commission in Kumase observed sagely that "it will take time."

65. M. Chanock, *Law, custom and social order: The colonial experience in Malawi and Zambia* (Cambridge: Cambridge University Press, 1985), 46–47; and Chanock, "Paradigms, policies and property: A review of the customary law of land tenure," in Mann and Roberts, eds., *Law in colonial Africa*, 82.

66. A late colonial report on land tenure in southern Asante concluded that since customary court rulings "turned on questions of historical fact . . . rather than . . . legal principles . . . , it has not proved possible to abstract . . . any general principles of Akan tenure" from court records. Quoted in Kyerematen, *Inter-state boundary litigation*, 36. See also Berry, "Hegemony," 336ff.; and Berry, *No condition is permanent*, 32ff.

67. For instance, Edwesohene Yaw Awuah's disputes with Beposo and Doyina, first brought before the commissioners in 1907, were still under adjudication in 1927 and 1955 respectively. NAGK 721, Land dispute between Kumase and Ojesu, 1907, 1927; NAGK 943, Chief Yaw Nimo, Doyina, v. Omanhene Kojo Buaten, Ejisu, 1927; NAGK SCT 211/4/694, Kwaku Ware, Gyasehene, Ejisu, v. Kwabena Boateng, Donyina, 3/30/53–2/9/55.

68. NAGK 796. CWP to Chief Seketia, 1/8/13.

69. Ibid., Minute by CCA. The year before, Fuller told Belfield that "any member of the tribe" could cultivate cocoa free of charge, as long as he gave a tenth of the crop to the chief. NAGA ADM 5/3/13, Belfield Report, 1912, 14.

70. NAGK 797, Correspondence between CCA and CEP, July–Sept. 1913. See also NAGK 814, Penny per cocoa tree, 1914.

71. All quotations in this paragraph are from NAGK 2743, Police Magistrate to CCA, 8/29/13.

72. Ibid., CS to CCA, 10/6/13 and CCA to CS, 7/6/14.

73. Fuller's ruling was cited as a precedent in a number of subsequent cases. See, e.g., NAGK 1507, Correspondence between CCA and PCs, 6–7/24; Memo on the history of cocoa tribute, 10/27. Applications of the ruling varied, however: farmers often avoided the labor of counting trees by agreeing to an annual lump sum payment. NAGK 780, Payment of cocoa rent . . . , 1915; NAGK 898, Cocoa tribute, 1916; MRO ACC, Cocoa tribute, 1949–53.

74. NAGK 1507, DCs' Conference, Kumase, 10/15–18/24. Compare Mann & Roberts, eds., *Law in colonial Africa*, "Introduction."

75. Ibid., PCEP to CCA, 12/13/24.

76. Ibid., CS to CCA, 2/20/25. The Native Jurisdiction Ordinance of 1924 had introduced provisions permitting chiefs to enact by-laws on a limited range of issues.

77. NAGK 1507, Memorandum, October 1927.

78. Ibid., CCA to CS, 3/19/26.

79. Ibid., CS to CCA, 1/25/28. The search for an "orderly" solution to the question of stool finances is discussed in ch. 2 below.

80. Rattray, *Ashanti law*, 64, listed eight matriclans. Pointing out that Bowdich identified twelve in 1817, Wilks suggests that the matriclans "not only came into existence in specific historical circumstances but also are slowly passing out of existence as circumstances change." Wilks, *Forests of gold*, 78. I was told on several occasions that nowadays, many people "don't remember" what clan they belong to. In 1994, however, the Ministry of Local Government and Chieftaincy Affairs circulated a list of clans and their respective animal totems to Asante stools, asking senior chiefs to identify their clan(s) and those of their subordinate chiefs.

81. Rattray, *Ashanti law*, 63.

82. Acknowledging that evidence on land use and tenure in the sixteenth and seventeenth centuries is virtually nonexistent, Wilks explains that "it is necessary to extrapolate from more recent practice, described by Rattray, Busia and Fortes." Wilks, *Forests of gold*, 99. A. N. Klein has criticized his argument as ahistorical, but it has proved popular with other historians. See Klein, "Slavery and Akan origins," *Ethnohistory* 41, no. 4 (1994) 627–56; I. Wilks, "Slavery and Akan origins? A reply," *Ethnohistory* 41, no. 4 (1994) 657–65; McCaskie, "State and society," 482ff.; McCaskie, *State and society*, 25; Akyeampong and Obeng, "Spirituality," 490.

83. Wilks, *Forests of gold*, esp. ch. 2.

84. Ibid., 99. Wilks's argument may strike some readers as technologically determinist. People have farmed in other West African forests without developing corporate matriclans.

85. McCaskie, *State and society*, 88. *Abusua* refers to a matrilineage or lineage segment; *abusua kesee,* or big lineage, to a matriclan.

86. Ibid., 89.

87. Arhin, "Rank and class," 12.

88. In 1820, Dupuis learned that "many thousands of Fantes, Assins and Gamans" were kept as slaves or prisoners of war in villages around Lake Bosomtwe and suggested that "the territory thereabouts may be considered the Siberia of the Court." Quoted in McCaskie, *State and society*, 89.

89. Ibid., 99. In 1920, Kumawuhene Kweku Boaten filed a complaint against a man who, he alleged, had referred to him in public as the child of an Anwa, or northerner. NAGK 27, Enquiry into the Kumawu Omanhene's complaint, 5/31/20. See also Rattray, *Ashanti law*, 40; Arhin, "Rank and class," 11–12; and Klein, "Inequality."

90. NAGK 1507, Memorandum on cocoa tribute, October 1927.

91. Most non-Asantes who worked in the cocoa-farming sector were employed as laborers or, at best, sharecroppers. Before the 1940s, when migrants whose cocoa had been destroyed by swollen shoot disease began to move into Asante from the Eastern Region, most cocoa farmers in Asante appear to have been of Asante origin. W. H. Beckett, *Akokoaso* (London: Percy, Lund Humphries, 1944), 5; Austin, "Emergence," 263; J. Adomako-Sarfoh, "Migrant cocoa farmers and their families," in C. Oppong, ed., *Domestic rights and duties in southern Ghana* (Legon: Institute for African Studies, 1974); P. Konings, *State and rural class formation: A comparative analysis* (London: Kegan Paul), 63–64.

92. NAGK 2743, CCA to CS, 10/6/13.

93. NAGK 862, Chief Yao Boaten v. Chief Kobina Safu and others, 7/4/17. As often happened in such disputes, Fuller asked the district commissioner to negotiate a compromise, which he did.

94. After a period as cantonment magistrate in Kumase during the early years of Fuller's tenure as chief commissioner, Harper served as chief secretary to the governor in Accra, where he conducted much of the governor's correspondence with the Asante administration. See also Wilks, "On which foot . . . ?"; J. Brown, "Kumasi, 1896–1923: Urban Africa during the colonial period" (Ph.D. diss., University of Wisconsin, 1972), 170.

95. NAGK 1507, Memorandum on cocoa tribute, 10/27.

96. NAGK 1507, DCs' Conference, 10/15–18/24.

97. This particular incident occurred in 1915. Around that time, similar administrative rearrangements "settled"—or aggravated—land disputes between Patriensa and Juaso, Asokore and Kumawu, and Esienmpon and Doyina. NAGK 1507, passim.

98. NAGK 942, Juaben-Effiduase Boundary Dispute, NAGK 1264, Acting District Commissioner to CCK, 3/19/36. Justified officially as a return to the *status quo ante pax Britannica*, the "restoration" marked yet another reorganization of the chiefly hierarchy in Asante. I will discuss this episode in ch. 3 below.

99. NAGK 1231, Warrington's Comments on the Minutes of the Confederacy Council, 11/30/38.

100. NAGA ADM 11/1/1338, Constitution and organization of Ashanti stools, 1924. See also K. Arhin, "A note on the Asante *akonkofo*: A non-literate sub-elite, 1900–1930," *Africa* 56, 1 (1986): 25–31; Austin, "No elders"; Lewin, *Asante*, 215; and McCaskie, *State and society*, 69ff.

101. NAGA ADM 11/1/1900, Part I, Ashanti rising, 1900–1901, Governor to SSC, 3/3/01.

102. T. McCaskie, "Accumulation, wealth and belief in Asante history. II. The twentieth century," *Africa* 56, 1 (1986): 12–13.

103. NAGK 2149, Indenture, 1/1/1915; NAGK 2372, Kumasi Chiefs Lands, 1926.

104. NAGA ADM 11/1/1338, Report on Enquiry into the Tribal Organization of the Adonten Abrempon of Kumasi, 3/24/25: 26. See also NAGA ADM 5/3/13, Belfield Report; NAGA ADM 11/1/1902, Chief Commissioner's Diary, 4/7/22; NAGK 2372, Chief Frimpon to CCA, 7/5/26; Tordoff, *Ashanti*, 161, 192, 230ff.; Brown, "Kumasi"; McCaskie, "Accumulation II," 12–13.

105. NAGK 2149, Indenture, 1/1/1915, and correspondence, 2/28/29.

106. Two of his nephews, Isaac and Edward Asafu-Adjaye, who were educated in England at Chief Frimpon's expense, also figured prominently in Asante's political elite from the late 1920s.

107. NAGK 875, Chief J. Q. Frimpong v. Chiefs Kweku Dua and Kwamin Adabor, 1915. Chief Frimpon also claimed land and people outside Kumase, including a dozen villages at Eduabin, ca. 10 miles south of the city near Feyiase. NAGA ADM 11/1/1338, Report, 3/24/25. In 1918, Chief Frimpon was involved in a dispute with the Kokofuhene over the land at Eduabin, and his successors are involved in litigation there today. NAGA ADM 12/5/160, Chief Commissioner's Confidential Diary, 1/19/18; and interviews with Adontenhene Agyeman Nkwantabisa III, July 24–26, 1996.

108. NAGA ADM 11/1/1338, Report, p. 26.

109. NAGA ADM 11/1/1905, Governor's secret memo, 2/12/25.

110. NAGK 2585, Chief Frimpon to CCA, 10/29/06.

111. NAGA ADM 11/1/1338, Report, p. 25.

112. NAGA ADM 5/3/13, Belfield Report, 1912.

113. Ibid., PM to CCA, 3/9/12; NAGK 2372, Kumasi Chiefs' lands, 7/27/26.

114. NAGA ADM 11/1/1902, Chief Commissioner's Diary, 12/8/21. See also F. Fuller, *A vanished dynasty: Ashanti* (London: John Murray, 1921).

115. NAGA ADM 11/1/1338, Report, Appendix A.

116. NAGA ADM 11/1/1902, Chief Commissioner's Diary, 12/8/21 and 1/11–30/22.

117. NAGA ADM 11/1/1338, Constitution and organization of Kumasi stools, 1924.

118. NAGK 2372, Minute by President, KPHB, 7/27/26.

119. Ibid.

120. A complete transcript of the testimony, as well as Furness-Smith's report, is contained in NAGA ADM 11/1/1338, Constitution and organization of Kumasi stools, 1924, from which the excerpts quoted here are taken.

121. Chief Frimpon also served as a key informant for other colonial inquiries into Asante history and customs, such as NAGA ADM 5/3/13, H. C. Belfield Report on legislation governing the alienation of native lands in the Gold Coast Colony and Ashanti, CD 6278, 1912. See also Tordoff, *Ashanti*, 230ff.

122. Tordoff, *Ashanti*, 182–83.

123. Ibid., 184–86. Official debates over the timing and terms of Prempeh's return are extensively documented in, *inter alia*, NAGA ADM 11/1/1899, Nana Prempeh and others, 1910–1932; ADM 11/1/1901, Ex-King Prempeh—return of, 1911–1925; and ADM 11/1/1902, Chief Commissioner's Diary, 10/31/19–4/30/22.

124. NAGK 2449, Chief Kofi Sencherey et al. to CCA, 4/3/12; see also NAGA ADM 11/1/1905, Deputy PC to CCA, 8/11/25.

125. NAGA ADM 11/1/1338, Constitution and organization of Kumasi stools, 1924.

126. NAGA ADM 11/1/1901, Frimpon to CCA, 7/6/24.

127. NAGA ADM 11/1/1899, Chiefs to CCA, 1/10/25. As a member of Prempeh's "maintenance committee," Frimpon was instrumental in raising money to build his house and buy him a car. NAGA ADM 11/1/1905, Secret memo from PC Duncan Johnstone, 3/13/25.

128. NAGA ADM 11/1/1905, Governor's secret memo, 2/12/25. The Kotoko Society, a group of "youngmen" led by members of the royal family, saw Prempeh as a counterweight to the Kumase chiefs and lobbied energetically for his reinstatement as Asantehene. By July, Chief Frimpon had turned against them, urging the government to break the power of the "young Bolsheviks," and mended his fences with the other Kumase chiefs. Ibid., Duncan Johnstone to CCA, 7/28/25; CCA to Governor, 7/29/25.

129. Ibid., PC Duncan Johnstone's secret memo, 3/13/25. Duncan Johnstone accompanied Prempeh on his return voyage from the Seychelles and was assigned to keep a close watch on his activities during his first few months in Kumase.

130. NAGA ADM 11/1/1342, Akyaw-Brempong to Colonial Secretary, Accra, 6/12/31.

131. When the Native Jurisdiction Ordinance was first enacted in 1924, all of Kumase was placed under a single customary court, presided over by the newly repatriated "Kumasehene" Prempeh I. The volume of cases proved far too great for one court to handle, however, so in 1928, the government established a separate native tribunal for each of the *fekuo* (military divisions of the precolonial Asante state). They were referred to, confusingly, as "clan courts." See, e.g., Tordoff, *Ashanti*, 252ff. On Chief Frimpon's role in the Adonten Clan Court, see NAGK 1077, Kumasi District–Handing over reports of, 1931–1941.

132. Chief Frimpon was eventually destooled and died soon afterwards, in 1948. NAGK 2854, Asantehene to CCA, 3/7/47; NAGK 1231, Ashanti Confederacy Council Digest, 1935–49.

2

UNSETTLED ACCOUNTS: STOOL DEBTS, CHIEFTAINCY DISPUTES, AND THE QUESTION OF ASANTE CONSTITUTIONALISM

In a recent study, Fred Cooper argues that strikes and other forms of labor protest had a clarifying effect on official thinking not only about labor policies but also about the aims and, ultimately, the viability of colonial rule.[1] As Africans went on strike, from the Copperbelt to the docks of Mombasa and the Gold Coast Railway, to demand better wages and working conditions, colonial administrators first envisioned and then embraced the idea of an African working class and the possibility that African workers could be managed with the same kinds of labor codes and social welfare policies that obtained in Europe. Of course, the image of a working class applied only so far in Africa. Colonial officials never fully understood the way African workers lived or the place of wage employment in African society, and they were dismayed when their newly acquired understanding of Africans as universal workers was challenged, in the 1950s, by former strike leaders who began to insist on Africans' rights to political autonomy. Nonetheless, as Cooper shows, the effects of recurrent, often highly effective strikes were far-reaching. As officials confronted the financial and political implications of providing *all* Africans with social welfare benefits and economic development comparable to those of Europe, they decided it was time to abandon the imperial enterprise.

Chieftaincy disputes had an even longer history in colonial Africa
than strikes but did far less to clarify officials' thinking. Embedded in
systems of governance that colonial administrators regarded as "customary," chieftaincy disputes bore little obvious resemblance to forms
of political contestation in Europe. Their ubiquity tended to reinforce
rather than challenge the official presumption that Africans were different—backward, childlike, and unfit to master the methods of modern
administration or withstand the temptations of expanding commercial
opportunity. Convinced that the vast majority of their colonial subjects
would never approach European levels of political and organizational
sophistication, administrators did not question the necessity of colonial
rule, but they worried a good deal about how to implement it. To this
end, chiefs were crucial. Lacking the means to organize and operate
large establishments of European officials to govern colonial peoples as
well as to exploit their resources, colonial regimes had to rely on the
labor and cooperation of Africans. Understanding traditional systems of
authority and social order was essential to strategies of colonial governance in Africa, yet custom proved frustratingly elusive. This was not
because African ideas about authority and social conduct were beyond
European comprehension; rather, to the extent that power was, in practice, shared, or at least dispersed, among colonizers and those they
claimed to rule, it was also subject to negotiation, contest, and debate.
Chieftaincy disputes were neither symptoms of the "breakdown" of traditional order and morality nor simple manifestations of newly emerging patterns of class conflict, but part of an ongoing struggle to define
and exercise legitimate authority in a society both transformed and de-
stabilized by the imposition of colonial rule.

In the following pages, I will explore this point with specific reference to the early period of colonial rule in Asante. Though the position
of the chief in colonial Asante was a relatively privileged one, it did not
go unchallenged.[2] Contests among rival contenders for office and popular protests against the conduct of incumbents were frequent, often prolonged, and sometimes violent. At first, colonial officials treated them,
with a mixture of contempt and tolerance, as inherent in traditional culture. "By a fortunate coincidence," wrote Chief Commissioner Fuller in
1907, "it appears to be part of an Ashanti chief's duties to dislike all
other chiefs." The resulting divisions being stronger "than mere patrio-
tism or hatred of our rule," he added, the government could afford to
reduce the size of the Kumase garrison.[3] Later, as increasingly formal
codifications of custom failed to stem the tide of disputes, officials worried that *they* were to blame—for having disrupted the orderly hierarchy
of traditional society in their haste to dismantle the precolonial state,

depose and deport rebellious chiefs, and reward colonial sympathizers with office, land, and subjects. As we shall see, their reinterpretations led to shifts in policy that helped to keep debates going rather than bring them to a close.

For Asante chiefs and commoners, struggles over chiefly succession and destoolment were linked to pursuit of wealth, legitimacy, and influence, but in complex ways. Access to land and labor and the division of income were important issues but not the only ones, and attitudes toward the colonial state were not one-sided: both chiefs and commoners were as likely to appeal to the administration for support in their struggles with one another as to combine in opposition to colonial rule. In the profusion of chieftaincy contests, which continued, unabated, throughout the colonial period, struggles over wealth and influence took the form of conflicting accounts—disputed accounts of stool finances and contested accounts of custom and historical precedent. Debates over stool debts, in particular, were not straightforward contests over chiefly greed or integrity but multifaceted struggles to determine who was accountable to whom and for what. These debates revolved, in turn, around questions of historical precedent, and they led to further debate over what was known about past events and by whom. Chiefs, commoners, and commissioners did not agree, among themselves or with one another, as to how such questions should be answered, but they all took part in the debates, whether or not they approved of or even admitted to doing so. Taken together, their debates and struggles were no passing phase in Asante's transition to modernity but rather the core of the colonial political process.

This chapter explores interrelations among stool debts, chieftaincy disputes, and the production of knowledge about Asante "custom," through a case study of conflict in Kumawu—a stool that, like those of other outlying provinces of the precolonial state, enjoyed considerable autonomy from Kumase under colonial rule. I begin by discussing some of the causes of stools' indebtedness in the early colonial period, and the place of stool debts within broader debates among colonial officials, chiefs, and commoners over where to draw the line between public finance and private income and wealth. I then describe a series of disputes over destoolment and chiefly succession that kept Kumawu in an uproar for most of the decade from 1915 to 1925, and prompted debate between the governor and the Asante administration over "the principles of Twi constitutionalism"[4] and the practice of indirect rule. Stemming directly from struggles over stool accounts and chiefs' accountability, the crisis in Kumawu contributed to the government's decision, in 1935, to "restore" the Asante Confederacy.[5] In the years following the restoration, stool treasuries were established, many stool debts were written off, and the issue subsided as a central point of contention in chieftaincy disputes. But the struggles continued.

THE CHIEF'S POCKET AND THE PUBLIC PURSE

Most colonial administrators agreed with Chief Commissioner Maxwell that "ninety percent of stool troubles in Ashanti are caused by reckless finance."[6] Stools were frequently in debt, and chiefs' efforts to pay off their debts by imposing levies on their subjects were a source of perennial friction. By reducing or, better yet, eliminating stool debts, officials hoped to assuage popular discontent, reduce the number of disputes, and strengthen the edifice of chiefly authority on which indirect rule was predicated. Administrators were convinced that the long-term solution must be institutional: the creation of native treasuries, wrote Maxwell in 1926, is "the most important work in Ashanti today."[7] But this was easier said than done. The necessary legislation was in place by the late 1920s, but getting chiefs to follow the rules was another matter. The district commissioner of Mampon voiced a common complaint when he wrote, in 1937, that the Asokore stool "is hopelessly in debt and [its] finances . . . a jumble of unintelligent accounting. . . ."[8]

How did stools get into debt? To colonial officials and their scholarly contemporaries, the crux of the problem was litigation. Tempted by the rewards of colonial commerce and bewildered by bureaucratic procedures, chiefs, they felt, had been drawn into an escalating cycle of competition over land, money, and office, which rendered them unable (or unwilling) either to refrain from litigation or to control its costs. As early as 1912, a chief in Kumase told a government investigator that most stools were in debt because of land litigation, adding candidly, "mine is."[9] A colleague disagreed: since lawyers were prohibited from practicing in Asante, he argued, chiefs only spent money "on entertainment."[10] But the implied distinction was not clear-cut. In 1916, after winning a boundary dispute with the chief of Pekyi, Chief Kwame Ashanti of Tredeh sued his former rival, hoping to recover the £275 that he had spent in litigation over their mutual boundary. Most of the money, he explained, had been used to transport twelve stool elders, eighteen subjects, and an unspecified number of witnesses from Tredeh to Kumase and maintain them there for four months while the case was pending before the chief commissioner.[11] Even without lawyers, litigation could be expensive.

In 1933, lawyers were finally admitted to Asante courts and Asante chiefs' outlays on legal fees began to rival those of their counterparts in the Colony. In 1945, a government inquiry into the costs of stool litigation found that

> the majority of states in the Colony and in Ashanti have been, and many still are, in debt. Though there are other contributing factors, litigation is undoubtedly the main cause of the indebtedness. Stool debts caused by litigation generally arise out of litigation over land and particularly out of boundary disputes.[12]

In the thirty-two disputes for which the commission collected detailed information, the costs of litigation ranged from £40 to over £20,000, with a median of £1,700 per case.[13]

These data are dramatic, but they provide only partial support for the commission's conclusion that litigation was the principal source of stool debts. In the mid-1930s, for example, an official review of accounts for the chronically indebted (and disputed) stool of Asokore showed that roughly half of the stool's expenditures from 1934 to 1936 had gone for litigation.[14] But what about the other half? In neighboring Nsuta, no one mentioned litigation in 1933 when, following the installation of a new chief after a decade of dispute, a debt of £2499 suddenly "appeared."[15] Chiefs' outlays on litigation were substantial, sometimes ruinous, but they were not the whole story.

For some contemporary observers, colonial rule was as much to blame as chiefs. "Stool litigation," wrote Meyer Fortes in 1948, "exemplifies . . . the incompatibility between the old social structure and modern development. [A chief] is no longer primarily the servant of the community and their intermediary with the ancestors. He is as much or more the servant of the White Man." Chiefs' "direct relationship with the administration," he added, "stimulated their desire to aggrandise themselves at the expense of their neighbors. . . . "[16] Expanding on Fortes' critique, Simensen and Grier argue that conflicts over stool debts and destoolments were a sign of capitalist exploitation. With the backing of the colonial state, chiefs operated as both landlords and capitalists—extracting rent from the expanding production of cocoa, rubber, timber, and gold; keeping down the cost of labor by limiting ordinary farmers' and farm workers' opportunities to accumulate property;[17] and participating directly in the rising class of "cocoa capitalists," as farmers and traders on their own account.[18]

If chiefs often behaved as rentiers and capitalists, however, it does not necessarily follow that their subjects comprised an emerging class of peasants and workers. Opponents of a particular chief were likely to include an assortment of people—subchiefs and commoners, women and men of all ages and lineages, prosperous as well as poor. Grier acknowledges this point but insists that "at the heart of the conflict was the struggle between the traditional ruling class of royals and other privileged lineages, on the one hand, and the 'commoners' or 'young men,' persons of unfree or poor lineage, on the other."[19] To read "youngmen" as a synonym for the poor and disadvantaged is, however, misleading: in Asante parlance, "youngmen" refers simply to free persons without office, or the majority of the population. Moreover, privilege was as likely to adhere to particular people as to entire lineages, and protests were usually directed at unpopular chiefs rather than the institution of chieftaincy *per se*. Subjects rarely repudiated a chief's right to make demands on them and were more likely to complain if s/he failed to litigate in defense of the stool's lands than if s/he spent money in doing so.[20] Popular anger was roused less by chiefs' spending more money than they collected than by their refusal to explain what they had spent it for.[21]

To commissioners struggling with the conflicts and confusions of the present, it was tempting to see the past as a golden age in which Asante beliefs and institutions functioned smoothly, to the benefit of all. "In former days," rhapsodized the assistant chief commissioner, in 1934, "disputed elections were unknown and bribery in connections with election [*sic*] was unknown."[22] In 1921, the Asante administration established its own Anthropology Department, hoping to rediscover the virtues of the past in order to reinstate them. After his first few weeks with the new department, Captain Rattray assured his superiors that "no opportunity has been missed of instituting a propaganda among these people . . . [to convince them that] our culture, . . . dress, ideas, arts and customs should not be embraced and superimposed upon their own to the entire extinction of what is just and good in their own national institutions."[23]

For Rattray, what was just and good about Asante institutions was, in part, their functionality. Public finance was a case in point. In the past,

> everything a Chief brought with him when he came upon the Stool became sunk in the Stool property. If he were destooled, he could not take anything away without special permission, even what had been his own property before he became Chief. In consequence of this law a Chief never regarded his tenure of office as a possible occasion on which he might enrich himself.[24]

Writing in the late 1940s, the Asante scholar K. A. Busia went even further, reflecting nostalgically on a precolonial past when "the chief's social personality was completely merged in his office"[25] and chiefly aggrandizement was unheard of. By virtue of his office, a chief was obliged to maintain a large household of wives, offspring, kin, and retainers, and he also "provided food and drink for those who visited him, rewarded the services of his subjects, and distributed presents at religious festivals."[26] Redistribution, in other words, did not depend on individual altruism but flowed automatically from the structural logic of Asante's constitution, and chiefly aggrandizement was a modern invention.

Rattray's and Busia's encomiums on precolonial fiscal practice have not been borne out by subsequent historical research. As Wilks, Arhin, McCaskie, and Austin, among others, have shown, social status in precolonial Asante was closely related to wealth. Rank often followed wealth—the coveted title of *ɔbirempɔn*, in particular, was reserved for those who could afford the lavish ceremonies of installation[27]—but "relative affluence or deprivation was [also] a reflection of one's political position. . . . "[28] McCaskie describes the case of Yamoa Ponko, a successful trader who began in the 1760s to invest in land and subjects. He donated land at Anyinasu to his father's stool, as a kind of down payment on the office;[29] then he leased the land back from the stool and settled his subjects there to trade on his behalf. Over the course of his career, Yamoa Ponko amassed a fortune. He was rewarded with two of the most senior stools in Asante and, shortly before his death in about 1785, achieved the rank of *ɔbirempɔn*. After he died, the state claimed most of his gold as *awunnyadeɛ*—the "death duties" that were levied on personal wealth—but as stool property, the land at Anyinasu was exempt from taxation. Far from performing a kind of constitutional alchemy that turned chiefs' private wealth into public property, stools in precolonial Asante could be bought, sold, mortgaged, and used to shelter individually acquired wealth from inheritance taxes imposed by the state.

By the early twentieth century, then, the notion that a chief's property was indistinguishable from the stool's was probably anachronistic. It was certainly impractical. If, on succeeding to office, a chief's income and assets became one with the stool's, the reverse was also true: whatever the occupant of a stool decided to do with its resources was, by definition, for the stool's benefit. If chiefly aggrandizement was unthinkable, so was chiefly accountability: a chief could hardly be held *personally* accountable for property that belonged to the stool. Indeed, by insisting it was customary for a chief to merge his/her personal property with that of the stool, officials tended to defeat their own efforts to prevent chiefly aggrandizement. Rather than eliminating stool debts and forestalling disputes, the conflation of private with public property encouraged chiefs to evade accountability and provoked their subjects to try to unseat them.

It also contributed to stool debts. While commissioners and commoners held to the view that, according to custom, when a chief took office, his property became indistinguishable from that of the stool, chiefs insisted that the tribute, fees, and gifts accruing to their office were theirs to dispose of as they saw fit. In effect, both sides tended to conflate public and private accounts: the difference was that while commissioners thought chiefs should devote their personal resources to the public good, chiefs were more inclined to treat the perquisites of office as personal income. The result was a standoff. In 1912, Fuller assured his superiors that chiefs would use "their rents" to maintain the roads.[30] Twenty years later, his successors were still trying to convince stoolholders that "cocoa tribute for land access ought to be treated as a form of public money."[31]

The ambiguities of chiefly finance emerged clearly during a revealing set of exchanges in the Gold Coast Colony between the administration, the chiefs of Akyem Abuakwa, and a group of settlers, known as the New Juabens, whose forebears had fled Asante during the British invasion of 1874 and settled in Akyem. Though physically scattered throughout Akyem, the New Juabens maintained allegiance to a common chief and claimed separate but equal political status vis-à-vis the Akyems. Unlike the migrant cocoa farmers[32] who came later, the New Juabens did not purchase land in Akyem, nor did they pay tribute on the cocoa farms that they eventually planted. In 1918, the Akyem State Council resolved that, like other strangers, descendants of the New Juaben settlers should pay cocoa tribute at the going rate of one-third of the crop. The New Juabens refused, and the government backed them up, arguing that chiefs were not authorized to impose taxes. The Akyem State Council was obliged to settle for a "voluntary rent" of £1 per farm.[33]

In 1927, taking advantage of a new native administration ordinance,[34] the paramount chief of Akyem Abuakwa, Nana (Sir) Ofori Atta, reasserted his right to tax the New Juaben settlers—this time demanding 1d per cocoa tree, the rate that had been officially approved in Asante in 1913.[35] By the late 1920s, however, cocoa prices had fallen substantially and the real burden of the tax had risen accordingly. More determined than ever to resist the chiefs' demands, the New Juabens insisted that they were Asantes and hence under no obligation to pay taxes to the Akyem stool. But they also claimed that, as long-term residents of Akyem, they were "naturalized with the Okyeman from the time immemorial" and, like indigenes, were entitled to farm on Akyem land without paying tribute to anyone.[36] Ofori Atta countered that they could not have it both ways and insisted that, as "strangers," the New Juabens owed cocoa tribute to the stool.[37]

Official opinions were divided.[38] The secretary for native affairs insisted, as a matter of principle, that chiefs had no authority to levy taxes independently of the government. The governor was willing to allow the stool to collect cocoa tribute from the New Juabens, to help defray its debts, but only if the chief would agree to establish a stool treasury. Ofori Atta was eager to raise revenue but unwilling to submit stool expenses to government audit. Beating a strategic retreat on the issue of taxation, he suggested that cocoa tribute was not a "tax" but a "private" arrangement between settler farmers and the indigenous "owners" of the land, in which government had no right to interfere.[39] Like the New Juabens, Nana Ofori Atta sought to have his cake and eat it too—invoking the history of the Juabens' migration and the principle of stool ownership to support his claims to tribute, but rejecting the government's view that tribute was a form of public revenue that belonged to the *oman* rather than the *omanhene* and must be publicly accounted for.

Throughout the debate, key participants articulated their positions in ambiguous, even contradictory terms. Colonial officials both upheld and restricted chiefs' authority; Ofori Atta defined cocoa rents as both public and private income; and the New Juabens claimed to be both Asantes and citizens of Akyem. Viewed in the context of these ongoing struggles, efforts to appropriate cocoa income appear less as a sustained attempt to define and enforce a single system of property rights[40] than as moments in a continuing proliferation of rules and historical precedents. Rent-seeking was a matter not of clarifying and enforcing the rules but of participating in their ongoing reinterpretation. A similar dynamic was at work in Asante.

CRISIS IN KUMAWU

In 1916, after a reign of twenty years, Kumawuhene Kwame Afram was destooled. He had been the target of disaffection before, but Chief Commissioner Fuller and the district commissioner, Alex Norris, who admired the Kumawuhene, were inclined to dismiss his critics as jealous upstarts. Both men understood chiefly power in Asante as authoritarian and hierarchical, and they sought to uphold it as a cornerstone of British rule. In 1915, for example, when one of the Kumawuhene's drummers defected to the Basel Mission in Akwapem, Norris fetched him back, "explain[ing] to the Mission that we could not allow this kind of thing as it would lead to any man who does not want to serve their masters [*sic*] running away and saying they are Christians."[41] Both Norris and Fuller considered Kwame Afram an exemplar of traditional authority: "the finest chief we have . . . , loyalty personified. . . . "[42]

The commissioners' enthusiasm for Kwame Afram was not universally shared by his subjects. In May 1915, when disaffection was already rife in Kumawu, the chief was accused of having embezzled money from the

government's War Fund. At first, Norris dismissed the charges as slander-
ous but later, after riots broke out in the town, he investigated and found
them to be true. Hoping to save face for the chief as well as his superiors,
Norris persuaded Kwame Afram to repay the money *and* to add £300 from
his own pocket, as a gesture of loyalty and reconciliation.[43] He then informed the chief commissioner that the *omanhene* had made peace with the
"youngmen" and deserved to "avoid disgrace."[44]

The rioters did not get off so easily. Norris "removed the five Princi-
pals," locking them up in the Sunyani jail to keep them out of trouble while
he went on leave to England.[45] For good measure, he also arrested three
clerks and banished them from Kumawu. The hapless clerks had not taken
part in the riot: their principal offense appears to have been that they "knew
book palaver" and had promised that if the rebels "listened to their guidance—they would shew them how to win their cause."[46] On the eve of his
departure, Norris warned Fuller that a party of Kumawu "youngmen" was
en route to Kumase to appeal his decision, adding that "I trust you will
uphold my order, whatever you think of it."[47]

Fuller obliged, but the chief's opponents were not mollified. In January
1916, perhaps emboldened by the commissioners' backing, Kwame Afram
indulged in "an outburst of passionate abuse" against his detractors, which
was followed by further riots.[48] Norris, by then returned from England,
quelled the disturbances but did not succeed in silencing demands for the
chief's destoolment. In April a group of "Elders and youngmen" petitioned
the government to remove Kwame Afram from the stool. In addition to
embezzlement, they charged the chief with levying heavy fines for trivial
offenses, "misconducting himself with the youngmen's wives," "marrying
women of close kin and affinity," insulting both "youngmen" and elders,
and generally indulging in "tyrannical rule and . . . improper conduct."[49]

As news reached Accra of the depth and duration of the crisis in Kumawu,
the governor grew alarmed, then annoyed. In May, he was dismayed to
discover that the acting chief commissioner's report on the January riots
had failed to mention either Norris's finding of embezzlement or the changes
made by the "youngmen" against the chief. Norris was rebuked for accepting financial restitution from the Kumawuhene while ignoring popular demands for his destoolment: "Government had allowed itself to be bought
off by a contribution to the War Fund."[50] By the end of the month, Norris
had "requested" and received a transfer to another district.

While the governor deplored Norris's poor judgment in making light of
the Kumawuhene's financial peccadillos, he was more disturbed by the
Asante commissioners' apparent disregard for political principle. "An
Omanhene in Ashanti is an elected Chief of his people who have a perfect
right, according to native custom, to destool him if he has betrayed his

trust."[51] In Kumawu, he concluded, the people rioted because they believed
that

> the Omanhene was secure of the support of the local Government in any
> circumstances, and that it would be vain to address a petition for his
> deposition to you through the D.C. This impression was strengthened by
> the extravagant eulogies of this Chief which were delivered in His
> Excellency's presence by Mr. Norris, who described him as "the best
> chief in Ashanti," and scouted the idea of allowing him to be deposed.[52]

In all, the governor expressed "deep displeasure" not only with Norris but
also "with the attitude assumed by the Government of Ashanti towards native questions, as that attitude is revealed by an examination of its dealings
with the people of Kumawu."[53] Norris and Fuller, he concluded, had shown
not merely poor judgment but "an apparent failure to grasp the basic principles of Twi constitutional law and customs"—adding that "the real delin-
quent in this case is the CCA."[54]

In October, the "malcontents" prevailed: Kwame Afram was destooled
and banished to Efiduase. Accompanied by more than seventy wives,
offspring, kin, and retainers, the ex-chief left Kumawu "unbroken in
spirit, . . . as arrogant as ever," and vowing to return.[55] Fuller acqui-
esced in his protégé's downfall but vigorously defended his own understanding of Asante custom. After Prempeh I was deported, he reminded
his superiors, chaos reigned in Asante until Stewart took command, in
1902, and the role of Asantehene "devolved upon the British administration."[56] As the ranking representative of that administration, the chief
commissioner was, in effect, the modern successor to the Asantehene. If
government failed to appreciate this fact, Fuller intimated, the people of
Asante were not so obtuse: they had never claimed "democratic powers" and deferred to the administration in all matters of "internal politics." Two Kumawu subchiefs and their "youngmen," he added, had actually written to thank him for his role in destooling Kwame Afram.
"Had they for a moment considered that the power of destoolment rested
with them, they would never have addressed me such a letter."[57]

In short, the political crisis in Kumawu set off a debate over constitutional principles, which reverberated throughout the Gold Coast administration. The depth and persistence of opposition to the Kumawuhene raised
questions not only about the conduct and capability of individual officials
but also about the principles of chiefly succession in Asante. Brushing aside
Fuller's claims that the malcontents in Kumawu were aberrant troublemak-
ers—"youngmen" who had no right under customary law to unseat a chief—
the governor argued that social order had been jeopardized in Kumawu

because the Asante administration had ignored legitimate popular demands. His doubts did not, however, extend to the merits of colonial rule itself. Instead, he concluded that what was needed to make indirect rule work was a better understanding of Asante custom.

THE STRUGGLES CONTINUE

If Kwame Afram's destoolment satisfied the governor that justice had finally been done, it did little to restore tranquillity in Kumawu. The new Kumawuhene, Kweku Boaten, proved no less controversial than his predecessor. Within a year of his accession, fresh disturbances broke out. Once again, controversy focused on the stool's finances, and the commissioners were faced with a choice between suppressing dissent and sacking the chief.

Kweku Boaten, a successful cocoa buyer, was not a member of Kumawu's royal family. The elders accepted his bid for the stool primarily because he promised to take personal responsibility for the stool's outstanding debt. Sources give different figures for the amount of the debt, but officials and townspeople agreed that much of it stemmed from the riots that led to Kwame Afram's destoolment in 1916.[58] In effect, Kweku Boaten purchased the stool by undertaking to pay the fines of stool subjects who, in their efforts to unseat his predecessor, had been convicted of riot and assault—and had also paved the way for his own succession.

Having accepted Kwame Afram's downfall, Fuller wasted little time on regrets. Within a week of his erstwhile protégé's departure from Kumawu, the chief commissioner was ready to welcome the new chief: "slippery, astute and sycophantic, . . . he is, nonetheless, a firm believer in the Government and has invariably rendered me assistance when called upon to do so."[59] While admitting that Kweku Boaten had probably intrigued and bribed his way to office, Fuller "confessed to a feeling of relief" that the elders had chosen him, "instead of some nonentity without brains or influence."[60] He even produced a geneaological table purporting to show that Kweku Boaten "was descended from former Kumawu Omanhins on his mother's side . . . "—a story that officials carefully preserved as long as Kweku Boaten remained on the stool and abandoned as soon as he left it.[61]

Once assured of the commissioners' approval, however, Kweku Boaten set out to profit from his office rather than endow it. He seized farms and houses belonging to his predecessor, claiming that they were stool properties; confiscated the goods of traders who incurred his displeasure; and imposed heavy fines for trivial offenses.[62] He even tried to back out of his promise to pay off the stool's debt—imposing a levy on his subjects to cover the cost, rather than absorbing it himself.[63] His audacity cost him the support of two of Kwame Afram's most outspoken opponents. One, Bodomasehene Kwame Toa, was a lifelong activist in Kumawu politics, who boasted of having destooled both Kwame Afram, in 1916, *and* his predecessor, Kwesi Krapa, in 1896.[64] The other, Yaw Kusi, a trader from Ofinso, was one of the men whom Norris had sent to jail in 1915 for rioting against Kwame Afram. Kweku Boaten rewarded Yaw Kusi's opposition to Kwame Afram by appointing him to the office of Gyasehene but, when Kweku Boaten reneged on his promise to pay off the stool's debt, Yaw Kusi turned on his patron and began a campaign to destool him. In May 1918, Kumawu was again shaken by rioting and, in June, Yaw Kusi was banished from the town. Less than a week after his departure, two "youngmen" took up the cause, charging Kweku Boaten with a list of offenses that ranged from illegitimacy and greed to attempted murder.[65] Like the clerks whom Norris had arrested in 1915, they too were banished for having gotten above themselves—in this case, for contravening the "custom" that only elders had the right to press destoolment charges against a chief.[66]

Like his initial endorsement of Kweku Boaten, Fuller's subsequent handling of the stool debt question was more opportunistic than principled. The alacrity with which he welcomed the new chief[67] suggests that the chief commissioner was more concerned to get the stool's debts paid than worried about where the money came from. Although he had questioned the legitimacy of the debt, declaring at one point that debts incurred to pay the fines of rioters were not the responsibility of the stool,[68] in approving Kweku Boaten's candidacy, Fuller tacitly endorsed the elders' decision to sell the stool to a nonroyal—in order to defray a "debt" the legality of which he denied! Consistency, to say nothing of constitutional principle, was evidently not the chief commissioner's primary concern in managing the affairs of the Kumawu stool.

Elders and subjects were also ambivalent toward the stool's debt. In agreeing to pay the debt out of his own pocket, Kweku Boaten may have had no other motive than personal aggrandizement—an argument borne out by his subsequent behavior—but the elders' eagerness to have it paid is somewhat harder to explain. In accepting Kweku Boaten's offer to purchase the stool by paying the rioters' fines, the elders implied not only that the chief's wealth and political ambition qualified him for office but also that the stool was financially responsible for the cost of political protest. In general, Asante stool elders jealously guarded their "constitutional" prerogative to appoint and destool their chiefs, insisting that the only acceptable way for "youngmen" to express dissatisfaction with a chief was by politely informing the elders of their grievances. Ostensibly, the subchiefs and elders of Kumawu subscribed to this dictum, but their willingness to sell the stool (even to a pretender) in order to avoid having to hold riotous "youngmen" to account for their actions suggests that they did not always find it expedient to practice what they preached.

Though the administration supported Kweku Boaten, as they had Kwame Afram, by punishing his detractors, the chief eventually bowed to popular pressure, canceled the levy, and paid the stool's debt himself. Tensions in the community subsided and, toward the end of 1919, some of the exiled rioters petitioned to be allowed to return to their homes and farms, though Kweku Boaten complained that members of Kwame Afram's family—notably his mother, his queen mother, and several of his sisters—continued to intrigue against him.[69] Early in 1920, however, a scandal erupted that even Kweku Boaten was unable to face down.

Three laborers, engaged to dig a grave, discovered objects at the gravesites of some of the town's earliest settlers which suggested that the graves themselves might contain gold.[70] The news was conveyed to the Kumawuhene, who sent the gravediggers packing and despatched two of his associates to investigate. What happened next is not clear, but the treasure—comprising, by some accounts, three large vessels of gold dust worth £11,000—disappeared, and the townspeople whose forebears occupied the graves in question accused the Kumawuhene's messengers of stealing it. On 22 January, the two men were charged before the Kumawuhene and elders, found guilty, and imprisoned. That night they "escaped" from jail—the door was later said to have been left unlocked—and, six days later, their bodies were found hanging from a tree in the forest near Bodomase.

In the ensuing uproar, the Kumawuhene fell under suspicion for complicity (if not outright responsibility) in the prisoners' deaths and the disappearance of the gold, and his opponents seized the occasion to renew their efforts to destool him. At first the commissioners defended him but, after the chief's house was attacked by a mob and Kweku Boaten himself beaten severely enough to require hospitalization, they withdrew their support. On 10 September, Chief Commissioner Harper destooled Kweku Boaten without even bothering to investigate the charges against him: the chief's position, he declared curtly, had become "untenable."[71]

Following the Kumawuhene's disgrace, the commissioners moved unilaterally to stabilize the stool's finances. They drew up a "Kumawu Constitution," which directed that the stool create court and financial records, keep them up to date, and open a bank account. However, they backed away from imposing a political settlement, preferring to place the onus of consensus on the community by insisting that they would not confirm a successor to the stool unless the choice was "nearly unanimous."[72] By 1921, the stool's debts had been paid and the remaining exiles returned home without incident, but the elders remained deadlocked over the choice of a new chief. A campaign to reinstate Kwame Afram drew support from prominent chiefs in Kumase, as well as from his friends and relatives in Kumawu,[73] and Harper expected that they would prevail. However, led by Kwame Afram's old adversaries—Bodomasehene Kwame Toa and Kweku Boaten's queen mother, Adwoa Serwaa—the "opposition [proved] stronger than expected."[74]

Two years later, with no end to the deadlock in sight, the district commissioner intervened and a new chief, Kwabena Kodua, was installed.[75] Although the elders gave formal assent to his candidacy, the new chief owed his position entirely to the government. When asked, in 1923, to sign a petition urging the administration to repatriate the ex-Asantehene from exile in the Seychelles, Kwabena Kodua begged the district commissioner to advise him, as "he did not know what course to take."[76] His tenure in office lasted less than two years and, in December 1925, Kwame Afram was finally reinstated, fulfilling his defiant promise of 1916.

To be sure, the district commissioner imposed conditions.[77] Kwame Afram had to promise to retain Adwoa Serwaa as queen mother and furnish the district commissioner with an account of his private debts, which were to be kept separate from the stool's. He also promised to refrain from repeating any of the offenses with which he had been charged in 1915. Finally, the chief and his supporters agreed to make "a free gift"—amounting to £1065 10s of their own money—to defray the stool's accumulated debts.[78] Once again, the commissioners put solvency ahead of principle and proved themselves complicit in what Chief Commissioner Harper condemned as "a practice of buying and selling stools."[79]

"THE POWER IN THE STORY"[80]

Throughout the decade of political turmoil in Kumawu, both combatants and peacemakers appealed to history to advance and defend their claims. Between 1920 and 1925, colonial officials made at least four separate attempts to compile authoritative versions of the geneaology of Kumawu's royal family and the structure and functions of its offices—consulting the chief and selected elders when the stool was occupied and their own files and colleagues when it was not.[81] Individual chiefs and elders also furnished historical briefs to substantiate their respective agendas. Ohemaa Adwoa Serwaa, who opposed Kwame Afram's reinstatement on practical grounds,[82] buttressed her position with a lengthy history of Kumawu, in which she claimed, *inter alia*, that Kwame Afram was "grandson" to a former Kumawuhene whose disgraceful conduct had led to his descendants being forever barred from the stool.[83] The views of her ally, Bodomasehene Kwame Toa, on royal geneaology are not recorded, but he liked to recount his own history as a kingmaker whenever the opportunity arose.[84] Kwame Afram's supporters also stressed the importance of history to good governance and the welfare of the community. As Kumawuhene, they pointed out, Kwame Afram had successfully defended stool lands against rival claimants but, under his successor, Kumawu lost a land case with Asokore because "we had no one capable of giving the history of the disputed land. . . . [N]o one else knows the history."[85]

In Asante, it is said, "the chief speaks with the voice of the ancestors."[86] In conversation, chiefs often refer to their predecessors in the first person: "I fought with Osei Tutu at Feyiase," as if the famous battle of about 1700 had occurred within living memory. Like the ubiquitous formula "from time immemorial" (which is as likely to be heard today in arguments before the high court as in casual conversation), chiefs' syntactic identification with sometimes distant ancestors conflates history with custom, suggesting that authority gains legitimacy in the present from the fact of its exercise in the past. Similarly, colonial officials, chiefs, and commoners often invested particular historical events with the weight of constitutional principle, invoking a timeless past to construct a charter for the present. In citing Kwame Afram's knowledge of history as evidence of his suitability for office, the chief's supporters portrayed him as a living repository of both historical and constitutional knowledge.

If chiefs, who "know custom," often tell conflicting stories, then the very premise that history constitutes a single corpus of shared constitutional knowledge embraces the possibility of multiple versions and future reinterpretations. In colonial Asante, chiefs' and commissioners' avowed commitment to custom allowed them to claim certainty while simultaneously entertaining doubts; to invoke the authority of constitutional principle without resolving the question of *which* historical precedents merited the status of custom. In effect, "custom" embraced both a set of constitutional principles and an ongoing practice of historical narrative and interpretation. If the former was unchanged, in theory, "from time immemorial," the latter clearly entailed an interactive and performative process, in which rules and social relations were continually reaffirmed and redefined through the (re)production of history. When told in a judicial venue or some other public forum—whether as family history, legal testimony, royal pronouncement, praise poem, or political ritual—historical accounts and allusions claimed authority for both narrator and narrative.[87] Neither reactionary nor visionary, custom in colonial Asante was a process of active engagement between past and present.

While chiefs told many stories, colonial officials alternated between portraying custom as fixed and timeless and lamenting its vagaries and elusiveness. Their efforts to compile definitive statements of custom were punctuated by expressions of doubt that such a project was feasible, and each official enquiry was followed, sooner or later, by another.[88] When Kwame Afram returned to the stool of Kumawu, at the end of 1925, Rattray was collecting material for *Ashanti Law and Constitution.*[89] He "had the honor to be present at the ceremony"[90] when Kwame Afram was reinstated, and soon afterwards he returned to Kumawu to gather data. Although Rattray's enquiries in Kumawu were completed in a couple of weeks, the evidence he collected there figured prominently in the book. On the subject of land tenure in particular, Rattray's conversations in Kumawu led him to make substantial revisions in his own earlier thinking.

As its title suggests, *Ashanti Law and Constitution* was intended as an authoritative compendium of customary law. Rattray rarely mentions individuals by name in the book, and he never enumerates his informants.[91] His field notes make it clear, however, that his inquiries in Kumawu consisted primarily of conversations with Kwame Afram, supplemented by a few exchanges with the chief's mother, Yaa Amponsa, and the ex-Krontihene, Kweku Kodua. Both Yaa Amponsa and Kweku Kodua had remained loyal to Kwame Afram during his exile, challenging his detractors and organizing repeated petitions to the government for his reinstatement.[92] Yaa Amponsa, at least, was rewarded for her efforts: not long after his installation, Kwame Afram reneged on his promise to retain Adwoa Serwaa as queen mother and appointed Yaa Amponsa in her place.[93] Rattray makes no mention in the book of either the decade of turmoil that preceded his inquiries in Kumawu, or the parts played therein by his informants. On the contrary, he describes Kwame Afram (without mentioning his name) as a living repository of customary knowledge—"one of the most learned exponents of the old Ashanti law," whose words "may . . . be accepted as more than the mere *obiter dicta* of a learned custodian of the law and be taken as a fairly accurate statement of the traditional rules upon this subject."[94] Like Fuller and Norris, Rattray was evidently prepared to accept political success as presumptive evidence of historical expertise.

During his first twenty years on the stool, Kwame Afram had worked energetically to defend and advance the stool's claims to land and revenue. He contested the stool's boundaries with Kwahu and Mampon; he intervened in a land dispute between Kwaman and Beposo, and a quarrel between the Manwerehene and Tafohene over land and subjects at Drabonso; and he lost no opportunity to press his own stool's claims to homage, fees, and tribute.[95] In his conversations with Rattray, however, the Kumawuhene glossed over his own history of efforts to defend or extend stool territory,

stressing instead the antiquity of the stool's rights to land. Most stools, he explained—his own included—had originally acquired their land either by settling their people in an unoccupied area or by fighting for it. In the case of Kumawu, the people had followed his ancestors to their present site long before the founding of Asante. "In olden times, the *Oman* (tribe) all resided in one large town"[96]—people went out into the surrounding countryside to hunt and farm but returned to town to sleep. Later, the stool allocated portions of its land to subchiefs and heads of families who, in turn, distributed land among their followers.

From Kwame Afram's stylized account of the way stool lands came to be partitioned, Rattray constructed an explanation of their origin that reversed his own previous conclusions. In an earlier work, Rattray had postulated that stool lands were a relatively recent innovation, having emerged toward the end of a gradual process in which isolated, self-contained families (or "kindreds") had evolved into larger social units ("clans" or "tribes").[97] Stool lands and chiefs emerged gradually, as families chose one family head to preside over the others. In *Ashanti Law and Constitution*, Rattray repudiated this theory and declared, largely on the basis of Kwame Afram's testimony, that stool lands had come into being at a moment of "revolutionary" social change brought on by the transition from hunting to agriculture.[98]

When Asantes took up farming, Rattray declared, they gave up "roaming" and settled permanently on portions of stool land allocated to them by the head chief. The subdivision of stool lands did not lead to political instability: subjects continued to serve their chief and, indeed, risked losing their land rights if they did not. With the advent of "our beneficent rule," however, subjects were freed from "the most onerous" of their traditional obligations to the chief, namely, military service. "Stool revenues have correspondingly diminished . . . [together with] respect, discipline and obedience."[99] Because they had already allocated most of their lands to subchiefs, *head* chiefs in particular found themselves excluded from the benefits of rising land values and the spread of commercial agriculture in the colonial era. Thus, Rattray concluded, the chronic indebtedness of Asante's principal stools was directly attributable to the partition of their lands. "Unless steps are taken soon," he warned, "we shall find Stools and all the wonderful organization they represent broken and, at least metaphorically, bankrupt."[100] To avert such a calamity, he recommended that government allow head chiefs to recoup their finances by imposing taxes on their subjects![101]

In the culminating volume of his corpus on Asante custom, then, Rattray revised his earlier views on land tenure to make the case that Asante chiefs should be granted powers of direct taxation in order to defray their debts. And, in justifying so radical a departure from established government policy, he relied almost exclusively on testimony that (despite his disclaimers) was far from disinterested. In depicting Kumawu as a polity whose members had spread over the countryside from a single point of origin, receiving allocations of land from his own ancestor, Kwame Afram offered a version of the stool's history that clearly served to underscore his own claim, as head chief, to control its lands. Whether his subjects would have agreed, in 1926, we do not know: Rattray did not ask. Among their descendants, history is by no means a matter of consensus. In 1994, conversations with more than fifty Kumawufoɔ yielded substantial agreement that the chief controlled stool land but many different accounts of how the stool had been founded and portions of its land settled.[102]

Rattray not only limited his inquiries in Kumawu to three informants, but his reading of their testimony was decidedly selective. In describing how he allocated land to his subjects, Kwame Afram explained that he never *said* "I present this land to you," but rather "I give you this land to eat on" or "to look after for me."[103] He added, however, that he really *meant* "I present it to you," because both he and the land seeker understood that he would never try to take it back—unless, of course, a subject refused to continue to serve the stool. From this somewhat enigmatic statement, Rattray singled out the idea that land, once allocated to a subchief or a subject, *would* not be reclaimed, and he argued that the stool was thereby *precluded* from any share of its produce in the future. Although Kwame Afram explained that his words were intended to safeguard, rather than relinquish, the stool's continued right to receive revenue from allocated land,[104] Rattray chose to ignore this part of the chief's testimony, preferring to advance his own interpretation and its corollary, a case for direct taxation. After years of ethnographic enquiry, Rattray appears to have considered his own understanding of constitutional matters superior to his informants'. In the final chapter of *Ashanti Law and Constitution*, he chided head chiefs in general for "forfeiting much of their old authority over Sub-Chiefs and their people, because they are themselves losing sight of what was their real position under the old Constitution. . . . "[105]

SETTLING ACCOUNTS?

Rattray's three volumes on Asante culture established a benchmark for subsequent generations of ethnographers. As a "guide for Political Officers,"[106] however, *Ashanti Law and Constitution* was obsolete almost as soon as it was published. By 1932, the chief commissioner was lobbying to "restore" the Asante Confederacy in order to make indirect rule work—an argument that directly contradicted Rattray's conclusion that "*[d]ecentralization* . . . was [a] fundamental of the Ashanti Constitution," on which "lay the whole success and wonder of this loosely bound confederacy. . . . "[107] Two years later, on the eve of restoration, the assistant chief commissioner convened a committee of linguists to help him prepare a digest of "old Ashanti custom as it obtained prior to 1900 . . . and any recognized modifications [to serve] as a guide to Political Officers" in dealing with constitutional disputes and stool treasuries. [108] It was as if *Ashanti Law and Constitution* had never been written.

In 1943, the "restored" Asante Confederacy Council formally endorsed the complete separation of chiefs' personal income and property from that of their stools.[109] It was already common practice to distinguish them informally, as Hobbs had done in 1925, when he laid down conditions for Kwame Afram's return to the stool. By publicly ratifying the principle, the council probably helped to dissipate some of the discursive ambiguity that allowed Kwame Afram and many of his colleagues to demand that their subjects reimburse them for the costs of campaigning for and remaining in office. In the depressed economic conditions of the 1930s, it had become increasingly difficult for chiefs to raise levies[110] or to maintain their demands for high levels of tribute from "stranger" farmers. Colonial officials also took a firmer line on the question of stool accounts. Stool treasuries were created in increasing numbers, "native clerks" were engaged to keep accounts, and commissioners began to reduce burdensome stool debts through the simple expedient of disallowing most of the expenses claimed by chiefs and elders.[111] As the commissioners did this, chiefs' resistance to stool treasuries subsided, and they were established with little fanfare. Stool debts declined in the latter part of the colonial period, not because they were repaid or sold to private creditors but because they were written off.

Settling stool accounts on paper did not, however, resolve the question of chiefly accountability. After 1935, chiefs were no less interested in turning office to profit than they were before. But the terrain of contest had shifted, from struggles over stool debts to the administration and adjudication of rights to land. With the establishment of native tribunals in the mid-1920s, the growing number and jurisdiction of customary courts gave chiefs an increasing role in the adjudication of land disputes. In 1930, the government also created the Lands Department, headquartered in Accra, with responsibility for preparing town plans and recording and administering formal leases.

Chiefs were not slow to see the importance of these developments. In 1930, Kwame Afram and the elders of Kumawu requested that government prepare a layout for the town. Within three years, the demarcated plots were taken up, and the district commissioner called for a new survey, urging prompt action since "the Kumawus are keen on the improvement of their town."[112] In 1935, the "restored" Asantehene was given expanded judicial responsibilities, especially with regard to disputes over land and "'constitutional' offences against Native Law and Custom. . . . "[113] Eight years later, the Asantehene acquired his own Lands Office, housed in the royal compound at Manhyia, and the right to review every new lease issued in Kumase.[114]

Thus, with the wholehearted support of the colonial state, the reinstated Asantehene presided over an expanding apparatus of "customary" and bureaucratic institutions concerned, among other things, with the allocation of land rights and the adjudication of conflicting claims to land and landed property. Seated at the apex of the reconstituted "traditional" state, Prempeh II occupied a pivotal spot in the apparatus of indirect rule where, under a government committed to upholding "custom," he presided, in effect, over the interpretation of the past. As layouts replaced levies as prime instruments of chiefly rent-seeking, chiefs learned to navigate the corridors of bureaucracy as well as palace courtyards, bureaucrats contested for stools, and Prempeh I's successors set to work to furnish the Golden Stool with land as well as subjects.

NOTES

1. F. Cooper, *Decolonization and African society: The labor question in French and British Africa* (Cambridge: Cambridge University Press, 1996).

2. B. Grier, "Contradictions." Grier argues that the colonial state reinforced and strengthened chiefly power in colonial Ghana—a point Mamdani has recently made for the entire continent. M. Mamdani, *Citizen and subject: Contemporary Africa and the legacy of late colonialism* (Princeton, NJ: Princeton University Press, 1996). In contrast, Roger Gocking has explored the contradictory implications of stool disputes—though not stool debts—for the political viability of indirect rule in the Gold Coast Colony. Gocking, "Indirect Rule."

3. NAGK 6, Reorganization of Ashanti, 1906, CCA to Chief Secretary, 1/4/06.

4. NAGA ADM 11/1/1307, Kumawu Native Affairs, 1915–1925, Governor's comments on Chief Commissioner's Diary, 5/30/16.

5. In 1932, Chief Commissioner Newlands argued that "restoring" the confederacy was essential to the success of direct taxation: "no revenue will be paid to any Head Chief's Stool which is not the Stool which, by Asante native custom, is the overlord to whom such revenue is due." Quoted in Tordoff, *Ashanti*, 322–23. Because it reinstated the Asantehene, the "restoration" of the Asante Confederacy Council is sometimes referred to as the beginning of indirect rule in Asante. Inasmuch as the Asante administration sought to maintain order through upholding "custom" and chiefly authority, however, it may be said to have practiced indirect rule from its inception.

6. NAGA ADM 11/1/1906, Ex-King Prempeh, 1926–1927, CCA to SSC, 9/10/26. Scholars who have endorsed this view include Grier, "Contradictions," 37, 44; R. Rathbone, *Murder and politics in colonial Ghana* (New Haven, CT: Yale University Press, 1993), esp. ch. 3; J. Simensen, "Commoners, chiefs and colonial government" (Ph.D. diss. University of Trondheim, 1975), chs. 7, 11; and Simensen, "The Asafo of Kwahu, Ghana: A mass movement for local reform under colonial rule," *International Journal of African Historical Studies* 8, no. 3 (1975): 400.

7. NAGA ADM 11/1/1906, CCA to SSC, 9/10/26.

8. NAGK 2348, Asokore Stool Levy, 1934–1942, Acting District Commissioner, Mampong, to CCK, 5/7/37.

9. His testimony was confirmed by the Nkawiehene. NAGA ADM 5/3/13, H. C. Belfield, Report on legislation governing the alienation of native lands in the Gold Coast Colony and Ashanti, Cd 6278, 1912, 93, 95.

10. Ibid., 94. The second speaker, Adontenhene John Kwame Frimpon, was an influential figure in Asante politics from the turn of the century to the late 1940s. McCaskie, "Accumulation II," 12–13.

11. NAGK 850, Pekki-Tredeh Boundary Dispute, 1916–29. See also NAGK 954, Omanhene of Juaben v. Omanhene of Ejisu, 1925–35.

12. Gold Coast Colony, *Report of the Commission of Inquiry (Havers) on expenditures connected with litigation* (Accra: Government Printer, 1945), 31. In addition to contemporary sources, a number of more recent studies have cited costs of litigation as a major source of stools' chronic indebtedness. See, e.g., Tordoff, *Ashanti*; M. Owusu, *Uses and abuses of political power: A case study of continuity and change in the politics of Ghana* (Chicago: University of Chicago Press, 1970); Kyerematen, *Interstate boundary litigation*; Simensen, "Commoners"; Grier, "Contradictions"; Rathbone, *Murder*.

13. Gold Coast Colony, *Report*, Appendix B. These figures are based on cases from the Colony as well as from Asante.

14. NAGA 2348, Asokore Stool Levy, 1934–1942.

15. NAGA 975, Nsuta Native Affairs, 1921–36.

16. M. Fortes, "The Ashanti social survey: A preliminary report," *Rhodes-Livingstone Journal, Human problems in British Central Africa* 6 (1948): 22–23. Similar arguments were made by Rattray, *Ashanti law*; K. A. Busia, *The position of the chief in the modern political system of Ashanti* (London: Frank Cass, 1968); and many colonial officials. See, e.g., Gold Coast Colony, *Report*; also Arhin, "Some Asante views."

17. Grier, "Contradictions," 37ff., points out that, in the Colony, the decision to vest land in stools represented a reversal of the colonial government's earlier policy of condoning or even encouraging the development of individual ownership. She argues that this policy was designed to keep labor cheap by limiting Africans' opportunities to accumulate wealth.

18. G. Austin, "Emergence," 267ff.; and Austin, "Capitalists and chiefs," 78 and passim. See also Grier, "Contradictions"; and Simensen, "Commoners" and "The Asafo of Kwahu."

19. Grier, "Contradictions," 36–37. The term "youngmen" refers, in Asante parlance, to the majority of the population who do not hold office—i.e., occupy a stool. Use of this generic term has sometimes, I think, served to exaggerate the degree of collective solidarity or common class interest among those challenging a chief's quali-

fications to remain in office. Allman argues, for example, that "youngmen" played a catalytic role in the Asante nationalist movement of the mid-1950s, but her argument that what began as an upsurge of mass protest was quickly hijacked by members of the chiefly and western educated elite suggests that forces leading to collective action from below were not very strong. J. Allman, "The youngmen and the porcupine: Class, nationalism and Asante's struggle for self-determination, 1954–57," *Journal of African History* 31 (1990): 263–79; R. Rathbone and J. Allman, "Discussion: The youngmen and the porcupine," *Journal of African History* 32 (1991): 333–38; and Allman, *The quills of the porcupine*.

20. See, e.g., Busia, *The position of the chief*, 207; Austin, "Capitalists and chiefs," 88.

21. NAGK 1264, Petition from Twafohene, Akwamuhene and over 400 Youngmen of Asokore, 1/18/33.

22. NAGK 1231, A digest of the minutes of the Ashanti Confederacy Council, 67.

23. Quoted in NAGA ADM 11/1/1907, Annual report, Ashanti, 1921.

24. Rattray, *Ashanti law*, 116. See also Busia, *The position of the chief*, 51.

25. Busia, *The position of the chief*, 199. Based on research carried out in 1941–42, Busia's manuscript was submitted to Oxford University as a Ph.D. thesis, and first published in 1951. Busia cites Rattray as his "main source" on Asante history and chose to do his fieldwork in Mampon because Rattray had worked there. Busia, *The position of the chief*, x. Rattray did not, however, believe that a chief's person was inseparable from his/her office: "In Ashanti, the stool is greater than the King or Chief who sits upon it." Rattray, *Ashanti law*, 85.

26. Ibid., 199. According to this argument, chiefs who accepted bribes were guilty of violating custom.

27. Wilks, *Forests of gold*, 136ff.; McCaskie, *State and society*, 42–49. Anyone receiving the rank of ɔbirempɔn was expected to make a public display of his wealth. In addition to showing off the candidate's achievements, this ritual enabled the state to make a preliminary assessment of his fortune and what might be demanded as death duties.

28. Arhin, "Rank and class," 9.

29. Under the rules of matrilineal succession, Yamoa Ponko would not normally be eligible to succeed to his father's stool. In this case, however, strategic generosity eventually gained him the office. See McCaskie, *State and society*, 59–64; also Wilks, *Forests of gold*, 136–38.

30. NAGA ADM 5/3/13, Belfield Report, 1912, 87.

31. J. Dunn and A. F. Robertson, *Dependence and opportunity in Ahafo* (Cambridge: Cambridge University Press, 1973), 53.

32. Beginning in the 1890s, many Akwapim, Krobo, Ga, and Shai farmers bought land and established cocoa farms in Akyem Abuakwa. P. Hill, *Migrant cocoa farmers of southern Ghana* (Cambridge: Cambridge University Press, 1963).

33. Simensen, "Commoners," 106.

34. This native administration ordinance applied to the Colony. Legislation for Asante was kept separate from that of the Colony until 1934. W. H. (Lord) Hailey, *Native administration in the British African territories*, Part III. *West Africa* (London: Oxford University Press, 1951), 229. For an absorbing account of Nana Ofori Atta's career and the complex political aftermath of his death, see Rathbone, *Murder*.

35. In making this claim, Ofori Atta was testing section 40 of the new native administration ordinance, which extended chiefs' authority to make by-laws to all matters pertaining to "good government and the welfare of the inhabitants." Quoted in Simensen, "Commoners," 200.

36. NAGA ADM 1/1/184, Cocoa farming tribute.

37. Ibid., Ofori Atta to DC Akyem, 4/10/28.

38. Simensen, "Commoners," 201–2. Simensen has traced the long history of Ofori Atta's debates with the colonial administration on these and other issues in great detail. Briefer accounts are also given in Rathbone, *Murder*, ch. 13 and Firmin-Sellers, *Transformation*.

39. NAGA ADM 11/1/184, Cocoa farming-tribute . . . by-laws, Ofori Atta to DC Kyebi, 9/12/29.

40. Firmin-Sellers, *Transformation*, ch. 4. I am not persuaded by Firmin-Sellers' argument that Ofori Atta set out to introduce a new system of property rights in Akyem Abuakwa, complete with institutions of enforcement, in a manner consistent with "new institutional" economic theory. Specifically, Firmin-Sellers argues that Ofori Atta gained the support of colonial authorities by controlling their access to information about events in Akyem, and he gained the support of his subjects by convincing them that the stool would use its revenues for their benefit. The former claim is not borne out by the lively debates within the colonial administration over Ofori Atta's motives and policies, explored in detail by Simenson, "Commoners." The latter claim depends on reading Ofori Atta's and J. B. Danquah's rhetoric as evidence of their accomplishments, and a modest increase in "customary" tax payments to the stool treasury (from £110 in 1941–42 to £362, or 9 percent of total revenue, in 1942–43) as "a remarkable story," which shows that "citizens paid their taxes to the treasury and, in return, rulers enforced property rights, refusing to appropriate the farmers' profits." Firmin-Sellers, *Transformation*, 84. Cf ch.5, n59.

41. NAGK 413, Kumawu candidates for baptism forced to beat drum, 1915, DC, Juaso, to CCA, 9/27/15.

42. NAGA ADM 11/1307, Kumawu Native Affairs.

43. NAGA ADM 11/1307, Governor's comments on Fuller's diary, 7/11/16; CS to ACC, 6/23/16.

44. NAGK 935, Boundary demarcations—Chief Commissioner's instructions, 1915–1931, DC, Juaso to CCA, 5/23/15.

45. NAGK 62, Kumawu politics, DC, Ashanti Akyem to CCA, 3/25/18; NAGK 935, DC, Juaso to CCK, 5/23/15.

46. NAGK 935, Assistant District Commissioner, Juaso, to CCK, 5/23/15.

47. NAGK 935, DC, Juaso to CCA 5/23/15.

48. NAGA ADM 11/1307, CCA to CS 8/29/16.

49. NAGK 64, Kumawu elders and young men—petition for destoolment of Omanhin Kwame Afram, 1916.

50. NAGA ADM 11/1307, CS to Acting Chief Commissioner of Ashanti, 6/23/16.

51. Ibid., CS to Acting Chief Commissioner of Ashanti, 5/30/16.

52. NAGA ADM 11/1307, CS to Acting Chief Commissioner of Ashanti, 5/30/16.

53. Ibid., CS to Acting Chief Commissioner of Ashanti, 6/23/16.

54. Ibid., Governor's comments, 7/11/16.

55. Ibid., CCA to CS, 10/14/16; and personal communication, Nana Osei Bediako Firaw, Kumawu.

56. Ibid., CCA to CS, 11/16/16.

57. Ibid.

58. NAGK 31, Kumawu disturbances, 1920, CCA to CS, 9/10/20; NAGK 62, DC, Ashanti Akyem, to CCA, 1/17/19; Kojo Nsiah and Kofi Wurai to Governor, 6/16/18. According to Harper, Kweku Boaten had agreed to pay off a debt of £1100. In April, 1919, the chief himself claimed to have paid £1310 towards the stool's debts, leaving a balance of £90 owed to Chief Frimpon. See also NAGA ADM 11/1307, CCA to CS, 10/14/16, and Minute by Secretary for Native Affairs, 6/7/29; also NAGK 23, Petition praying for their return to Kumawu, 4/21/19.

59. NAGA ADM 11/1307, CCA to CS, 10/14/16.

60. Ibid.

61. Compare NAGK 31, CCA to CS, 9/10/20; NAGK 29, Kobina Kodia, Omanhene of Kumawu—election of, 1922; NAGK 34, Enquiry into the constitution of the Kumawu Stool, 1924; Rattray, *Ashanti law*, fig. 50.

62. NAGK 62, Kumawu Native Affairs, 1918; NAGK 68, Enquiry into a complaint against Omanhene of Kumawu by one Kwesi Nuama, DC, Juaso, to CCA, 1/30/18.

63. NAGK 62, Report on Kumawu Palaver, 12/24/17; NAGK 31, CCA to CS, 9/10/20.

64. NAGK 28, Re Kumawu Exiles wishing to return to Kumawu . . . , Kwame Tua to CCA, 3/12/21; NAGA ADM 11/1307, DC's Report on Kumawu Disturbances, 1918. Kwame Toa was often at odds with whoever happened to be occupying the Kumawu stool. In 1916, he was jailed for his part in the riotous protests against Kwame Afram; in 1920, he was arrested and fined for taking part in the riots against Kweku Boaten. NAGK 64, Kumawu elders and youngmen—petition by for destoolment of Omanhin Kwame Afram of Kumawu, 4/4/16; NAGK 31, DC, Juaso to CCA, 7/14/20; NAGK 62, Acting District Commissioner's Report on Kumawu palaver, 12/24/17. He boasted of having installed Kwame Afram on the stool for the first time in 1896, after ousting his predecessor Kwesi Krapa, and later of having unseated Kwame Afram in 1916. NAGK 28, Kwame Tua, Bodomasehene, to CCA per DC, Juaso, 3/12/21. NAGK 31, Yaw Djibin, Worasohene and 11 other elders to CCA, 7/9/20. When Chief Commissioner Harper visited Kumawu and surrounding villages in December 1921, he was surprised to find that "Kwame Toa, the chief king maker and king breaker of Kumawu does not seem to have much honor or support in his own country," adding hopefully that Kwame Toa looked old and ill and that, "if he were to disappear from the scene," opposition to Kwame Afram's reinstatement might diminish. NAGA ADM 11/1/1902, Chief Commissioner's Diary, 3/12/21.

65. NAGK 62, Report on Kumawu Palaver, 12/24/17; K. Nsiah and K. Wurai to Governor, 6/16/18.

66. Ibid., CCA to CS, 9/4/18.

67. Kweku Boaten's appointment appears to have been made in haste. Four years later, Fuller's successor could find no record that Kweku Boaten had ever been formally installed as Kumawuhene. NAGK 31, CCA to CS, 9/10/20.

68. Cited by Chief Commissioner Harper in a memorandum that reviewed the history of Kumawu's stool debt. Idem. See also NAGA ADM 11/1/1307, CCA to CS, 10/14/16.

69. NAGK 28, DC, Juaso, to CCA, 9/18/19; NAGA ADM 11/1307, Skene's Report, 9/8/20.

70. Except where noted otherwise, my account of this incident is based on NAGK 27, Notes of an inquisition into the death of two Kumawu men—stealing gold dust valued at £11,000, 1920.

71. NAGK 31, CCA to CS, 9/17/20. In an earlier moment of compromise, the elders had agreed to repay the stool's outstanding debt themselves if Kweku Boaten died on the stool, but not if he abdicated. Apparently the chief commissioner hoped that, by removing the chief unilaterally, he could prevent the elders from evading "their share" of the stool's debts. NAGK 24, Petition in favour of Kweku Boaten . . . as Omanhin of Kumawu, Agreement between Kweku Boaten and Elders of Kumawu, 4/21/19.

72. NAGA ADM 11/1/1902, Chief Commissioner's Diary, 4/12/21.

73. In August 1921, Harper noted that the prominent Kumase chief Kwesi Nuama had come to plead Kwame Afram's case, explaining that Kwame Afram was "marked out by Providence to return as Chief to Kumawu. No elephant has been killed since he was destooled, but no sooner does he set foot on Kumawu land that [*sic*] two elephants are killed and so on." Ibid., 8/15/21.

74. Ibid., 4/12/21.

75. NAGK 29, Kobina Kodia, Omanhene of Kumawu—election of, 1922.

76. NAGA ADM 11/1/1901, Ex-king Prempeh—return of, 1911–1925, Precis of correspondence, entry for 12/18/23.

77. NAGA ADM 11/1/1307, Acting Chief Commissioner of Ashanti to CS, 9/1/25.

78. Ibid.

79. NAGA ADM 11/1/1902, Chief Commissioner's Diary, 12/14/21.

80. With apologies to M.-R. Trouillot, *Silencing the past* (Boston: Little, Brown, 1995), 1. Trouillot's subtle exploration of the various ways that power may be expressed or exercised through stories and silences about the past has been an inspiration in my efforts to think about the abundance of historical narrative in debates over property and power in Asante. I am, of course, entirely responsible for the resulting use—or misuse—of his insights.

81. See n. 61 above.

82. She warned that Kwame Afram's reinstatement was likely to cause further turmoil, since he could be expected to take revenge on the youngmen who had insulted him and seduced his wives while he was in exile. NAGK 28, Enquiry . . . re election of candidate to Kumawu stool, 4/20/22.

83. NAGK 62, Adjuah Serwah, Ohimba Kumawu to CCA, 12/2/21.

84. See n. 73 above.

85. NAGK 28, Enquiry . . . re election of candidate to Kumawu stool, 4/20/22.

86. K. Yankah, *Speaking for the chief: Ɔkyeame and the politics of Akan royal oratory* (Bloomington: Indiana University Press, 1995), 95. He explains that to use the first person in public speech is a royal privilege: others, notably *akyeame* or royal spokespersons, must use the third person. Ibid., 130.

87. Yankah, *Speaking for the chief*, 49ff. See also K. Arhin, "The Asante praise poems: The ideology of patrimonialism," *Paideuma* 32 (1986):163–97; McCaskie, *State and society*. Additional examples of the power of speech and song in African politics are given in K. Barber, *I could speak until tomorrow: Oriki, women and the past in a Yoruba town* (Washington, DC: Smithsonian Institution, 1991); L. Vail and L. White, *Power and the praise poem: Southern African voices in history* (Charlottesville: Uni-

versity of Virginia Press, 1991); and D. Coplan, "History is eaten whole: Consuming tropes in Sesotho auriture," *History and Theory* 32 (1993): 80–104.

88. As one observer concluded, after a lengthy review of land disputes in Adanse, since judgments in the native court "turned on questions of historical fact . . . rather than Court decisions on legal principles," it was not "possible to abstract . . . any general principles of Akan land tenure" from court records. Quoted in Kyerematen, *Inter-state boundary litigation*, 36.

89. *Ashanti law and constitution*, the final volume of Rattray's ethnographic trilogy on Asante, was first published in 1929, following Ashanti (1923) and *Religion and art in Ashanti* (1927).

90. Rattray, *Ashanti law*, 222, n. 5.

91. At times Rattray cites his Kumawu informants by name, but he also quotes them without attribution at several other points in the book. See, e.g., Rattray, *Ashanti law*, esp. chs. 28–33, and R. S. Rattray Collection, Royal Anthropological Institute, Herskovits Library, Northwestern University, MS106, nos. 21–22.

92. NAGK 62, Kweku Boaten and others to CCA, 6/17/18; NAGA ADM 11/1/ 1307, Acting Chief Commissioner of Ashanti to CS, 9/1/25.

93. Interview with Panin Yao Mensah, Kumawu, 7/11/94. In 1930, her signature appears on a petition addressed to the chief commissioner by the chiefs and elders of Kumawu, requesting that a surveyor be sent to·prepare a layout of the town. NAGK 1683, Kumawu Township, 1/5/30.

94. Rattray, *Ashanti law*, 1969, 355. Compare T. C. McCaskie, "R.S. Rattray and the construction of Asanti history: An appraisal," *History in Africa* 10 (1983): 192.

95. NAGK 682, Strangers in Kumawu lands, 1906–08; NAGK 684, Land dispute between Kumawu and Okwahu, 1907–1912; NAGK 726, Report on tour—re land dispute between Mampong and Kumawu, 1908; NAGK 829, Chief of Kwamang—assault on his subjects by Chief of Atebubu, 1914; NAGK 856, Chief Kofi Nti—his subjects at Drabonsu, 1917–1921; NAGK 8/73, Committee of Privileges, 1935. The Kumawu stool was a prime beneficiary of the colonial boundary, established in 1906, between Asante and the Gold Coast Colony. As Fuller reminded the chief, "the Kumawus are not numerous, but you are none-the-less left in possession of a vast territory, which you cannot properly look after for want of people. It does not, therefore, behoove you to claim more land than has been granted you. . . . I shall inform all settlers *north* of the Obosum [River] that they are in Ashanti territory and that they will have to obtain your permission to remain there." NAGA ADM 11/242, Kwahu-Kumawu Land Dispute, 1909– 1912, CCA to Omanhene of Kumawu, 5/16/07. Despite, or perhaps because of, Fuller's imperious tone, the lesson was not lost on Kwame Afram or his successors. Fuller's letter has figured prominently in litigation between the Kumawu stool and its neighbors ever since.

96. Quoted in Rattray, *Ashanti law*, 344.

97. Rattray, *Ashanti*, ch. 21.

98. Reacting to Rattray's earlier "evolutionary" interpretation of Akan history, Wilks has also proposed a "big bang theory," which associates the origins of Akan matriclans with the development of forest agriculture. Wilks, *Forests of gold*, 94.

99. Rattray, *Ashanti law*, 359.

100. Ibid.

101. Ibid., 365.

102. During two months' residence in Kumawu, in June and July, 1994, I discussed matters of land and local history with men and women of varied backgrounds, including a number of subchiefs and family heads.

103. Specifically, the chief explained that he would not say "*me de asase yi me kye wo* ('I present, make a gift of, this land to you')" but rather "*me de asase yi, me ma wo didi so* ('I take this land [i.e., soil] and give it to you to eat upon'), or sometimes *Me de asase yi ma wo, fwe so ma me* ('I take this land and give it to you to look after for me')." Rattray, *Ashanti law*, 354–55.

104. "'I would never give land to any man using the words *me de kye wo* (I make you a gift), for if I did so, that would mean the donee could sell the actual land; if he found a nugget upon it he could keep it, and he need never give me anything from it.'" Ibid.

105. Ibid., 409.

106. See n. 108.

107. Rattray, *Ashanti law*, 405. McCaskie argues that this is a better description of the colonial order than of the precolonial state. McCaskie, "*Ahyiamu.*"

108. NAGK 1231, Asante Confederacy Council Digest, 1935–1949, 52.

109. Ibid., 13.

110. In 1937, the stool of Asokore succeeded in raising only 18 percent of the amount needed to pay off the stool's debt. Two years later, another levy was imposed, with even more meager results. Fewer than one fourth of the assessed men and women paid voluntarily, and the amount realized was little more than half that collected in 1937. After prosecuting fifty-five delinquents for a return of only £20 10s, the stool gave up the attempt. NAGK 2348, Asokore Stool Levy, 1934–42; NAGK 1858, Asokore Stool Levy, 1936–37.

111. Hailey, *Native administration*, 240; NAGK 2348, District Commissioner's memorandum on the enquiry into the Asokore Stool debt, 5/17/38.

112. NAGK 1683, Kumawu township, 1930–1933, Acting District Commissioner to Assistant Chief Commissioner, Kumasi, 2/25/33.

113. Hailey, 1951:244.

114. The Asantehene's steadily expanding role in the allocation and adjudication of land claims in and around Kumase since 1935 is discussed in ch. 3.

3

WHO OWNS KUMASE?

By the early 1930s, the Ashanti administration had come to the conclusion that indirect rule would work in Asante only if it were based on a full restoration of the traditional state. Accordingly, in 1935, Osei Agyeman Prempeh II was promoted from Kumasehene to Asantehene, presiding over an Asante Confederacy Council composed of senior Kumase chiefs and provincial *amanhene*. Echoing official thinking at the time, scholars have portrayed the restoration of 1935 as a moment of decisive transition from direct rule by the colonial commissioners to a system of indirect rule, in which colonial authority operated through the medium of traditional government. Even the most outspoken critics of the authenticity of the restored Asante Confederacy tend to agree that the Asantehene's reinstatement marked a decisive change in relations between the chiefs and the colonial state.[1]

In practice, of course, British officials had treated Asante chiefs (absent the Asantehene) as agents of colonial rule from the outset. As we have seen in the preceding chapters, indirect rule did not stand or fall on the authenticity, or otherwise, of officials' understanding of custom but involved continual reorganization, as administrators experimented with different methods of harnessing traditional authority to the cart of colonial rule. None of the institutions that were put in place between the mid-1920s and mid-1940s—native tribunals, native treasuries, native administrations—either replicated the structures of the eighteenth and nineteenth centuries or went uncontested by Asante citizens and chiefs in the twentieth. The restoration itself capped a decade-long process in which chiefs and commissioners renegotiated, sometimes uneasily, the prerogatives of Edward Prempeh[2] and his successor, and their position in the colonial order. When Edward Prempeh's status as a private citizen became increasingly untenable, the government assigned him to the invented office of Kumasehene. The decision to restore the office of Asantehene was taken only in 1932, when it was hoped that the prestige of the Golden Stool would soften Asantes' reluctance to pay taxes in the midst of the depression.[3] And after Prempeh

II's elevation from Kumasehene to Asantehene, negotiations over precedence and jurisdiction continued—in sittings of the Committee of Privileges, in meetings of the Asante Confederacy Council, through further reorganization of the customary courts, and, above all, in ongoing debate over the Asantehene's authority with respect to land.

Once taken, the decision to reinstate the Asantehene was portrayed as a response to overwhelming popular demand. In considering the matter, the governor insisted that he had "refused to listen to outside voices" and agreed to act only when assured of the "unanimous" support of the Ashanti chiefs.[4] But official enthusiasm could not silence an undercurrent of anxiety. However one might read the past, it was clear that in 1935, the Golden Stool had no land. As chiefs throughout the region were keenly aware, a paramount stool without land was an anomaly, and it stood to reason that the newly restored Asantehene would seek to do something about it.

As we shall see in the following pages, the "restoration" of 1935 opened a new chapter in the history of land claims in Asante—one whose conclusion has yet to be written. Well aware of chiefly sensitivities on the issue, Prempeh II approached the land question cautiously but persistently and his successor continued to pursue the matter with the combined advantages of the prestige of his office and his own professional training as a lawyer.[5] Both men played adroitly on their position as guarantors of the customary principle of stool ownership to consolidate their authority over other Asante chiefs, while steadily expanding the Golden Stool's claims to land at the other chiefs' expense. Their success in turning land claims to political advantage, and vice versa, has contributed in no small measure to the remarkable resilience of chieftaincy in postcolonial Ghana. Despite sweeping legislative efforts, under Nkrumah and, later, Rawlings, to abrogate the formal administrative and judicial powers that chiefs held under colonial rule and relegate their statutory prerogatives to the largely ceremonial realm of "chieftaincy affairs,"[6] chiefs remain a force to be reckoned with in the actual mobilization and deployment of both property and power. In the following pages, I argue that the dramatic discrepancy between chiefs' prerogatives *de jure* and their influence *de facto* in contemporary Asante is firmly anchored in the political economy of making claims on land.

RECONFIGURING KUMASE:
LAND, THE MARKET, AND THE STATE

Walking on Two Legs

By the late nineteenth century, the once-flourishing capital of the Asante state had been much reduced, in population and appearance, by political turmoil and warfare. Visitors in the late 1880s and early 1890s described Kumase as run-down and overgrown.[7] The city began to revive, however, after the turn of the century, as peace, cocoa, and colonial rule brought increased trade and population. From an estimated 3,000 inhabitants in 1903, the population of Kumase grew to almost 19,000 by 1911.[8] Chiefs and merchants put up buildings in the city to be close to the center of commercial and administrative activity. Growing opportunities for trade and employment also attracted ordinary people, from Asante and beyond, and the rising demand for residential and commercial accommodations acted as a further stimulus to building construction. A few people built "storey houses" before 1902 and, in the following decade, "many of the old thatch-covered houses were replaced by European-style, solid brick buildings with iron or shingle roofs, often leased to the business firms at a handsome rental."[9]

Colonial policy toward land in Kumase walked on two legs: controlled use and collective ownership. Land was vested in the stools but the state intervened actively in stool land management and administration, setting the terms on which chiefs could allocate land and directing patterns of land use. As Kumase's population grew and the accompanying building boom spawned an active market in claims on urban land, commoners, chiefs, and colonial officials struggled over the control of land allocation. For strategic reasons, the state appropriated all land within a one-mile radius of the Kumase Fort (later extended to a mile and a half) for the Crown but hesitated to provoke further unrest by taking any more.[10] What the Crown's land lacked in extent, however, was more than made up by its location. Set squarely in what was to become the commercial heart and most affluent residential areas of the city, the Kumase Town Lands were some of the most valuable in Asante. Africans complained repeatedly of having to pay high allocation fees and ground rent to the government, but the authorities were unmoved. For the next four decades, the Asante administration defended its property aggressively against rival claimants—including other branches of the government—and used its authority to compete in the urban land market as well as to regulate it.[11]

Part of the Kumase Town Lands were set aside for administrative use and housing for Europeans,[12] but plots were also let to commercial firms and to individual Asantes and "immigrants" who wanted to build on them.[13] Demand was brisk. After the railway was completed in 1903, cocoa cultivation spread rapidly in Asante, and Kumase became the commercial hub of an expanding regional economy.[14] Within a few years, several expatriate firms had built stores along Kingsway and Harper Road. To make way for them, Kumase's principal market was moved from Harper Road to the vi-

cinity of the palace[15] and, in the following years, the slope between the fort
and the Nsubin River (Adum) gradually filled with commercial and residential buildings. In 1920, a second market was established in Zongo; five
years later, the railway station and the main market were moved to their
present location at Kejetia.[16]

As commercial activity expanded and the population of Kumase grew,
government derived increasing amounts of revenue from the Kumase Town
Lands. The importance of these rents in the eyes of the Asante commissioners was enhanced by the fiscal structure of the Gold Coast as a whole.
The wealth of the colony was built on cocoa. Virtually unknown in West
Africa before the 1870s, cocoa was introduced to southern Ghana from
Fernando Po.[17] Farmers in the Gold Coast were quick to perceive its commercial value and the crop spread rapidly, moving into southern Asante in
the early 1900s. By 1920, the Gold Coast had become the largest supplier
of cocoa on the world market, deriving more than 80 percent of its total
export earnings from the crop.[18] Since duties on exports and imports were
collected at the ports, the bulk of the colony's revenues accrued to the
central administration at the coast: Asante and the Northern Territories received their shares in the form of remittances from the colonial treasury.
Perennially aggrieved at receiving less than they felt entitled to,[19] administrators in Kumase clung jealously to the rents that they collected directly
from the Kumase Town Lands.

Indeed, although further additions to Crown Land were deemed politically and legally inexpedient,[20] the commissioners were not above enlarging
their holdings by other means. By law, the government was empowered to
appropriate portions of stool land as needed "for public services,"[21] and they
often did so without paying even token compensation to the owner(s). If
government failed to build within a reasonable period, the land was supposed to revert to the original owners, but officials in Kumase were loath to
part with valuable urban sites and sometimes resisted doing so. In 1921, for
example, the railway declined to return a portion of unused land to the Tafo
stool, noting with more confidence than logic that land for the railway "was
expected to be acquired free of compensation" and could not be reclaimed
by the stool just because the rail line had "deviated" from its projected
course.[22] Conversely, when tenants objected to paying rent to the government for plots at Kejetia that had been allocated to them by the Omanhene
of Juaben, they were told that the chief had "relinquished" the land in 1922,
and it had "reverted" to the government.[23] When the state's interest as landlord was at stake, it required the persistence and savoir faire of a Chief
Frimpon to hold the commissioners to the letter of the law.[24]

However aggressively they defended their own proprietary interests,
Asante administrators were also keenly aware of their stake in protecting

those of the stools. Commissioners were not above squabbling with chiefs over the terms of leases, or even over particular parcels of land, but they understood clearly that the chiefs, on whom their own administrative system depended, needed income, and that the lion's share of most chiefs' revenue came in the form of rent and tribute collected from users of stool lands. If colonial officials expected that by vesting land in the stools and proscribing land sales they would forestall disputes, they were quickly disillusioned.[25] That they adhered, nonetheless, to the principle that the inalienability of stool rights was "customary" and therefore sacrosanct had more to do with the fact that stool lands underwrote indirect rule than with any false consciousness about the inherent beneficence of traditional authority.

Protecting stools' rights over land did not mean that chiefs were given carte blanche in making decisions about land use. In Kumase, officials took steps early on to make some provision for sanitation.[26] Building plots were laid out in rectangular lines and separated by alleys, to facilitate waste collection. Following an outbreak of plague in 1909, the government took steps to improve drainage in Kumase and strengthen the enforcement of sanitary regulations.[27] After a second epidemic, in 1924, parts of Zongo were demolished and the residents moved to another site.[28] A year later, the city's main market was moved to its present location at Kejetia, after the area had been made habitable by draining swamps along the Nsubin River.[29]

Concerns over sanitation also provided a rationale for segregating residential neighborhoods on racial and ethnic lines.[30] In the interests of raising revenue, the Asante administration was prepared to lease portions of the Kumase Town Lands to anyone, African as well as expatriate, who could afford to pay for them. But the terms on which leases were issued varied according to the race and "citizenship" of the tenants.[31] During the first decade of the century, for example, Europeans paid £24 per annum for a fifty- to ninety-nine-year lease on a plot of 940 square meters while, for Africans, tenancies were limited to seven years and plots to 233 square meters. Rents were lower for African than for European tenants and also differentiated according to colonial ideas of citizenship: Asantes paid £2 per annum per plot, whereas non-Asantes were charged £4.[32]

Neighborhoods were demarcated according to officials' understanding of the structure of African society. Zongo and Aboabo, where immigrants from the north had congregated before British occupation, were now reserved for non-Asantes.[33] In 1913, Fante New Town was laid out for what were expected to be more affluent and westernized immigrants from the Colony: the plots were larger than those in the older "strangers'" quarters and rents were also higher, although still differentiated by colony of origin. Asantes were charged £3 17s. per annum for a plot of 520 square meters, non-Asantes twice as much.[34] Three years later, officials noted with satisfaction that Fante New Town was developing into a "high class native residential quarter" and began a survey of Bantama, to prepare for its transformation from a "muddled mass of huts" to a "credit to the town."[35]

Over time, as planners' perceptions of African social structure changed, they developed more elaborate classificatory schemes. In 1935, the administration announced plans to lay out a new residential area at Mbrom "for the accommodation of barristers, lawyers, professional men, well-to-do traders and all others whose standard of living approximates to that of Europeans."[36] Applicants for leases had to meet stringent building standards, including the requirement that each house must cost at least £800. This measure was justified by the need to prevent "speculators"—that is, "Syrian entrepreneurs"—from buying up the plots and reselling them, at a profit, to their intended tenants. Despite these stringent criteria, by 1939, applications for fifty-two plots had been filed by forty-one members of the city's non-European elite.[37] Development was delayed, however, when the government announced that residents would be expected to foot the bill for providing their new neighborhood with paved roads, piped water, and electricity—amenities that were furnished by the state in the European residential area. The debate dragged on for years: by 1946, the government had agreed to pay for water and electricity but was still trying to get the Asantehene to put up part of the money needed for road construction.[38]

After World War II, class differences emerged as the primary basis for defining and developing urban neighborhoods, and the colonial regime invested in a limited amount of low-income housing.[39] In 1945, a new master plan proposed "to wrap new African housing areas around the centre" of Kumase, dividing them into "high class" areas with spacious plots for "storey houses," and "working class estates" composed of single-room row houses for laborers and "two to three-roomed dwellings for artisans and clerks."[40] Exceptions to this scheme were vigorously resisted. In 1950, for example, the acting lands commissioner "strenuously opposed" a plan to build flats for African nurses on Pine Avenue Extension, arguing that they "would destroy the character of what is intended to be a high class residential area."[41] After independence, racial categories disappeared completely from the lexicon of urban planning, but neighborhoods continued to be laid out along class lines. A study carried out in the mid-1970s described Kumase's residential areas as divided into five categories: high-, middle-, and lower-income areas—the last being further subdivided according to residents' areas of origin.[42] Detailed building codes have been drawn up for each category, although there is considerable evidence that they have not been widely enforced.[43]

Commerce and Custom

As we have seen, the colonial administration's insistence on upholding and formalizing "customary" principles of land ownership and access in Asante neither discouraged the use of land for commercial purposes nor inhibited the development of an active market in land rights. Within a few years of the British occupation, Kumase chiefs began to emulate the colonial practice of issuing formal leases to urban tenants. In 1905, it was still possible for the Wesleyan Mission to express pained surprise when the administration claimed land on the Kintampo Road that Chief Obuabasa had assigned to the mission in 1896. The mission director admitted that the chief's grant was undocumented but, he wrote indignantly, Captain Stewart confirmed the arrangement verbally in 1902, and the mission had assumed "that the word of a British officer . . . would be duly ratified."[44]

Warned, perhaps, by such experiences, chiefs began to issue written leases themselves—transactions that often provoked disputes rather than precluding them. On New Year's Day, 1915, Amakomhene Kweku Atta placed his mark on an "indenture" agreeing to lease a parcel of Amakom stool land to the Society for the Propagation of the Gospel, in exchange for £100 down, and £3 annual ground rent.[45] The document was co-signed by Adontenhene John Kwame Frimpon, who received a share of the proceeds in exchange for his services. Chief Frimpon later claimed that his signature betokened the Adonten stool's authority over Amakom, a charge that the latter hotly denied: "we received [land rent] through him because he understands English and arranged the sale."[46]

Rising land values in Kumase led to the development of a market in mortgages as well as in building plots. In 1931, the chief commissioner noted that commercial firms accepted Kumase leases as collateral, and that farmers were beginning to follow suit, often hiring surveyors (at "exorbitant" rates) to make plans of farms they intended to mortgage.[47] In Kumase, building plots and houses were mortgaged, sometimes repeatedly, and the frequency and complexity of such transactions increased as the urban and regional economy became increasingly commercialized. An illustrative case is provided by the history of house B171 in Bantama, details of which emerged in court in 1951.[48]

The plaintiff in the dispute, Kofi Akyeampong, worked as a cocoa buyer for the United Africa Company. In 1916, he told the court, he leased a plot of land at Bantama from the government, and built a four-room house on it at a cost of £300. In 1927, after pledging three of the four rooms to Adjuah

Nsiah for £90, Kofi Akyeampong traveled to the Ivory Coast, where he remained for many years. During his absence, Adjuah Nsiah died and her successor, Ama Awusu, sold the house for £180. (This claim was corroborated by Ama Awusu, a cloth trader, who was the first defendant in the case.) Over the course of the next few years, the house was resold twice, the second time to the uncle of the second defendant, Kwaku Addai, who testified that his uncle had paid £445 for the house and that he had inherited it when his uncle died. Despite this evidence that the value of the property had risen substantially, Kofi Akyeampong insisted that since he had never intended to sell the house but only to mortgage it, he was still entitled to redeem it for £90.

Emmanuel Ocrah, an official of the Lands Department who was called as a witness, told a different story. The plot, he explained, had originally been leased out by the government in 1919. In 1930, the administration reclaimed the land, together with the house, on the grounds that the lessee had "failed to fulfill the terms of the lease," and evicted the lessee's relative who was occupying it at the time. In 1934, the government leased the house to Adjuah Nsiah for twenty years, at an annual rent of £6/17s/6d. Four years later, with the government's consent, Adjuah Nsiah mortgaged the house for £160. When the mortgage was not paid on time, the government attached the house and sold it at auction, in 1939, for £180, to a woman who later resold it (to Kwaku Addai's uncle) for £445. Whether the court was swayed by Ocrah's official status, or the fact that he provided documents to substantiate part of his testimony, is not recorded. In the end, faced with contradictory statements by Ocrah and the first defendant as to when and how the house had been sold for £180, the court apparently chose to believe them both. As the presiding chief declared, in the idiom of the time, "I have weighed the evidence . . . , and consulted my legs and am perfectly of the firm opinion that the balance of evidence is overwhelmingly in favour of the defendants."[49]

From Village to Urban Neighborhood: Building Amakom

The rate of new construction slowed in Kumase during the global depression of the 1930s and World War II but revived after 1945, as trade restrictions eased and the world cocoa market began to recover from the war. For the next decade, cocoa prices rose steadily, reaching unprecedented heights in the early 1950s and unleashing a wave of investment in new cocoa farms. As recently planted trees came into bearing,[50] exports rose steeply. Although the resulting gains were concentrated in the hands of brokers, chiefs, and well-to-do farmers, the effects of the cocoa boom were felt by many. In areas where planting was

widespread in the late 1940s and early 1950s, farmers, brokers, trans-
porters, petty traders, even farm laborers enjoyed rising incomes into
the early 1970s.[51] Their expenditures, in turn, fueled the domestic market, generating an increased demand for local and imported commodities ranging from staple foodstuffs to furniture and motor vehicles. During this period, many people also invested in housing. From 1948 to
1970, the housing stock in Kumase tripled, from just over 4,000 to nearly
12,000 dwellings,[52] and entire sections of the city were completely transformed. A case in point is Amakom.

Together with Tafo, Buokrom, Kaase, and Ohwim, the Amakom stool
was settled in the vicinity of present-day Kumase long before Osei Tutu led
a confederation of chiefs in a successful rebellion against the neighboring
state of Denkyira, in about 1700, and founded the Asante state.[53] At that
time, Amakom's land is said to have stretched from Kumase (then known
as Kwaman) past Ejisu to the River Oda. Osei Tutu later requested and
received land at Ayigya for one of his wives (*aheneyere*), and the
Amakomhene gave permission to some people from Denkyira to settle at
Ayeduase.[54] Amakom also acquired land and subjects at Esaaso and Adujama,
northwest of Kumase, after helping Osei Tutu defeat Domaa Kusi. During
the reign of Osei Kwame (1777–1803), the Amakomhene was obliged to
surrender his authority over the inhabitants of Esaaso and Adujama, to help
defray a debt incurred by Adontenhene Kwaaten Pete, but his stool retained
rights to the land.[55] A map prepared by the town surveyor in 1914 shows
the Amakom stool controlling approximately 480 acres in the southeastern
corner of Kumase (Map 1.3).

During the early colonial period, a number of people sought accommodation on Amakom stool land. The site leased to the Anglicans in
1915 was subsequently acquired by the government for a secondary
school.[56] To relieve congestion in Zongo, a second parcel of Amakom
land was assigned to "strangers" (Aboabo), reportedly over the objections of Amakomhene Kweku Atta.[57] In 1935, the town planning authorities drew up a layout for Amakom-Aburutia but development was
postponed while the war in Europe was in progress. In the late 1940s,
residents recall, much of Amakom was still "bush" broken only by scattered villages.

Things began to change, however, as trade and cocoa revived in the late
1940s. Kojo Dura, who was born around the time that Prempeh I was arrested by the British, spent his youth as a cocoa farmer and broker at
Konongo. By the early 1950s, he had made "a lot of money" and decided
to build a house in Kumase and rent out rooms, in order "to get money and
spend it." At that time, he remembers, most of the surrounding area was
still "a forest," but it did not remain so for long. Cocoa farmers and buyers,

wholesale and retail traders, lorry owners, drivers, and mechanics all used some of their expanding earnings to acquire plots and put up buildings in Kumase. Those who could not afford to put up a large house all at once built little by little, often beginning with a row of rooms at the back of the plot (known, since colonial times, as "the boys' quarter"), then adding a "storey house" in front, one floor at a time. Today, the old village of Amakom, an irregular oval of single-story, tin-roofed buildings, is completely surrounded by large, solid, three- and four-story structures, which overshadow the modest dwellings of the old village and provide concrete testimony to the agrarian prosperity of the 1950s and 1960s. Traffic flows continuously along the major streets, and residents who gather in front of their houses to trade, converse, or play board games must shout to make themselves heard over the roar of motor vehicles.

Amakom's location, adjacent to the railway and the main road to Accra, proved attractive to institutions as well as individuals. In 1950, at the behest of the Asantehene, the Amakom stool donated 2,560 acres to the government, as a site for the future University of Science and Technology.[58] The Amakomhene also provided land for Kumasi Polytechnic, Ahmadiyya Secondary School, and the Kumasi Stadium. By the late 1950s, industries were moving into the area as well. A stream bed near the original village, where the ground was too soft to support large cement-block buildings, was filled in and leased out to a small army of auto mechanics, electricians, panel beaters, and vulcanizers, whose shops abutted multistory residential structures built on firmer ground. Further south, Ahinsan developed into a major industrial and commercial area, housing Kumasi Breweries, Ltd., a Coca-Cola bottling plant, a branch of Ghana Commercial Bank, and several sawmills and petrol stations. Both industrial and residential construction generated employment, customers, and traffic, adding to the area's attractions for commercial users and bringing revenue to the stool.

By the late 1960s, "Amakom proper" was largely built up. Among the residents whom I spoke with in 1993, those aged seventy or above said they had acquired building plots from Nana Mensah Yiadom, during his first term on the stool, and put up their buildings "in Kwame Nkrumah's time." (An outspoken supporter of the National Liberation Movement, Nana Mensah was destooled by the government in 1961 and imprisoned for eighteen months. He returned to the stool in 1966, after Nkrumah was overthrown, and remained on it until his death in 1980.) Among my younger informants, most had either inherited the rooms or houses they occupied or were living with relatives. In most houses, some rooms were rented out to nonfamily members, but I encountered no buildings that were wholly occupied by tenants—in contrast to newer working-class residential districts, such as Ayigya.[59]

Meanwhile, the adjacent areas of Asokwa and Amakom Extension, also under the Amakom stool, were developing into "high class" residential areas.[60] A few residents of old Amakom (principally those related to the chief's family by descent or marriage) obtained plots in Asokwa at well below market prices, but most of the land was allocated to the well-to-do, including some of Kumase's most prominent businessmen, chiefs, lawyers, and civil servants. Amakom "natives" who acquired plots in Asokwa insisted that they had merely acknowledged the stool's largesse with "drinks" and a token payment of £4 or £5 as *aseda* ("thanks"), but most of the stool's lessees paid much more. Informants quoted prices ranging from £150 to £400 for plots acquired in "Amakom proper" during the 1950s and 1960s, and larger amounts for more recent transactions in Asokwa. In 1990, for example, a plot containing the foundation of a new house changed hands for ¢ 6,700,000.[61]

During the 1970s, the Ghanaian economy suffered a series of reversals. The sahelian drought of 1968–73 was followed by a sharp deterioration in Ghana's external terms of trade[62] and rising deficits in the balance of payments. Mounting debt service obligations combined with inflationary levels of government spending and considerable mismanagement of state-owned enterprises and assets to erode the volume (as well as the value) of exports and levels of real income. By the late 1970s, many Ghanaians had emigrated in search of better economic opportunities, and the growing shortage of agricultural labor led to further declines in output and supplies of staple foodstuffs.[63] In Kumase, investment in public housing declined and, while private construction appears to have kept pace with population growth, it was skewed toward high-cost dwellings. According to one estimate, between 1960 and 1980, the number of high-cost houses in Kumase rose by 163 percent, compared to a 93 percent increase in the housing stock as a whole.[64] Construction revived in the 1990s, as structural adjustment policies stimulated trade, but the gains in income were concentrated at the upper ends of the scale.

LAND FOR THE GOLDEN STOOL?

Reassembling Asante

Although Prempeh I and his retinue of relatives and senior chiefs had been banished to the Seychelles, following the uprising of 1900, they did not disappear from the minds of their compatriots or the colonial administration. Efforts to negotiate the exiles' repatriation began soon after they left Kumase and continued for almost three decades. Prempeh himself petitioned colonial authorities repeatedly to allow him to return to Kumase, and some officials were sympathetic. Confident of his rapport with the Asante chiefs, Chief Commissioner Fuller made light of the risks. Prempeh's return might be "unsettling at first," he wrote, but in the long run it would allay "the general feeling of discontent" and reinforce the administration's "increasing sympathy with the Ashantis."[65] The issue was put on hold during the war in Europe but raised again in 1918—this time by leading chiefs and members of the intelligentsia in the Colony.[66] At first, officials declined to discuss the issue, but gradually the unfolding logic of indirect rule led them to soften their stand. In March 1924, after receiving a letter from the chief commissioner, which reviewed the history of appeals on Prempeh's behalf and assured him that Asante chiefs supported repatriation unanimously,[67] Governor Guggisberg agreed.[68]

Prempeh's return was seen as an opportunity to rectify what officials had come to regard as an inconvenient power vacuum in the "native administration" of Asante. Following Asantehene's exile, Kumase chiefs vied to position themselves to advantage in the colonial order, arguing over questions of precedence as well as land and subjects. Since the latter were scattered throughout the region, Kumase chiefs were soon embroiled in disputes with the provincial *amanhene* as well as one another. By the early 1920s, officials had come to regard chiefly contestation over status and jurisdiction as a major obstacle to their own efforts to rationalize the judicial system in Asante by creating a system of "Native Tribunals" (customary courts), presided over by paramount chiefs. Lacking a paramount chief of their own, members of the Kumase Council claimed that they *all* merited paramount status. The commissioners rejected this reading of "custom" but admitted that, in practice, the Kumase chiefs' position vis-à-vis the administration was not very different from that of the provincial *amanhene*. Unable to resolve the chiefs' quarrels, and stymied in their efforts to proceed with judicial reform, officials in Asante turned hopefully to Prempeh I as one figure with sufficient prestige to hold the Kumase chiefs to account. The governor was inclined to agree. The young men of Kumase, he wrote, are "sick of the maladministration by Chiefs—they look to Prempeh to rule them. . . . "[69] Chief Commissioner Harper endorsed the idea of Prempeh's return as early as 1922, although he recommended that it be delayed until the native tribunals were in place. In 1924, the Native Jurisdiction Ordinance cleared the way, and Prempeh set sail in November, at government expense, bound for Kumase via Liverpool and Accra.[70]

As colonial officials moved towards repatriation, both Kumase chiefs and provincial *amanhene* joined the bandwagon of public "demand" for his return, but it was no secret that their protestations were tinged with ambivalence. In a petition signed in December 1923, seventeen Kumase chiefs and eleven senior *amanhene* ostentatiously proclaimed their unanimous support for "the repatriation of King Prempeh," and offered to put up "a substantial security for the peace and loyalty of Ashanti" in the wake of his return.[71] Chief Frimpon, who had been on bad terms with the former Asantehene for some time and regarded Prempeh's impending return as a threat to Frimpon's own ambitions,[72] urged Chief Commissioner Maxwell to hold them to their promise. Officially, the former Asantehene was returning to Kumase as "private citizen" Edward Prempeh[73] but, Frimpon warned,

> Ashanti scholars in town [together] with the community of Ashantis have decided to raise up a petition for Prempe to be reinstated as a king, when he comes, and this will surely bring up an unrest of affairs, and I am sure that all this would not take place if the bond is signed.[74]

The administration took Chief Frimpon's advice, but more as a precaution against immediate unrest than because they meant Prempeh to remain a "private citizen" indefinitely. Within a few weeks of the ex-king's arrival in Kumase, Governor Guggisberg proposed in a secret memorandum that government create a new Kumase Division and install Prempeh as its *omanhene*. With a paramount chief of their own, he argued, the chiefs of Kumase would be placed on an equal footing with subordinate chiefs in the rest of Asante—an arrangement altogether preferable to the present situation in which they enjoy "direct access to the Chief Commissioner."[75] Guggisberg anticipated that Chiefs Frimpon and Kobina Kofuor would instigate resistance among their colleagues on the Kumase Council, but he thought that Prempeh's return "would . . . be so popular a move among the young men that . . . they would probably be able to over-ride the objections of any Chief, probably destooling him."[76] In the event, Chief Frimpon retained his stool but lost the battle to prevent Prempeh's reinstatement as a chief. In 1926, the Kumase Division was formally established, and Prempeh was installed in the newly invented office of "Kumasihene."[77]

That the administration had envisioned some such arrangement from the outset is suggested, *inter alia*, by their exceptional concern for Prempeh's personal financial security. At first, officials made a show of holding the chiefs responsible for Prempeh's expenses. At the administration's behest, chiefs raised a subscription of £6,000, to build a house for Prempeh and his family and provide him with a modest annual allowance of £200.[78] Within a few weeks of his return, however, it was clear that the house alone would cost more than the amount the chiefs had collected, and that nothing would be left toward an annual allowance. The governor not only offered to make up the difference but also proposed that government provide Prempeh with an allowance of £1,000 per annum "on condition of good behavior."[79] He dismissed out of hand Acting Chief Commissioner Ballantine's concern that such generosity might violate the conditions under which the "ex-king" had been allowed to return to Kumase, observing condescendingly that Captain Ballantine had done very well as a district commissioner—building roads and rest houses with assiduity—but lacked "competence" in handling more senior administrative responsibilities.[80]

Two years later, as preparations got underway to install Prempeh as "Kumasihene," the governor's deputy suggested that he should keep his £1,000 per annum (although no other *omanhene* received an allowance from the government), "to relieve any grievance that may be felt" over the administration's monopoly of rents from Kumase Town Lands.[81] The chief commissioner concurred: "I understand that Prempe intends, when reinstated, to raise the question of the Government's title to the Kumase Town Lands. It would be a very serious matter if this question was ever raised by the Ashantis," he warned, adding that if there was any reason to doubt the legality of the government's title, the Kumasehene's "annual allowance of £1,000 . . . might be given as a *quid pro quo* for our present rights."[82] A thousand pounds, to say nothing of a potentially inflammatory breach of administrative precedent, was evidently a small price to pay for tenure security.

The Kumasehene moved easily into his new role as head of the customary courts in Kumase Division, but the establishment of native tribunals did not solve the problem of stool finances. British colonial administrations in Africa tended to shy away from direct taxation, preferring indirect forms of revenue collection where these were feasible.[83] In the Gold Coast, the alacrity with which African farmers took up cocoa growing for the world market allowed the colonial regime to rely primarily on import and export duties, but officials still worried about meeting expenses. As we have seen, commissioners in Asante were keen to get the chiefs to shoulder part of the cost of governing their subjects.[84] Officials' demands played no small part in provoking disturbances over stool debts, and the government's campaign to "stabilize" stool finances by establishing native treasuries was repeatedly thwarted, or delayed, by fears of popular protest. The question was still unresolved when the global economic depression of the early 1930s plunged the colonial administration into fiscal crisis. Like the chieftaincy disputes of the 1910s and 1920s, the economic crisis of the early 1930s prompted much official soul searching, which culminated, once again, in a renewed effort to bring colonial administrative practice more closely in line with "authentic" Asante custom.

Commissioners in Asante had long suspected that their administrative and fiscal problems were, in part, of their own making. In the 1920s, chiefly rivalry over the allocation of native tribunals was blamed, in part, on "the creation of artificial divisions, a policy which pursued in the past has caused much tribulation in Ashanti."[85] In the early 1930s, as trade and incomes fell and the popular mood soured, officials became increasingly convinced that the future viability of the colonial order depended on undoing the mistakes of the past. As before, crises led not to a questioning of the merits of indirect rule itself but to efforts to improve it through a better understanding of custom. By the early 1930s, officials had the benefit of access to Rattray's three volumes, reporting the results of his extensive inquiries into Asante culture, law, and history. However, although Rattray's research had been commissioned by the colonial administration, officials did not always find it expedient to follow his advice. In 1926, for example, Maxwell conceded that Rattray's findings were "valuable from a historical point of view" but that he "totally ignores the difference of the position of affairs in Ashanti today as compared with . . . 1896."[86]

Neither Maxwell nor his successors were convinced by Rattray's argument that direct taxation by Asante chiefs could be justified as a *de facto* revival of ancient custom,[87] but they shared his conviction that the keys to the effective governance of Asante in the present lay in an accurate reading of the past. By the early 1930s, Chief Commissioner Newlands was arguing that the only way to make indirect rule financially viable in Asante was to restore the Asantehene. Since "no revenue will be paid to any Head Chief's Stool which is not . . . , by Ashanti native custom, . . . the overlord to whom such revenue is due,"[88] the solvency of the Native Authority system depended on reinstating its supreme ruler.

This was just what many Asantes were afraid of. As Kwame Arhin has shown, members of Asante's mercantile and professional classes had objected strenuously to the idea of reviving death duties or other forms of precolonial taxation,[89] and the prospect of a restored monarchy rekindled their apprehensions. Some outlying *amanhene* were opposed to conceding any of their authority to a reinstated Asantehene, and even those who were willing to consider it on political grounds worried that a reinstated monarch might lay claim to their lands. Convinced that the key to stability was "tradition," the administration assigned Assistant Chief Commissioner Warrington to compile a digest of "old Ashanti custom as it obtained prior to 1900 [together with] any recognized modifications [to serve] as a guide to Political Officers [in dealing with] constitutional disputes and Stool Treasuries."[90] On most issues, the tone of Warrington's report was confident, but on the question of land rights, he was almost apologetically vague:

In former times, all land in Ashanti belonged to the Ashantihene by right of conquest and he gave the land to the various Chiefs. Such at any rate

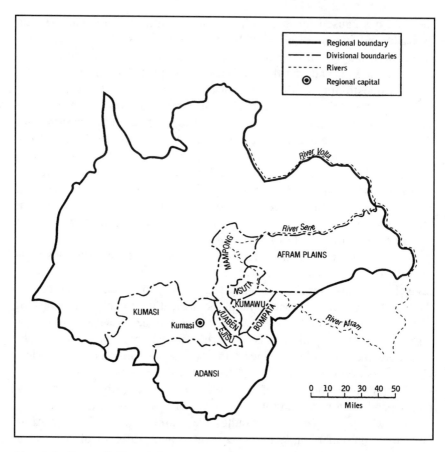

Map 3.1 Some divisions of Asante, 1934.
Source: NAGA ADM 5/3. Papers relating to the restoration of the Ashanti Confederacy, 1935.

was the general principle but it is difficult now to say what were the legal rights of the Ashantihene in respect of the lands of the Abrempon or to what extent such rights were exercised if indeed they were ever defined. There was no land which belonged to the Golden Stool as distinct from the land occupied by the Chiefs who served the stool.[91]

In all probability, he concluded, the situation was fluid: the *abirempon*

served the Ashantihene with their lands and . . . the rights he exercised in respect of such lands depended upon the relations existing at any particular time between the Ashantihene and the Birempon concerned.[92]

From the moment of his installation, both Prempeh II and the administration were at pains to reassure Asante chiefs that their newly reinstated
monarch had no designs on their lands. At the installation ceremony, the
governor promised that the "domestic affairs and property rights of properly constituted divisions will not be interfered with. . . . "[93] Three years
later, to reaffirm the point, the Asante Confederacy Council resolved that
"all land in Ashanti is the property of the Stools of the various Chiefs.
. . . "[94] In 1941, the Asantehene again assured the council that "I do not
intend to interfere with the right of any chief to his land. You may all know
that custom does not permit me to litigate with any chief for his land."[95]

Anxious to avoid an open confrontation with his colleagues, Prempeh II
instead directed his quest for land to the architects of his "restoration." At
the second session of the Confederacy Council, the Adontenhene raised the
question "of the Kumasi land and its restoration by Government to the
Asantehene, the original owner of the Kumasi land."[96] Officials were loath
to confront the issue. When the Lands Commission asked for a list of stools
for whom "the consent of the Asantihene is a requisite formality in order to
ensure that a gift of land by such stools would be duly and completely
effectuated," the chief commissioner prevaricated. Such a list existed, he
explained, but he "could not vouch for its accuracy . . . [especially] at this
time when the Confederacy is in its infancy. . . . "[97] Two years later, when
the Mamponhene brought the issue before the council again, the chief
commissioner's condescension barely concealed his desire for caution. Since
government had already turned down a similar request, the issue was moot—
although he granted that the chiefs might not be ready to concede the point.
"[A]s constant dripping wears away a stone I suppose you think if you
keep on asking perhaps you may succeed someday."[98]

In the event, that is just what happened. Prempeh persisted, evidently
well aware that the administration had pegged the viability of indirect rule
to his office. As more stool treasuries were established, and the administration grew less dependent on the revenue they derived from the Kumase
Town Lands, officials began to relent. In 1941, the government announced
its intention to hand over the Kumase Town Lands to the Golden Stool and,
after protracted haggling over terms, the transfer was completed in 1943.[99]
History had come more than full circle.

The Position of the Chief in Modern Asante[100]

As head of the first African state to win independence from colonial
rule, Nkrumah and his colleagues set out to transform the former Gold
Coast into a progressive modern nation. Nkrumah was determined both
to dismantle the archaic apparatus of indirect rule and to nip political

opposition to his own power in the bud. Chiefs were suspect on both counts, and none more so than those who had openly supported the National Liberation Movement (NLM), the Ashanti-based party that had mounted a fairly successful challenge to the Convention People's Party (CPP) in the elections of 1954. Although the Asantehene and other senior chiefs had backed away from the NLM, after the party fared poorly in the elections of 1956 and Britain rejected an Asante bid for secession,[101] Nkrumah was not prepared to forget the past. In 1958, he appointed a commission, headed by Justice Sarkodie Addo, to investigate allegations of financial misconduct by the Kumase State Council. The commission's findings were not particularly damaging, but Nkrumah decided to punish the chiefs anyway. Several outspoken supporters of the NLM were destooled and a few, including Amakomhene Nana Mensah Yiadom, were imprisoned. Nkrumah did not risk a direct challenge to the Asantehene: instead, in a move designed to weaken him financially, the state took over the Kumase Town Lands "to be held in trust for the Golden Stool and the natives of Kumasi."[102]

Nkrumah's attack on the structures of indirect rule was not limited to Asante. Chiefs throughout Ghana were relieved of the judicial and administrative powers they had held under colonial rule, and the Administration of Lands Act (1962) affirmed the state's unchallengeable right to acquire stool lands, as needed, "for public purposes."[103] To contemporary observers, it appeared that chieftaincy was doomed. By "divorc[ing] the chief from the land," wrote one, the new laws "struck directly to the heart of the institution of chieftaincy itself [and] it is . . . difficult to see how the chiefs can long remain a significant factor in the social, political or governmental life of the country."[104]

Thirty years later, this prediction remains unfulfilled. If anything, chiefs in Asante have extended their authority over land in the years since independence, and they continue to exercise a good deal of influence *de facto*, if not *de jure*, in politics and administration as well. Although it confirmed and extended the state's power to acquire and regulate stool lands, the Administration of Lands Act of 1962 was studiously vague on the question of ownership. In Kumase, land is divided into two categories: Part I (Kumase Town Lands and additional state acquisitions) is "controlled" by the government but "owned" by the Golden Stool, while the rest (Part II) is "administered" by the Lands Department but "managed" by the stools.[105] Thus, the language of the act avoids outright abrogation of the Golden Stool's authority over Part I and remains silent on the question of who *owns* Part II.

For the colonial state, as we have seen, the main purpose of resurrecting "the Asante Confederacy" was to achieve a more effective centralization of "native authority," and the Asantehene's office was central to that strategy. As Asantehene, Prempeh II wielded far greater judicial authority than he had as "Kumasihene." Beginning in 1935, the Asantehene's Grade A Court could hear appeals from any paramount chief's court in the region, as well as from all native tribunals in Kumase. In addition, the Asantehene exercised jurisdiction over all land disputes in which stools' interests were at issue, through a special Asantehene's Lands Court until 1940, and the Grade B Divisional Court thereafter.[106] Although the customary courts were disbanded after independence, the Asantehene has continued to play a major role in the adjudication of land disputes—"calling" cases from court for arbitration; giving, or strategically withholding, evidence in court;[107] and, it is alleged, often shaping litigants' strategies offstage. In addition, his continued jurisdiction over chieftaincy affairs has allowed the Asantehene to exercise far-reaching influence over stool land matters as well.

When the Kumase Town Lands were transferred to the Golden Stool in 1943, a special Asantehene's Land Office was created, adjacent to the palace at Manhyia, with responsibility for administering the former Crown Lands. Though formal administrative authority was transferred to the Lands Department after independence, the Asantehene's Land Office has continued to play an active role in the process of land allocation, reviewing all applications for leases before they are approved by the Lands Commission.[108] A study carried out in the mid-1970s reported that

> In Kumasi and the whole of Ashanti, the Asantehene is, by courtesy, referred to as the absolute owner of the land, and the sub-chiefs of Kumasi and the chiefs of the various towns in the region are referred to as caretaker chiefs who can only transfer land to strangers with the concurrence of the Asantehene.[109]

When a chief allocates land, the author added, one-third of the proceeds are remitted to the Asantehene "to signify his absolute title to the land," while the remaining two-thirds are divided equally between the "caretaker chief" and "the maintenance of the stool."[110]

In the years since independence, chiefs and citizens throughout Asante have engaged in vigorous debates over the bounds of "courtesy" and the practical rights and responsibilities of a "caretaker." Despite Nkrumah's statutory assault on traditional authority, disputes over chiefly jurisdiction continue to flood the courts. In 1973, the Acheampong regime created a special tribunal, the Stool Lands Boundaries Settlement Commission (SLBSC), with jurisdiction equivalent to that of a high court, to handle disputes over stool land. Like the Committee of Privileges convened by the chief com-missioner in 1935 to clear up any disputes over chiefly jurisdiction that might interfere with the smooth workings of the restored Confederacy, the commission was intended to put itself out of business by resolving disputed stool boundaries once and for all. In 1993, the commission had a substan-tial backlog of cases, and there was little reason to expect that its doors would close any time soon. Cases often lie in the commission's docket for years, and ways have been found to circumvent its decisions, even on ap-peal.[111]

The vitality of ongoing debate over stool lands is reflected in the con-tinuing elusiveness of their boundaries. In 1975, a report prepared at the University of Science and Technology's Land Administration Research Cen-ter included a map of stool lands in the Kumase metropolitan area, but the author cautioned that

> mapping the boundaries between the various sectors of Kumasi is not so easy. . . . In many cases, it would appear that no definite boundaries have been agreed upon between the various stool lands, and in other cases, litigation as to the location of the boundary is in process. . . . [T]he exact boundaries between these villages [which predate Osei Tutu] are not de-fined, and people do not want to hazard the approximate boundaries since it might lead to dispute among the chiefs.[112]

Twenty years later, the task was no nearer completion. In 1993, I was told that, at the request of the World Bank, the Lands Commission was prepar-ing an up-to-date map of stool boundaries in Kumase. Further inquiry re-vealed that the project had been underway for several years and was not likely to be completed soon. The demarcation of stool boundaries, begun with such enthusiasm by colonial commissioners at the beginning of the twentieth century, continues at the century's end with no denouement in sight.

First Families of Kumase

In the years since independence, the men who occupied the Golden Stool have waged a steady campaign to extend their authority over land.[113] Struggles over the Asantehene's claims to land, in and around Kumase, have lent new energy to debates over the interpretation of Asante history. Although many Asantes—lawyers and chiefs, as well as ordinary citizens—hesitate to challenge the Asantehene directly, some have been galvanized into open defiance. Several of the most bitterly contested land disputes in Kumase today turn on conflicting claims by the occupant of the Golden

Stool and the descendants of some of the city's "first families," whose ancestors were established in the area before the time of Osei Tutu.

In 1949 or 1950, Oheneba Boakye Dankwa, a son of Prempeh II and the
Akyempimhene of Kumase, took a farmer named Kwame Kobi to court.[114]
The chief accused Kwame Kobi of insubordination,[115] alleging, among other
things, that Kwame Kobi had cut down trees at the village of Apaasu without asking the chief's permission or paying him tribute. In his defense,
Kwame Kobi declared that he had bought land at Apaasu from the Kaasehene
and was only exercising his legitimate rights.

In rebuttal, Boakye Dankwa outlined the history of his own claim to the
land. When Osei Tutu first returned to Kumase from Denkyira, where he
had spent much of his youth, the area was already occupied by a number of
petty chieftaincies, including Kaase and Amakom.[116] Osei Tutu fought against
some of these chiefs, establishing his power in Asante by conquest before
he led their combined forces in a successful bid to break away from
Denkyira. Having fought with the Kaasehene and driven him to Bekwai,
Boakye Dankwa explained, Osei Tutu took control of the Kaase stool lands
and gave part to his wife and sons. The Akyempimhene sent people to
settle on his portion of the land, and their descendants had served his stool
ever since. When the ancestor of the present Odikro (village head) of Apaasu
migrated to Asante from Denkyira, he added, it was the Akyempimhene
who settled him at Apaasu and made him *odikro*. Having been driven from
the land by Osei Tutu, the Kaasehene had lost all claim to it and Kwame
Kobi's "purchase" was therefore invalid. Although the chief's testimony
dwelled on Kwame Kobi's insubordination, the historical narrative on which
he based his accusations implied a further claim—namely, that by conquer-
ing the Asante chiefs, Osei Tutu had acquired authority over their lands as
well as their subjects.

Twelve years after Akyempimhene's dispute with Kwame Kobi, in
1963, Nana Owusu Yaw Ababio succeeded to the Kaase stool. In 1968,
Nana Owusu quarreled with members of the Kumase Traditional Council and, in Justice François' vivid phrasing, was "pushed off the stool
and constrained to wander in the wilderness for thirteen years."[117] Nana
Owusu complained to the National House of Chiefs, which ruled, in
1981, that he had been improperly destooled and ordered him reinstated.
The chiefs also issued a restraining order, which forbade Nana Owusu
Domie (the man who had taken his place) from acting as chief or "dealing with Kaase Stool lands."[118]

Nana Domie defied the chiefs' orders and refused to relinquish either the
stool or its properties. When a second ruling by the National House of
Chiefs failed to dislodge him, Nana Owusu Yaw Ababio took his case to
court and, in 1985, obtained a writ of delivery for the return of the Kaase

stool properties. Two years later they were handed over, together with a set of plans for a new *ahenfie* (palace) and layouts for two new industrial areas to be sited on Kaase stool land, and the case appeared to have been re- solved. But Nana Owusu was not permitted to resume control of the Kaase stool lands. Instead, the Asantehene appointed a committee, composed of the Nsumankwahene of Kumase and several others, which took possession of the land and "started disposing of portions thereof."[119] The Kaasehene then sued the Asantehene and members of the committee for possession and declaration of title to the Kaase stool lands.

In the ensuing litigation, the defendants tried to reopen the destoolment case against the Kaasehene, but the courts refused to entertain their plea, arguing that the stool dispute was *res judicata*, and the only issue be- fore the court was the question of title to the land. Judgments given in the Kumase High Court and, later, the Supreme Court of Appeals turned on four principal points: (1) whether Osei Tutu's conquests had given him (and his successors) authority over land as well as people; (2) whether the Kaase stool lands were included in the Kumase Town Lands, which the colonial government had handed over to the Golden Stool in 1943; (3) whether the Asante Confederacy Council's resolution of 1938 (quoted above, p. 79) applied to both paramount and subordinate stools, or to paramount stools only; and (4) whether the fact that the Kaasehene had once remitted part of his stool revenue to the Asantehene, as a ges- ture of "courtesy," showed that the Golden Stool owned the land from which the revenue had been derived.

The trial judge ruled that the Kaase stool lands lay outside the boundary of the former Kumase Town Lands;[120] that what the defendants/appellants referred to as the Asante Confederacy Council's "alleged restatement of Ashanti custom on land ownership" in 1938 applied to subordinate as well as to paramount chiefs; and that Prempeh II's promise not "to interfere with the right of any chief to his land" applied to Kaase. The judge also considered it "doubtful" that when Osei Tutu "subjugated lesser stools in and around Kumase, . . . the conquered stools were divested of their title as absolute owners of the lands they had toiled for and had attached to their stools."[121] Although the Asantehene normally confirms allocations of stool land and receives one-third of their revenue, he argued, the stool retains the remaining two-thirds and "it is illogical to imagine how the 'owner' takes the lesser share and the 'caretaker' takes the larger share."[122] Accordingly, he awarded title to the Kaasehene and ordered that he should take posses- sion of the land.

The Supreme Court, which heard the case on appeal, agreed that the Kaase stool lands lay outside the Kumase Town Lands (which the Crown had transferred to the Golden Stool in 1943) but was divided on the question of title. Justice François affirmed the trial judge's ruling that the Kaasehene should take possession but declined to rule on the question of "absolute ownership," intimating instead that because of the Kaasehene's gesture of courtesy, the issue might never be resolved. Justice Adjabeng went further. Agreeing with the plaintiff's counsel that Osei Tutu did not "take the lands" of conquered chiefs,[123] he went on to argue that paramount stools—of which the Golden Stool is the supreme example—may not deprive "subordinate stools" of their rights to allocate land, citing the Asante Confederacy Council resolution of 1938 and several other cases in which the courts had upheld allocations of land made by subordinate stools. He also quoted extensively from the writings of Justice Ollenu, Casely Hayford, and J. B. Danquah, to show that land ownership by subordinate stools "is not a custom of land tenure peculiar to Ashanti." In short, Justice Adjabeng not only dismissed the defendants' case but also suggested that the Asantehene's attempt to claim ownership of Kaase stool land was contrary both to Asante precedent and to national traditions.

The Supreme Court's ruling drew national attention. One informant recounted gleefully that lawyers for the defendants huddled in Accra after the court's judgment was read, wondering how to break the news in Kumase. Another suggested that the Kaase case helped to precipitate the government's decision, announced in 1993, to undertake a pilot program of land registration in selected areas of Kumase and Accra. A lawyer in Kumase expressed grudging admiration for François' agile evasion of the question of allodial title—"he is a terrible man . . . so intelligent!"—but added that "he doesn't understand Ashanti customary rights."

Indeed, the exact import of the Kaase case remains open to debate. On the crucial question of title to stool lands, the appeals court ruling was ambiguous: the justices gave varied opinions and no attempt was made to reconcile their differences. Moreover, the Kaasehene's troubles did not end with the court's judgment. Several months later, the chief submitted his first allocation papers to the Lands Commission "on a trial basis," only to learn that the Ministry of Lands and Forests had issued an instrument compulsorily acquiring the land for public purposes. His lawyer[124] promptly challenged the acquisition as serving no demonstrable public purpose and threatened to sue. The ministry backed off, and the chief and his lawyer were persuaded to adopt a less confrontational approach. As of mid-1994, they were "negotiating inside [the government]" over the Kaasehene's ability to *exercise* the rights he had won in court.

It is not only chiefs who have found themselves at loggerheads with the Golden Stool over land. Another case, much discussed in the mid-1990s, involved the Asaman Kani family—descendants of Obiri Yeboah, the last of the local chiefs to preside over the loose confederation of petty chieftaincies that occupied Kumase before Osei Tutu came to power in the late seventeenth century.[125] During the 1990s, representatives of the Asaman Kani family became involved in a dispute over a large area on the southwestern side of Kumase, including Kwadaso Layout (a sprawling, middleclass residential area) and the suburbs of Kwamase, Apre, and Fankyenebra.[126] Some years ago, the government acquired a piece of land at Kwadaso as a site for a research institute and, as required by law, offered to compensate the rightful owner(s) for the loss of their property. The Asantehemaa claimed the money on behalf of the Golden Stool but was challenged by Obaapanin Yaa Tiwaa, the head of the Asaman Kani family. Later, when Yaa Tiwaa tried to lease out plots in another part of Kwadaso, she discovered that the Asantehemaa had already "sold" them. She offered to remit part of her land revenues to the Golden Stool if the Asantehene would acknowledge her family's claims, but the Asantehemaa refused. With neither party ready to concede the other's claim to title, the case was at an impasse.

Obaapanin Adwoa Adowaa, who succeeded Yaa Tiwaa,[127] continued to pursue the family's claims to land, both in and out of court. She issued leases; sued "unauthorized" holders of undeveloped plots, hoping to regain control of the land; and, on one occasion, tore down an uncompleted structure put up by someone else's tenant.[128] Some of her actions have been directed against ordinary citizens, who had acquired their plots in good faith and believed that their leases were valid. In 1974, for example, Osei Assibey acquired two adjacent plots at Kwadaso. He obtained allocation papers[129] but lacked the resources to develop the land at that time. Later, Adwoa Adowaa "sold" one of the plots to another lessee, and Osei Assibey challenged her in court. When he finally began to build on the second plot, the Obaapanin sued him—arguing that, as

> Head of the Asaman Kani Royal Family . . . from which the earliest recorded Kings of Ashanti, namely:—Twum Antwi, Oti Akenten, Kobia Amanfi and Obiri Yeboah were each in his turn nominated, elected and installed as Kings of Ashanti before its rebellion against the Denkyira overlords . . . , [she was] the only person . . . entitled to alienate, transfer lease out or deal with it as an exclusive owner thereof.[130]

Osei Assibey produced his lease in court, whereupon Adwoa Adowaa obtained an injunction, restraining him from entering the land (or completing his building) until the question of title was resolved. Though confident that the suit would fail on technical grounds,[131] Osei Assibey's lawyer admitted that there were larger issues at stake. Adwoa Adowaa should not have sued Osei Assibey at all, he said: "her case is with Otumfuo." The lawyer added that he hoped the court would hear the case and settle it, to protect leaseholders like Osei Assibey. "How can people build for their children with all this havoc?"

In both the Kaase and the Asaman Kani cases, the plaintiffs claimed ownership of land that their forebears had occupied (in present-day Kumase) before the time of Osei Tutu. In recent years, as economic recovery and urban growth have pushed up the value of land in a widening belt around the city, questions have also been raised about the Golden Stool's historical relationship to land outside the precolonial capital. In 1996, for example, two suits were brought against the Golden Stool itself over land at Baaman (east of Kumase off the Accra road) and Aputuogya (12 km to the southeast on the road to Lake Bosumtwi). Both areas are feeling the effects of urban growth. Buildings have sprung up rapidly, since the late 1980s, along the Accra Road,[132] and the area around Aputuogya has recently been zoned for industrial development.[133] In both of the suits, the principal plaintiff was Adontenhene Nana Agyeman Nkwantabisa III, the present successor to Chief Kwame Frimpon.[134]

Nana Nkwantabisa, who succeeded to the Adonten stool in 1966, has campaigned actively on behalf of his stool's rights over land. On a tour of Adonten stool properties, I was shown a building put up by Chief Frimpon on land which he had leased from the Crown in Adum. By the time of Nana Nkwantabisa's succession, the stool had lost control over the property. Acting on information that was revealed to him in a dream, Nana managed to track down copies of the relevant documents in Accra and recovered it. The original lease had expired in 1987, and Nana Nkwantabisa was still litigating, in 1996, with the tenants over the terms of its renewal. After thirty years on the stool, Nana Nkwantabisa is confident of his knowledge of history and his ability to defend the stool's interests. "I know my right from my left," he likes to say, "and I will not allow anyone to cheat me."

In his suits against the Asantehene, Nana Nkwantabisa has linked his claims to the history of his ancestors, who lived near Kumase before the founding of the Asante state, rather than to that of the Adonten stool, a military office that rose to prominence under Osei Tutu. In the Baaman case, Nana invoked the history of his ancestral stool, Eduaben, while at Aputuogya he emphasized that, as members of the Aseneɛ clan, the earliest settlers there were his kin.[135] A key source for his case at Baaman is a passage in *Ashanti Law and Constitution*, in which Rattray named Eduaben as one of five stools (*amantuo num*) who paid tribute to Denkyira before Osei Tutu led the Asante armies to victory over their imperious neighbor.[136]

As one of a group that includes Kumase, Mampon, Juaben, and Assumegya, Eduaben enjoys the status of a paramount stool.

Obeng Manu, the ebullient lawyer who was representing the Adontenhene in the Baaman suit, noted that on this point the chief's case was not airtight. After the war against Denkyira, the king's charismatic councillor, Komfo Anokye, advised Osei Tutu to bring Eduaben to Kumase where he could keep an eye on him. "Nobody could challenge Komfo Anokye, so he came." Unfortunately, the lawyer explained, this incident tends to "blur" Eduaben's historic status as an independent stool, equivalent to the other *amantuo num* in status and antiquity.[137] Fortunately, he added, there was other customary evidence to turn to. The Adontenhene is not required to remove his sandals when greeting the Asantehene—"a rare privilege," which the chief and his lawyer were counting on to offset any doubts the court might entertain on the question of Eduaben's status.

Arcane debates over chiefly protocol and ancient history are not, of course, the only basis for contemporary claims to land. The property and prestige of the Adonten stool today owe at least as much to Chief Frimpon's exploits in the twentieth century as to those of his seventeenth-century forebears. As the present chief's "grandson" pointed out, "Chief Frimpon was the one who developed the stool lands."[138] Chief Frimpon wielded considerable influence with the colonial administration, an advantage that he used to promote his own interests and those of his stool. He plied individual commissioners with information on Asante history and custom, testified in several official inquiries,[139] and had frequent recourse to the courts to press his claims against the colonial state, as well as his peers and compatriots. In 1915, he obtained judgment in the chief commissioner's court to a tract of land on the Mampon Road that is still held by the stool. Three years later, he was litigating over land at Eduaben.[140]

Like his redoubtable predecessor, Nana Nkwantabisa has come into close contact, sometimes conflict, with occupants of the Golden Stool. Chief Frimpon's opposition to the Prempehs was well-known, but he managed to avoid an outright break. Keenly attuned to the opportunities as well as the pitfalls of colonial interpretations of Asante custom, Frimpon opposed Prempeh II's reinstatement, but once the "restored" Asante Confederacy was in place, he accepted it as an accomplished fact, taking his seat on the Confederacy Council and playing a prominent role as a judge in the Asantehene's courts. When Nana Nkwantabisa was enstooled, he "met Prempeh II" and respected him: "Nana Prempeh knew history!" As his relations with Prempeh II's successor have frayed, Nana Nkwantabisa has also had frequent recourse to history. In his recent suits against the Asantehene, Nana has invoked episodes from his ancestors' domestic affairs as well as their dealings with the state. Tales of courtship, marriage, household management, and slavery mingle with accounts of migration and settlement, conquest, and oaths of office in his pleadings before the courts.

The dispute at Baaman began when Nana Nkwantabisa learned that the Asantehene, in a letter, had stated that the Amape stool lands (located at Baaman) were being looked after by his caretaker. The Adontenhene wrote to the Asantehene, asking him to withdraw the statement, but his letters went unanswered, so he decided to sue. In his statement of claim, the Adontenhene averred that the caretaker, one Obaapanin Afua Manu, was descended from the wife of a hunter, who was placed on the land by the Eduabenhene—and *not* (as Otumfuo had allegedly claimed) from a wife of the king (*oheneyere*).[141] In short, the chief argued, Obaapanin Manu was *his* caretaker, not the Asantehene's, and the land she was looking after belonged to him.

A number of lands in and around Kumase are claimed today by descendants of *aheneyere*,[142] in narratives that follow a common pattern. The king, having recently married, approached one of his chiefs to request land for his wife and her people. In some versions, the wife in question is said to have been the king's favorite, or so beautiful that he could not bear to be separated from her. Owing to distance or some natural obstacle such as a river, the place where she lived at the time of their marriage was difficult for the king to get to, and he wanted her closer to the capital. Invariably, the chief not only agreed to allow the woman in question to settle on his land but, because she was a wife of the king, ceded full authority over the land to her and her descendants in perpetuity.

Such narratives play on well-known themes, adding resonance to contemporary claims by multiplying their links to the past. In Akan communities, husbands and wives may reside separately for extended periods of time. Some couples remain with their respective families after marriage rather than establish a new conjugal household, and spouses often travel separately to conduct business or visit relatives and friends. Since polygyny has long been regarded as a marker of status, and a king's opportunities in this respect were almost unlimited, stories of descent from *aheneyere* may plausibly support a large number of claims to land. Moreover, the king's interest in conjugal proximity meant that lands given to *aheneyere* were likely to have been located fairly close to the royal capital. Thus, landholders whose claims derive from the matrimonial politics of the eighteenth century are often well placed to profit from urban growth in the twentieth. In the Bamaan case, the Asantehene's apparently casual reference to Obaapanin Manu as "his caretaker" tapped into a rich vein of historical allusion, which the Adontenhene evidently found sufficiently threatening to warrant the trouble and expense of a suit.

Nana Nkwantabisa's second case, at Aputuogya, turned not on the issue of royal marriage but on tales of kinship, servitude, and domestic organization. Initially, the dispute did not involve the Golden Stool at all. In 1994, the Adontenhene sued the secretary and chairman of the Aputuogya Town Development Council for title to "Aputuogya lands [which] have been the property of the Plaintiffs' Stool from time immemorial." His ancestors, Nana claimed, who belonged to the Aseneɛ clan, had settled some of their kinsmen on the land in question, and his stool therefore held allodial title "through its Aseneɛ Clan members represented by the second and third defendants."[143] He added, parenthetically, that Aputuogya was Gyaase (an office traditionally responsible for managing a royal or chiefly household) to the Adonten stool.

In response, the defendants averred that the Aputuogya stool "and its lands" had existed before the Denkyira wars; that Osei Tutu had promoted the stool to the rank of ɔbirempon after its occupant lost his life fighting with the Asantes against Denkyira; and that the question of Aputuogya's relationship to the Adonten stool, which had been submitted to the Kumase Traditional Council for arbitration in 1976, was unresolved. Since the Aputuogya stool was vacant, they argued, responsibility for managing its lands had devolved upon the town development council. As land values rose along Lake Road, the council sold several plots, using the proceeds to build "schools and places of convenience" for the benefit of the community. Casting themselves as agents of modernity, the defendants claimed that they had acted in a legitimate and public-spirited manner to ensure that the community was not excluded from the march of progress by the weight of archaic claims.

The defendants received a sympathetic hearing from the court. In a nicely balanced ruling, Justice Aninankwah of the Kumase High Court rejected the Adontenhene's request for an interim injunction, arguing that it would inflict hardship on the community as a whole by blocking further development for an indefinite period of time. To encourage the defendants' efforts on behalf of the community without prejudicing the question of title, the court ordered that the town development council be formally constituted as a land allocation committee, and that it open a bank account where the proceeds of future land allocations (net of funds invested in town development) would be held, pending the outcome of the court case.[144]

Two years later, a new statement of defense was submitted to the court, which differed significantly from the original in both form and content. The slate of defendants had been reorganized: the original codefendant was replaced by another, and the second defendant, though still listed in the suit, had been removed as chairman of the town development council.[145] In contrast to the original defense, which simply referred to "the Aputuogya lands," the revised defense began by asserting that "Aputuogya lands belong to the Asantehene as the occupant of the Golden Stool" and that the Aputuogyahene was his caretaker. The rest of the defendants' statement recapitulated, briefly, the town development council's efforts on behalf of the community but dwelled at length on questions of chiefly origins, succession, and precedence.

The codefendant traced in detail his ancestors' migration from Assin Adwafo to settle at Aduadin and Butuagya, and their relationships to Osei Tutu through marriage, oaths of allegiance, and support in the war against Denkyira. He then jumped to the twentieth century and the relationship between the Aputuogya stool and the Adontenhene. This, he declared, was of recent provenance, having begun "sometime after Prempeh I had been exiled to the Seychelles" when, in the Asantehene's absence, a newly appointed successor to the Aputuogya stool had taken his oath of office before Chief Kwame Frimpon, in Kumase.[146] After the Asante Confederacy was "restored" in 1935, there was some confusion over whether Aputuogya was subordinate to the Adonten stool or only to the Asantehene. Eventually it was "agreed that Co-defendant's family prepares to go and swear before Otumfuor," but various misfortunes prevented successors to the Aputuogya stool from acting on this decision. After a series of abdications, the stool fell vacant, and the Adontenhene "laid adverse claim to the lands of Aputuogya," asserting that the stool was his Gyaase. The matter was taken to the Kumase Traditional Council, where it had languished since 1976.[147]

Although the Asantehene was not named as a party to the revised defense, the Adontenhene saw his influence behind the case. Relations between the Adontenhene and the Golden Stool had already deteriorated to such a point that the Asantehene told Nana Nkwantabisa not to attend meetings of the Kumase Traditional Council, and asked the Amakomhene to take the Adontenhene's place on ceremonial occasions.[148] (In view of Chief Frimpon's long campaign to assert the Adonten stool's authority over Amakom, this gesture must have been particularly galling to the Adontenhene.) Concluding that the Asantehene was the moving force behind the whole dispute at Aputuogya, the Adontenhene filed suit against the Asantehene and the secretary of the Kumase Traditional Council for declaration of title to Aputuogya stool lands. In their statement of claim, the plaintiffs elaborated on the issue of Aputuogya's subservience to the Adonten stool.

During the reign of Opoku Ware I,[149] the Adontenhene led a successful military campaign in the north, in which the king of Yendi was killed and many captives taken. These captives were "brought down by the Adontenhene's contingents in the various Ashanti armies to work for and to serve the families and Stools of the plaintiffs," and their descendants "have no more title to any part of the said tract of land than their original captive predecessors. . . . "[150] Outraged to discover that the Asantehene was "inciting the townspeople to rebel,"[151] Nana Nkwantabisa escalated his attack, hoping perhaps to discredit the defendants once and for all by labeling them descendants of foreigners and slaves.

CONCLUSION

Throughout the twentieth century, the commercialization of land claims in Kumase has been embedded in struggles over authority. Absorbed into the colonial state as subordinate administrators and adjudicators, then stripped of their official functions by successive governments of Ghana, chiefs have remained remarkably influential in Asante. Chiefly control over land has allowed traditional officeholders not only to appropriate a significant share of the economic surplus generated by economic and urban growth but also to maintain an active hand in the mobilization and exercise of power, *de facto* if not *de jure*. Far from being relegated to the rural margins of colonial and postcolonial society, chieftaincy flourishes in Asante *because* it is anchored in the heart of the urban economy. State power may be hierarchical in Ghana, but it is not bifurcated.[152]

The social consequences of stool ownership of urban land in Asante are difficult to reduce to a single formula. The authority to allocate land has given chiefs a decided advantage in tapping the rents generated by urban growth and commercialization. By selling fifty- and ninety-nine-year leaseholds, Kumase stools have captured much of the increase in urban land values, and chiefs have managed to tap a good part of those funds for their own use. At the same time, under the prevailing interpretation of customary law, the sale of leaseholds does not terminate the stool's authority over the land in question. Thus, chiefs continue to assert and defend their claims on stool land, even after it has been allocated and built upon. In Kumase, this has meant that holders of long-term leases may find their land subject to dispute and their own access to it constrained by order of the courts, even though the validity of their own claim is beyond question. As a high court judge observed, in denying the Adontenhene's request for an injunction over the disputed land at Eduaben, "whenever two elephants fight, it is the ground that suffers."[153]

If stool lands have underwritten chieftaincy in Asante, it does not follow that chiefs are simply hereditary landlords with an unchallengeable monopoly over the rents generated by rising demand for fixed amounts of land. For one thing, while the supply of land within a given set of coordinates may be fixed, chiefly jurisdictions are not: both the boundaries of stools' lands and their place in the regional hierarchy of traditional offices have remained subject to contestation throughout the colonial and postcolonial periods. In addition, while many stools are controlled by particular families, succession is neither automatic nor guaranteed for life. To be selected for a stool, an individual must be able to mobilize support within the appropriate family or community and maintain it in order to remain in office. In general, the survival of chieftaincy in Asante has served both to reproduce a class of rent-seeking officeholders and to foster debate over their prerogatives and responsibilities. Preferential access to revenue from land has helped to sustain chiefs' influence and demands for their accountability.

As British officials soon discovered when they set out to govern Asante, Kumase has never been an urban enclave set apart, culturally or politically, from the surrounding peasant society. By the late nineteenth century, the lands and subjects of Kumase office holders were widely dispersed across the region, and occupants and subjects of provincial stools were linked to residents of Kumase by multiple ties of kinship, allegiance, and obligation. With the growth of trade and production, and the recentralization of authority in Kumase under colonial rule, historic links between city and countryside were replenished and intensified, as residents of Kumase invested in cocoa farms and rural trade, and successful farmers, traders, and chiefs from outlying areas built houses and cultivated connections in the capital. If wealth and power were to some extent concentrated in the capital, access to them and debates over their use were not. In the following chapters, I present case studies of two peri-urban villages and a rural stool, to compare changing patterns of land claims outside the city with those in Kumase, and explore the connections between them.

NOTES

1. Busia, *The position of the chief*; McCaskie, "Accumulation II"; McCaskie, "*Ahyiamu*"; and McCaskie, "R. S. Rattray and the construction of Asante history."

2. The name under which Agyeman Prempeh I returned from the Seychelles, as a private citizen, in 1924. See below, 73–75.

3. Tordoff, *Ashanti*, chs. xiv–xv; Hailey, *Native administration*.

4. NAGA ADM 5/4/32, *Papers relating to the restoration of the Ashanti Confederacy* (Accra: Government Printer, 1932).

5. For a sympathetic account of Opoku Ware II's career before his election to the Golden Stool in 1970, see I. Wilks, *A portrait of Otumfuo Opoku Ware II as a young man* (Accra: Anansesem Publications, 1995).

6. Harvey, *Law and social change*.

7. Tordoff, *Ashanti*, 31, 39.

8. Ibid., 193.

9. Tordoff, *Ashanti*, 193. See also B. Tipple, "Development of housing policy in Kumasi, Ghana, 1901–1981" (University of Newcastle upon Tyne, Centre for Architectural Research and Development Overseas, 1987), 5.

10. By 1912, officials were lamenting that their predecessors had not been bolder in claiming land for the Crown at the time of annexation, when British authorities were "in a position to dictate terms." NAGA ADM 5/3/13, "Report on the alienation of native lands . . . ," 8.

11. In 1921, for example, an official noted that land acquired for the railway in Tafo was "expected to be acquired free of compensation" and could not be returned to the stool simply because the railway was subsequently diverted from its intended course. NAGK 1587, Land acquisition Tafo-Coomassie, 1921. The administration also laid claim to prime commercial land near the railway station at Kejetia. NAGK 547, KPHB to CCA, 2/12/26.

12. Tipple, "Development of housing policy," 6.

13. Special areas of the city were earmarked by the colonial administration for African immigrants from the coast (Fante New Town) and savannah regions to the north (Zongo, New Zongo, Aboabo). Traders from the eastern Mediterranean (Greeks and "Syrians" or Lebanese) also established firms and leased plots in Kumase in the early years of the twentieth century. G. Clark, *Onions are my husband: Survival and accumulation by West African market women* (Chicago: University of Chicago Press, 1994), 111.

14. Tordoff, *Ashanti*, 172; Austin, "Emergence."

15. Brown, "Kumase"; R. Howard, *Colonialism and underdevelopment in Ghana* (London: Croom Helm, 1978), 63; S. A. Darko, "Changing settlement patterns in Ashanti, 1873–1966" (Ph.D. diss., University of London, 1971).

16. Clark, *Onions*, 111; Tipple, "Development of housing policy," 3; Darko, "Changing settlement patterns."

17. P. Hill, *Migrant cocoa farmers of southern Ghana*; Austin, "Emergence" and "Capitalists and chiefs."

18. G. B. Kay, *The political economy of colonialism in Ghana* (Cambridge: Cambridge University Press, 1972), 15, 27.

19. In 1921, for example, Ashanti revenue from local sources consisted of £7000 in rents, plus £3800 from licenses and fees. NAGA ADM 11/1/1907, Annual Report, Ashanti, 1921.

20. NAGA ADM 5/3/13, H. C. Belfield, Report on legislation governing the alienation of native lands in the Gold Coast Colony and Ashanti, Cd 6278, 1912.

21. Administration (Ashanti) Ordinance, 1902, cited in A. R. Edmundson, *Land ownership and acquisition in Kumase* (Kumase: Land Administration Research Centre, University of Science and Technology, 1975).

22. NAGK 1587, Land acquisition Tafo-Coomassie, 1921.

23. NAGK 547, Land in Kumasi leases, Kumasi Public Health Board to Chief Commissioner, Ashanti, 2/12/26.

24. See ch. 1, 21–23.

25. Ibid.

26. Some of the earliest municipal agencies established in colonial Kumase were the police and the Sanitary Committee, founded in 1909. Following the second outbreak of plague, in 1924, the Sanitary Committee was expanded and renamed the Kumase Public Health Board (KPHB). Composed of representatives of the town's elites—merchants and chiefs—the KPHB took on many of the functions of a town council—receiving revenue from ground rents and market and license fees, and issuing regulations concerning trade, building standards, and road maintenance, as well as drainage and waste disposal. Controlled by resident expatriates, the KPHB served as a "testing ground for local rivalries and alliances," within the European and African communities as well as between them. Clark, *Onions*, 111. In 1928, control over the allocation of plots was transferred to the newly established Lands Department and, in 1943, the board itself was replaced by the Kumase Town Council. NAGK 547, "Land in Kumasi Leases, 1925–29"; Arhin, *The city of Kumasi handbook: Past, present and future* (Legon: Institute of African Studies, University of Ghana, 1992). See also Tordoff, *Ashanti*, 154, 216–17; and Tipple, "Development of housing policy," 6–7.

27. Tipple, "Development of housing policy," 5.

28. E. Schildkrout, *People of the zongo* (Cambridge: Cambridge University Press, 1978), 76. Residents of Kumase Zongo came from all over West Africa and the Northern Territories of the Gold Coast. Immigrants from the Gold Coast Colony congregated in other parts of the city.

29. Clark, *Onions*, 111–12; Tipple, "Development of housing policy," 3.

30. As happened in other African cities under colonial rule. See, e.g., M. Swanson, "The sanitation syndrome: Bubonic plague and urban native policy in the Cape Colony, 1900–1909," *Journal of African History* 18 (1977): 387–410; A. L. Mabogunje, "Urban planning and the post-colonial state: A research overview," *African Studies Review* 33, no. 2 (1990): 137ff.

31. Colonial officials distinguished, in Kumase and elsewhere, between "natives" and "strangers," though the meanings of these terms varied from one context to another. See chs. 1, 15–20; 5, 150–55; and 6, 180–84.

32. Tipple, "Development of housing policy," 4.

33. K. Abankroh, "Aboabo: A study of an immigrant residential area in Kumasi" (B.Sc. thesis, Department of Planning, University of Science and Technology, Kumase, 1977).

34. Tipple, "Development of housing policy," 5.

35. Annual Reports on Ashanti, quoted in Tipple, "Development of housing policy." Official concerns over matters of health were sometimes carried to absurd lengths. In 1928–30, for example, when authorities in the Colony appropriated land "free of compensation" from the chiefs of Nkawkaw to establish a European residential area, African children were expressly barred from entering the area because they were likely to spread disease. NAGK 2395, "European residential areas acquired and paid out under agreement with Chiefs concerned–free of compensation, 1928–1930."

36. NAGK 1734, "Mbrom and Amakom-Aburutia layouts," Town Clerk, Kumasi, to Secretary of the Ashanti Health Board, 5/10/35.

37. Applicants included the Asantehene, ten farmers, four barristers, four clerks, three traders (one Syrian), three court officials, two storekeepers, two factors, two pub-

lic letter writers, an auctioneer, a Syrian surveyor, a government pensioner, an overseer from the Agricultural Department, and an Italian builder. NAGK 1734, "Mbrom and Amakom-Aburutia layouts," Asst. Commissioner of Lands to Chief Commissioner, 7/22/39.

38. NAGK 1734, "Mbrom and Amakom-Aburutia layouts," Memorandum, 1946.

39. Tipple, "Development of housing policy," 12.

40. Ibid., 14.

41. NAGK 1974, "Kumasi leases, 1948–1953," Acting Commissioner of Lands, 3/15/50.

42. Low-income areas were divided into those dominated by Asantes, by immigrants from the north, and by immigrants from southern Ghana. Cited in Abankroh, "Aboabo."

43. L. Nkansah, "Unauthorized development in residential areas in Kumasi" (B.Sc. thesis, Department of Planning, University of Science and Technology, Kumase, 1979); P.K.B. Asamoah, "The effect of city growth on land uses: Amakom Braponso and Atonsu-Kumasi" (B.Sc. thesis, Department of Planning, University of Science and Technology, Kumase, 1991); J. Buaduoh, "A study of large-scale acquisition of land by government and its impact on the urban fringes. A case study of UST and Ayeduase/Ayija" (B.Sc. thesis, Department of Planning, University of Science and Technology, Kumase, 1978); J. Bediako, "Impact of migration on low income housing in Kumasi" (B.Sc. thesis, Department of Planning, University of Science and Technology, Kumase, 1991); Abankroh, "Aboabo."

44. NAGK 577, "Wesleyan mission lands in Kumasi," Bartrop to Chief Commissioner, 1/25/05.

45. NAGK 2149, "Indenture between the Chief of Amakom and Rev. M. S. O'Rorke, Bishop of Accra, 1/1/1915."

46. NAGA ADM 11/1/1338, "Constitution and organization of Kumase stools." Undaunted, Chief Frimpon agreed that the lease was simply a business transaction, adding that the status of his stool was a matter of history, not business. See ch. 1, 21.

47. NAGK 1727, "Surveys of lands in Ashanti, 1931," CCA to DC, Kumasi, 1/10/31. Buildings, like cocoa farms, increasingly took the place of people as collateral for loans. Compare Austin, "Human pawning in Asante, 1800–1850: Markets and coercion, gender and cocoa," in T. Falola and P. Lovejoy, eds. *Pawnship in Africa: Debt bondage in historical perspective* (Boulder, CO: Westview, 1995).

48. MRO, Asantehene's Divisional Court B1 Record Book, vol. 53, 1950/51.

49. Ibid.

50. Until faster yielding varieties were introduced in the 1950s, most of the cocoa grown in Ghana took 7 to 8 years to mature.

51. H. Tabatabai, "Agricultural decline and access to food in Ghana," *International Labor Review* 127, no. 6 (1987): 717. A number of studies have shown that farm sizes and income are fairly unequally distributed among the minority of Ghanaian farmers who own any cocoa at all. See, e.g., Konings, *The state and rural class formation in Ghana*, 76; C. Elliott, *Patterns of poverty in the Third World* (New York, Praeger, 1975), 54; N. O. Addo, "Employment and labour supply on Ghana's cocoa farms in the pre- and post-Aliens Compliance Order era," *Economic Bulletin of Ghana*, 2nd series, 2, no. 4 (1972): 41–42; Ghana, Office of the Government Statistician, *Survey of cocoa producing families in Ashanti, 1956–57* (Accra: Government Statistician, 1960).

52. Official estimates of the housing stock in 1970 vary. According to the population census of 1970, the total was 12,000, while the Five Year Plan of 1975 gives a figure of 11,755. Tipple, "Development of housing policy," 34, 54.

53. Information on the early history of Amakom was collected in interviews with Amakomhene Nana Akusa Yiadom II, Buokromhene Nana Owusu Bempah, and Kwamohene Nana Amoako Mensah, and from sources in the National Archives. Details of Amakom's place in precolonial Asante may also be found in Wilks, *Asante*, and McCaskie, *State and society*. Unless indicated otherwise, information on the housing boom of the 1950s and 1960s was supplied by twenty-four residents of Amakom, whom I interviewed in October 1993.

54. Also reported in Buaduoh, "Large-scale acquisition of land."

55. NAGK 215/2, Chief Kweku Atta v. Kwami Panin; McCaskie, *State and society*, 40; interviews with Nana Akusa Yiadom II and the Odikro of Esaaso.

56. NAGK 2149, "Indenture. . . . ," 2/28/29.

57. Abankroh, "Aboabo."

58. The land included thirteen villages under the authority of the Amakomhene, but it was given to the state free of charge. Instead of compensation, residents were promised amenities and scholarships for some of their children. A study conducted in the late 1970s found that most of the villages had electricity and standpipes, though the latter were not very reliable. Toilets had yet to be built, however, and residents said that the scholarships had never materialized. Buaduoh, "Large-scale acquisition of land."

59. Tipple, "Development of housing policy," 56; Buaduoh, "Large-scale acquisition of land."

60. K. Awua-Peseah, "Kumasi—origin, growth and development of the city" (B.Sc. thesis, Department of Planning, University of Science and Technology, 1982).

61. Interview with the owner, 10/12/93. At the open market rate of exchange, ₡ 6,700,000 was worth ca. $US 19,200 in 1990.

62. Due, in large part, to external factors, including steep rises in world prices of oil and other commodities, and Ghana's declining share in the world cocoa market. For a useful summary, see J. Loxley, *Ghana: Economic crisis and the long road to recovery* (Ottawa: North-South Institute, 1988).

63. Tabatabai, "Agricultural decline," 721–24.

64. Tipple, "Development of housing policy," 52. He attributes the disproportionate growth of high-cost housing to the influence of rent control in low-income neighborhoods, but evidence on the actual enforcement of rent restrictions is slim. Ibid., 36–37.

65. NAGA ADM 11/1/1901, Ex-king Prempeh—return of, 1911–1925, Chief Commissioner to CS, 6/12/11.

66. Ibid., Chief Commissioner to Governor, 3/11/24. Advocates for the ex-Asantehene included Nana Sir Ofori Atta, Casely Hayford, and Nana Mate Kole, among others.

67. Ibid.

68. Ibid., Governor to Secretary of State for the Colonies, 3/15/24.

69. NAGA ADM 11/1/1905, Re King Prempeh, Governor's secret memo, 2/12/25.

70. NAGA ADM 11/1/1901, Confidential report from Duncan Johnstone to Chief Commissioner, 11/11/24. Johnstone was sent to accompany Prempeh on his homeward journey and assigned to gather intelligence on his activities for a year or so after he returned to Kumase. NAGA ADM 11/1/1906, Ex-King Prempeh, 1923–26.

The governor advised Johnstone to befriend Prempeh and prevent him from "revert[ing] to a purely native way of life." NAGA ADM 11/1/1905, Re King Prempeh, 1925–26, Governor's memo, 12/13/24.

71. NAGA ADM 11/1/1901, Petition dated 12/18/23.

72. See above, ch. 1, 24–25.

73. Agyeman Prempeh I took the name Edward after converting to Christianity during his exile in the Seychelles.

74. NAGA ADM 11/1/1901, Chief Frimpon to Chief Commissioner, 7/6/24.

75. NAGA ADM 11/1/1905, Re King Prempeh, Governor's secret memo, 2/12/25.

76. Ibid.

77. Official correspondence suggests that there was considerable tension in this period between a group of Kumase chiefs, led by Chief Frimpon, and members of the "Kotoko Society"—a group variously described in administrative correspondence as reformers (campaigning to rid Kumase of chiefly corruption), "intelligentsia," protonationalists, and junior members of the royal family who hoped to ride Prempeh's coattails to wealth and power. Chief Frimpon also intrigued with members of the Kotoko Society against senior Kumase chiefs. Relevant correspondence is contained in NAGA ADM 11/1/1901, Ex-king Prempeh—return of, 1911–1925; NAGA ADM 11/1/1905, Re King Prempeh, 1925–26; NAGA ADM 11/1/1906, Ex-King Prempeh, 1923–26; and NAGA ADM 11/1/1342, Edward Prempeh—Omanhene of Kumase, 1926–33. See ch. 1, 25.

78. NAGA ADM 11/1/1901, Minutes on Prempeh to District Commissioner Gosling, 11/27/24.

79. NAGA ADM 11/1/1905, Governor's Memo, 2/7/25.

80. Ibid., Governor to Chief Commissioner Maxwell, 4/3/25.

81. NAGA ADM 11/1/1906, Government Administrative Officer to Rt. Hon. L. S. Amery, M.P., 7/16/26.

82. Ibid., Chief Commissioner to SSC, 9/10/26.

83. J. Guyer, "Representation without taxation: An essay on rural democracy in Nigeria," *African Studies Review* 35 (1992): 41–79.

84. See ch. 2, 42.

85. NAGK 318, "Native Jurisdiction Ordinance, 1926–29," DC Bekwai to CEP, 6/2/28. See also Tordoff, *Ashanti*, 322ff.

86. NAGA ADM 11/1/1906, Chief Commissioner to Secretary of State, 9/10/26.

87. See ch. 2, 52–53.

88. Quoted in Tordoff, *Ashanti*, 323.

89. Arhin, "Some Asante views," 64–65.

90. Warrington, 1934, "Notes on Ashanti custom" (1934, revised 1941), in NAGK 1231, A digest of the minutes of the Ashanti Confederacy Council, 1935–49, 52.

91. Ibid., 72–73.

92. Ibid. Variations in spelling are found in the original.

93. NAGA ADM 11/1/1904, Secret No. 38. Asantehene—restoration of, 1932–35, Governor's speech, 1/31/35. See below, 83–89.

94. NAGK 1231, Digest of the Minutes of the Ashanti Confederacy Council [ACC], 1935–1949, 16.

95. Quoted in Kyerematen, *Inter-state boundary litigation*, 26.

96. Quoted in Tordoff, *Ashanti*, 363.

97. NAGK 1285, Acquisition of Government Lands, Commissioner of Lands to Chief Commissioner, 4/14/36.

98. NAGK 1231, ACC Digest, 1935–1949, p. 20.

99. Tordoff, *Ashanti*, 364. By 1946–47, when annual revenue of the Asante administration topped £260,000, the "loss" of some £15,000 realized in rents from the Kumase Town Lands was inconsequential. Hailey, *Native administration*, 248.

100. With apologies to Dr. Busia.

101. Allman, *Quills of the porcupine*, 183ff. See also NAGA ADM 11/1/194, *Report of the Commission appointed to enquire into the affairs of the Kumasi State Council and the Asanteman Council, by Mr. Justice Sarkodee-Addo* (Accra: Government Printer, 1958).

102. Ashanti Stool Land Act (Act 28) of 1958, quoted in A. R. Edmundson, "Land ownership," 9.

103. Harvey, *Law and social change*, ch. 2.

104. Ibid., 121–22.

105. Administration of Lands Act (123) of 1962. The Constitution of 1992 reaffirmed the principle of stool land ownership and prohibited the creation of any freehold interest in stool land. It also created the Office of the Administrator of Stool Lands to oversee the management of stool land revenues and mandated that 55 percent of such revenues be remitted to the district assemblies. Ghana, *Constitution of the Republic of Ghana* (Tema Press, 1992).

106. Appellant jurisdiction over stool land and chieftaincy disputes rested with the Asantehene's Grade A (Appeals) Court, but cases could be appealed all the way to the Privy Council until 1964, when the Supreme Court of Ghana became the final court of appeal. Harvey, *Law and social change*, 256, 403.

107. See ch. 4, 118. Chiefs in Asante frequently offer, or are called upon, to arbitrate disputes over land, but their decisions are nonbinding and any disputant is free to take a case to court, if s/he is not satisfied with a chief's decision.

108. Arhin, *Handbook*. Interviews with Mr. Sarpong, Senior Lands Officer, Lands Commission, Kumase, 9/23/93, 2/12/93; Mr. Agyen, Asantehene's Lands Secretary, Manhyia, 9/8/93.

109. Edmundson, "Land ownership," 10.

110. Ibid., n. 20. According to a prominent Kumase lawyer, the practice of remitting a third of the proceeds to the Asantehene was introduced by Otumfuo Opoku Ware II.

111. See below, 85–86, and chs. 4 and 6.

112. Edmundson, "Land ownership," i–ii.

113. Since its restoration in 1935, the Golden Stool has had only three occupants—Osei Agyeman Prempeh II, who reigned from 1935 until 1970, Otumfuo Opoku Ware II, 1970–99, and the present Asantehene, Osei Tutu II.

114. MRO, Asantehene's Divisional Court B1 Record Book, 1950/1.

115. In addition to cutting the trees, Kwame Kobi was said to have challenged the Akyempimhene's authority in Apaasu by refusing to accept part of the *aseda* ("thanks"), which the present Odikro distributed on the occasion of his accession. Ibid.

116. The others were Amakom, Buokrom, Tafo, and Ohwim. The exact sequence of struggles that led to the founding of the Asante state has been debated by historians. See, e.g., Wilks, *Asante*, ch. 9, and *Forests of gold*, ch. 3; also T. C. McCaskie, "Komfo

Anokye of Asante: Meaning, history and philosophy in an African society," *Journal of African History* 27 (1986): 317–39.

117. The phrasing is Justice François'. Superior Court of Judicature, Court of Appeal, Accra, Civil Appeal No. 128/90, Judgment, 7/31/91, 1. My discussion of the Kaase case is based on copies of the trial and appeals courts' judgments, a few of the documents submitted in evidence, and conversations with the Kaasehene and lawyers familiar with the case.

118. Ibid., Justice Adjabeng, 8.

119. Ibid., 10. The committee took possession of the Kaase stool lands in July 1988.

120. This is consistent with the map prepared by the town surveyor in 1914. See above, 71.

121. High Court of Kumase, Case No. LS. 1172/88.

122. Ibid.

123. Adjabeng pointed out that passages from Busia, *The position of the chief*, which were quoted by the appellants' lawyer, actually supported the plaintiff/respondent's case. In the first, Busia stated that in Brong states conquered by Asante, chiefs' rights over land "remained the same." In the second, he quoted Casely Hayford to the effect that Hayford had never encountered a case "where title of land has been based upon a right of conquest." Hayford, a barrister and leading spokesman for the Aborigines' Rights Protection Society, was writing to rebut British claims that unoccupied land in the Colony belonged to the Crown, by right of conquest. See Berry, *No condition is permanent*, 105ff.

124. W.A.N. Adumua-Bossman, a prominent lawyer based in Accra, has represented several clients involved in litigation with the Asantehene.

125. Wilks, who refers to Obiri Yeboah as Kumasehene, places his death sometime in the 1680s. According to one version of tradition, written under the direction of Prempeh I during his exile in the Seychelles, Obiri Yeboah's predecessor, Oti Akenten, purchased land at Kwaman (now Kumase) from its female owner. Wilks, *Forests of gold*, 65–66, 100–102, 244–45.

126. The following account is based on information and documents that were kindly supplied by lawyers W.A.N. Adumua-Bossman, E. Anaglate, and J. K. Koduah.

127. In 1999, however, when Adwoa Adowaa filed a petition with the National House of Chiefs challenging the Asantehemaa's nomination of her son, Barima Kwaku Dua, as successor to the Asantehene, elders of the Asaman Kani family dissociated themselves from her quest—evidently wishing not to place themselves at odds with the Asantehene-elect. *Daily Graphic*, April 5–6 1999.

128. Described, variously, by informants as "a wall" and "a nearly completed house," the destroyed structure gave rise to a criminal case against Obaapanin Adwoa Adowah. According to lawyer Anaglate, the court acquitted her in that case because of the larger issues of land ownership involved.

129. The allocation papers had been issued by one Opanin Kwadwo Forduor, approved by the Lands Commission, and co-signed by the Asantehene. One lawyer with whom I discussed the case described Kwadwo Fordjuor as a "caretaker" for the Asantehene.

130. Kumase High Court, Suit No. 107/92, Adwoa Adwoah v. Osei Assibey and The Contractor, Statement of Claim. Punctuation as in the original.

131. Interview with E. Anaglate, 7/25/96, in Kumase. Under section 25 of the Land Registration Act of 1962, registration of a lease constitutes actual notice of instrument and fact of registration to all persons and for all purposes.

132. See below, ch. 4, 124.

133. Aputuogya is near Feyiase, site of the famous battle at which Osei Tutu cemented his claims to rule over Asante by leading its forces to victory over their former overlord, Ntim Gyakari of Denkyira. See, e.g., Wilks, *Forests of gold*, 111. The area has been zoned for industrial development to accommodate the expected spillover as Ahinsan and Kaase become fully built up. When Nana Nkwantabisa decided to take up farming, in 1987, he leased land at Eduaben from the stool elders as a private person. In 1996, he had approximately 185 acres under cultivation and employed a work force of about seventy-five.

134. At least three other men occupied the stool, for varying lengths of time, between the end of Chief Frimpon's reign, in 1947, and Nana Nkwantabisa's accession two decades later—including Kwame Frimpon II, Nana Kofi Adonten, and an elder brother of the present chief. I first learned about the Baaman case from a brief announcement in *West Africa*, which I read en route to Ghana in 1996. Having read and heard a good deal about the Adontenhene's predecessor, Chief J. K. Frimpon, I was curious to learn more and began to make inquiries as soon as I reached Accra. Though unannounced, my queries elicited prompt and generous assistance from several people familiar with the case. W.A.N. Adumua-Bossman, J. K. Koduah, and P. Obeng Manu took time from their busy schedules to answer questions and facilitate my research, and Nana Agyeman Nkwantabisa III offered gracious hospitality as well as patient and informative replies to my innumerable questions.

135. Following a fairly standard legal formula, the chief has sued in both cases for declaration of title, damages for trespass, and a perpetual injunction restraining the occupant of the Golden Stool and his agents from entering the land or interfering with his rights to it. KHC Suit No. LS. 79/94, Nana Agyemang Nkwantabisa III and Obaapanin Afua Serwaa v. Kwasi Kwarteng alias Wahabu and Kwesi Sarpong alias Kwasi Dam, Statement of Claim, 6/17/94; and KHC Suit No. 114/96, Nana Agyemang Nkwantabisa III and others v. Charles Osei Bonsu, Secretary to Kumase Traditional Council, and Nana Otumfuor Opoku Ware II, Statement of Claim, 6/25/96.

136. KHC, Suit No. LS 150/96, Adonten Stool per occupant v. The Golden Stool per occupant, Statement of Claim, 6/17/96. The reference is to Rattray, *Ashanti law*, 235.

137. Interview with P. Obeng Manu, 7/24/96.

138. Gabriel Frempong, who formerly worked for the Lands Department in Accra as a land valuation officer, advises the chief on the management of his stool properties. By the matrilineal kinship terminology common in Asante, a man might use the term "grandson" to refer to a sister's son or a mother's sister's grandson.

139. NAGA ADM 5/3/13, Belfield Report, 1912; Fuller, *A vanished dynasty*; NAGA ADM 11/1/1338, Constitution and organization of Kumasi stools; NAGK 8/73, Committee of Privileges, 1935. Also see above, 75 and ch. 1, 22–23.

140. Copies of the judgments are in the Adontenhene's possession. The stool also claims land at Ebira (near Boanim), Wawase (near Swedru), and Boaman (near Bekwai).

141. Information about the possible historical basis of the defense in *this* case was drawn from the plaintiff's statement of claim (KHC Suit No. L.S. 150/96) and conversations with the plaintiff and his lawyer.

142. For other examples of claims based on descent from *aheneyere*, see ch. 4, 126–27.

143. KHC/LS 79/94, Statement of claim. The disputed land includes the seat of the Eduaben stool, which may explain why, in this case, the Adontenhene did not raise the question of the stool's historic status, as he has in the case at Baaman. The second and third plaintiffs were identified, respectively, as occupant of the Aputuogya stool and Obaapanin of Aputuogya—claims disputed by the defendants. Nana Nkwantabisa acknowledged that the Obaapanin is not the queen mother of his stool, but he explained that the woman who occupies that position has sided with his opponents. In acknowledgement of her status, the Adontenhene's representatives took me to greet her when we visited Eduaben.

144. KHC/LS 79 /94, Ruling, 9/19/94.

145. The slate of defendants in this case invokes the ambiguities surrounding questions of citizenship and nomenclature in contemporary Asante. The Muslim names/aliases of the two defendants and the substituted codefendants might be interpreted as supporting the Adontenhene's assertion that his stool had settled northern captives in the area, during the reign of Opoku Ware I, and that their descendants among the current residents could not possibly claim any authority over stool lands. It is also possible, of course, that the defendants are Muslims of Asante origin—though the fact that the two original defendants have Akan as well as Muslim names offers no stronger proof of this possibility than of its converse. See below, ch. 5, 153.

146. Chief Frimpon made use of the amorphous state of "customary" authority created by Prempeh's exile to preside over the enstoolment of several senior Adonten chiefs, as well as numerous subordinates. Chief Frimpon referred to Kofi Asante (by his alias Kofi Bomba) as "my present Jasi chief" but added that he was Jasi only in the sense of "those whose peculiar duty it is to guard the stool properly," not "those who serve the head stool direct," and declined to elaborate further on the Jasi's functions. NAGA ADM 11/1/1338, "Organization and constitution of Kumase stools." See above, ch. 1, 23.

147. By law, any ruling by the traditional council is considered a nonbinding arbitration. If the chiefs were to make a ruling, therefore, it is likely that the dispute would be continued in court.

148. These events, to which the codefendant made pointed allusion in his statement to the court, were confirmed by the Adontenhene. Interview with Nana Nkwantabisa, 7/24/96. See also KHC/LS 79/94, Statement of defence and counterclaim of codefendant, 3/18/96.

149. Opoku Ware I reigned ca. 1720–50. Wilks, *Forests of gold*, 385.

150. KHC Suit No. LS 114/96, Nana Agyemang Nkwantabisa III, Adontenhene, and two others v. Charles Osei Bonsu and Nana Otumfuor Opoku Ware II, Statement of claim. The second and third plaintiffs were described as Odikro and Obaapanin of Aputuogya, though, according to the defendants, the Aputuogya stool was vacant, and the Obaapanin was a pretender.

151. Interview with J. K. Koduah, 7/24/96.

152. Contrast Mamdani, *Citizen and subject*.

153. KHC/LS 79/94, Ruling, 9/19/94.

4

ON THE SUBURBAN FRONTIER: STORIES OF DISPOSSESSION, DEVELOPMENT, AND INDIRECT DEMOCRACY

As Kumase grew, it absorbed a number of villages many of which, like Amakom and Kaase, predated the establishment of Kumase itself as the capital of Asante. This process continued in the 1990s—not only in areas slated for industrial development, such as Aputuogya, but also in communities less strategically located, but close enough to Kumase to offer attractive sites for residential and smaller-scale commercial development. Beyond the current perimeter of urban construction and congestion lies a frontier of land acquisition, where those with the means to do so purchase long-term leases on plots for future building. The pace of actual construction has varied with the condition of the Ghanaian economy—expanding during the cocoa boom of the 1950s and early 1960s, declining sharply during the long period of economic stagnation and decline from the mid-1960s to the early 1980s, and reviving again since the mid-1980s under the impact of economic recovery and structural adjustment. By the mid-1990s, the effects of earlier land acquisitions were becoming increasingly visible.

The changing suburban landscape reflects the changing structure of the Ghanaian economy and society, as well as the overall growth of income. Many of the buildings going up on the periphery of Kumase in the 1990s were one- or two-story villas surrounded by walls and gardens, rather than the three- or four-story compounds[1] favored by the prosperous traders and cocoa farmers who built in Amakom during the 1960s. Villages once occupied almost entirely by farmers, traders, and their relatives are beginning to accommodate increasing numbers of contractors and salaried professionals, many of whom do not have established family ties in the communities where they have acquired plots and put up suburban villas. The story of land acquisition is one of social as well as economic change on Kumase's suburban frontier.

If the course of land allocation on the suburban frontier has been rapid since the late 1970s, it has not always been smooth. As we saw in chapter 3, farmers and traders who used profits from the postwar cocoa boom to build houses in Amakom made substantial payments to the stool just to obtain leases for their building plots. In contrast, those who used cocoa earnings to put up houses in their home villages often paid little or nothing for access to building sites, and many dispensed altogether with the cumbersome and costly process of obtaining a formal lease. By the mid-1990s, stools with land on the urban periphery had reaped substantial gains from the "sale" of building plots, a fact that did not escape the attention of their citizens.[2] In many communities, land allocation has created tension along several lines: between stools and individual citizens over the conversion of farmland into building plots; between chiefs, townspeople, and local government agencies over disposition of the proceeds of land allocation; and within and among families over the division of plots and proceeds among their members. In negotiating these tensions, both long-term residents and newcomers to peri-urban communities have drawn on economic, social, and political connections to Kumase, Accra, and towns and villages throughout the region.

FROM VILLAGE TO SUBURB:
PORTRAITS OF TWO COMMUNITIES

To explore the effects of urban expansion on land claims and social relations on the outskirts of Kumase, I interviewed chiefs and residents in two villages just east of the city: Asokore-Mampon and Kenyase (sometimes called Kenyase Kwabre, to distinguish it from Kenyase in Ahafo). According to the 1984 census, Asokore-Mampon had a population of 1,077, Kenyase 3,294.[3] In 1993, the Kenyasehene thought there were about 10,000 people in Kenyase. The Asokore-Mamponhene had suspended an enumeration of his subjects during a dispute with one of his subchiefs, but my rough count of occupied houses (about a hundred) suggested that the village may have accommodated about half as many people as Kenyase in 1993.

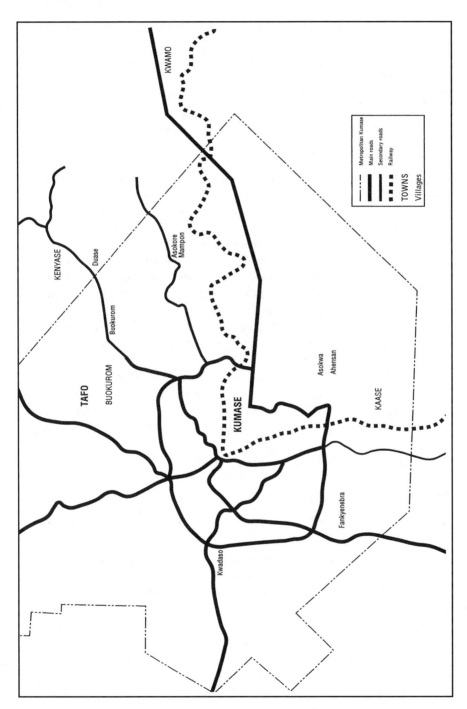

Map 4.1 Kumase and environs, 1973.
Source: Survey of Ghana.

Both Kenyase and Asokore-Mampon were founded before Asante. According to Wilks, the first settler at Kenyase was a grandson of Ankyewa Nyame, ancestress of Asante's royal family (the Oyoko Abohyen), who came to Kenyase from Kokofu.[4] Asokore-Mampon was also founded in the seventeenth century by a hunter from Kokofu, on land that was then under Amakom.[5] Though not related by blood to the royal family of Asante, Asokore-Mampon established close ties with the new state at an early date. Unlike Amakom, Kaase, and others who resisted Osei Tutu's early attempts to assert his leadership over the stools at Kwaman, Asokore-Mampon was one of the first to join the Asante union under Osei Tutu.[6] The Asokore-Mamponhene fought alongside Osei Tutu against Dormaa, and the stool gave land to his wives (*aheneyere*) at Ayigya, Yenyawso, Kantinkrom, and Sipe-Tinponu.[7] Towards the end of the eighteenth century, Asokore-Mamponhene Owusu Ansa fathered a son who later reigned as Asantehene Osei Tutu Kwame from 1803 to 1823.[8] In 1926, when Prempeh I was finally allowed to travel outside Kumase after his return from the Seychelles, he surprised British officials by choosing to visit Asokore-Mampon first. Officials speculated that he selected "this comparatively unimportant village" because portions of the royal treasure were stored in the vicinity, but they decided it would be impolitic to pursue the matter on the eve of Prempeh's installation as Kumasehene.[9]

As the world cocoa market rebounded in the late 1940s from global depression and war, residents of Asokore-Mampon and Kenyase joined the ranks of Asante farmers who opened up uncultivated forests in Brong-Ahafo and the Western Region for cocoa farming. Many people from Asokore-Mampon established farms around Tepa, Tachimantia, and Mim, traveling frequently between their farms and their home village to maintain family ties while reaping the rewards of the postwar cocoa boom. Kenyasefoɔ also planted cocoa, in Sefwi and Ahafo, and invested part of their earnings at home. Many of the solid, cement-block and sheet-roofed compounds that line the road through Kenyase today were built in the 1950s and 1960s, with farmers' and traders' earnings from cocoa. People also contributed to community projects: when Nana Owusu Agyeman first occupied the stool, from 1946 to 1952, Kenyasefoɔ provided money and labor to construct a reservoir and a handsome two-story school, both of which were still in use in 1993.[10]

In the 1970s, as the economy slid into decline and returns to cocoa growing dwindled, Ghanaians emigrated in increasing numbers, seeking employment and opportunity in the buoyant markets of Côte d'Ivoire and oil-rich Nigeria or, if they could afford to get there, Europe and North America. One study estimated that, between 1975 and the early 1980s, emigration led to a 15–20 percent drop in the agricultural labor force—enough to account for a significant proportion of the steep decline in food production that occurred during the same period.[11] The exodus is clearly reflected in people's recollections of the period. I met several people in Amakom, as well as Kenyase and Asokore-Mampon, who had worked abroad, or whose relatives had done so, at some point during the 1970s or early 1980s. Several people were receiving help from sons or daughters who lived in Europe and were hoping that others would follow them abroad.[12]

TABLE 4.1   Profile of Informants[13]

	Asokore-Mampon	Kenyase
Total Number of Informants	33	31
Men/Women	16/17	20/11
Citizen/Stranger*	18/15	23/8
Age: 70+	5	7
50–70	13	13
30–50	12	7
<30	3	1
Occupations:		
Farming	9	11
Trading, shopkeeping	10	7
Artisanal	5	16
Clerical, professional	10	5
Other**	9	7

Note: *Citizens = residents who consider this village to be their home town.

**Includes religious specialists, chiefs, laborers, and, in Kenyase, two people who described themselves as unemployed.

More than once in the course of fieldwork, I met Ghanaians who spoke no English but conversed readily in French. They had learned French not in school—most had no formal education—but in the course of working or trading in one or more of Ghana's francophone neighbors. (They did not need English to work in Ghana, where Twi is virtually a national language.) A case in point was Maame Fatima, an unschooled, highly articulate woman whom I met in Amakom. Maame Fatima, who gave her age as seventy-four, went to Abidjan after her second child was born, and she lived there for some time, traveling back and forth to Ghana to trade in provisions.

After her fifth child was born, she returned to Ghana and joined the cocoa rush, planting farms at two separate villages in the Central Region. During Nkrumah's time, she used some of the profits from her farms to acquire a plot in Amakom and put up the comfortable two-story house that she now shares with some of her children and grandchildren. She has continued to develop new business ventures, turning even the worst economic crises to advantage. During our conversation, she showed me a pile of well-seasoned lumber, stacked behind her house, which she had purchased in the early 1980s at rock bottom prices and was now preparing to sell in Kumase's booming construction market.

In 1993, Maame Fatima was building a second house in Amakom, up the street from the first, on a plot which she had bought at a bargain after the original leaseholder failed to develop it. She had also invested in land speculation, claiming to have "purchased" and resold more than a dozen building plots near Kumase and in her home town. A devout Muslim, Maame Fatima explained that many people attributed her success to hard work, but really "it was all up to God." As we walked away from her house to our next interview, my assistant shook his head in admiration. "She is a shrewd woman," he exclaimed. "Anything to do with money, she will get it!"

In the late 1980s, Ghana's economic recovery (and its neighbors' decline)[14] were reflected in new patterns of residence and mobility on the outskirts of Kumase. In the depressed economic conditions of the 1970s and early 1980s, some people took advantage of low prices to acquire building plots outside the city for future use. With the help of rain, devaluation, and structural adjustment loans, production and incomes rose, especially for those with professional degrees and/or commercial assets, and the government began a long-term effort to rebuild and upgrade the country's infrastructure. By the mid-1990s, the effects were becoming visible on the suburban frontier. The pace of land allocation had quickened, and the countryside was dotted with new or partly completed houses, electric poles and wires, and an increasing volume of traffic. Residents of both Kenyase and Asokore-Mampon noted that the number of taxis and "trotros"[15] available for travel to Kumase and nearby villages had increased dramatically since the mid-1980s. In late 1993, graders were at work on the secondary roads that linked both villages to Kumase and, by mid-1994, they had been transformed from badly eroded, untarred or seriously potholed side roads to well-paved thoroughfares. Both villages had electricity (Kenyase's was hooked up in May 1993), and plans to bring piped water from Kumase were under vigorous discussion.

Increasing accessibility to Kumase reinforced not only the pace of new residential construction but also the flow of commuter traffic between the city and its outlying suburbs. Residents of both villages traveled regularly to Kumase, some on a daily basis, to trade or work in town or to buy goods for consumption or resale at home. Comfort Buama, the widow of a former schoolteacher, recalled that when she and her husband first moved to Asokore-Mampon in the 1960s, transportation was scarce, there were no strangers in the village, and it was difficult to do business there. When they returned in 1985, after living in Kumase and Asaman, many people were acquiring land and putting up buildings, and trading was easy.[16] After her husband's death in 1987, Comfort divided her time between "preaching the good news" (she was a Jehovah's Witness) and hawking plastic buckets and bolts of cloth among her neighbors. By 1993, she had "grown tired" of going round the village to trade and was using her savings to build a small tavern in front of her house, overlooking the main road, so she could "sit down" and let the customers come to her.

In the early 1990s, Asokore-Mampon was also beginning to attract a new class of tenants—urban workers of modest means, who sought cheaper accommodations than they could get in town. I interviewed several such lodgers—a seamstress, a young man in his late twenties who worked as a technician for the Forestry Department, and a Pentecostal preacher who had left the Baptist Church after a disagreement and founded his own God's Overcomeness Ministry. Lacking the means to build a church, he held evening services for his flock in the local junior secondary school. All three had come to Asokore-Mampon to escape high rents in Kumase: they were pleased to be paying between ₵250 and ₵1,000 per month for rooms which would cost ₵5,000–6,000 in Kumase. Similarly, several informants in Kenyase said that rooms in their family houses had been let to tenants, and the local assemblyman noted that since the town got electricity, in May 1993, many people were coming there to rent rooms. In the mid-1990s, Kenyase and Asokore-Mampon were developing as suburban retreats for professionals and civil servants and as bedroom communities for the petty bourgeoisie.

FAMILY MATTERS

Claims on land in Asante are arranged in layers. Stools hold allodial title to their respective lands but cannot legally prevent the state from appropriating parcels of land (or land-based resources, such as mineral deposits or timber) for public use.[17] In addition, as we have seen, individuals may obtain rights to use particular portions of stool land for a variety of purposes, including farming, hunting, fishing, and building, without compromising the stool's simultaneous rights of ownership or the state's powers of appropriation. Use rights may be held exclusively by individual men and women, but more often they are subject to claims by a number of people whose relationships to property and to one another fall under the broad (and often ambiguous) heading of family ties. Before examining the relationship between property rights and local politics in Kenyase and Asokore-Mampon, it will be useful to take a look at families' rights to land.

Family membership in Asante is predicated on descent and reckoned matrilineally. People inherit from their mother's kin: thus, a man's wife and children are not entitled to a share of his estate, unless he has made special provision for them before he dies. Women are succeeded by their sisters or their "daughters"—a term that may refer to a woman's sister's daughters as well as to her own. But a family is more than a lineal descent group. People acquire family ties through marriage, adoption, fostering,[18] and, sometimes, servitude. In the nineteenth century, if a person died without a lineal heir, a slave or descendant of a slave who had been with the family for some time could inherit his/her estate.[19] In recent times, Ghanaian courts have sometimes ruled along similar lines. In 1989, the appeals court decided a dispute over succession to a family headship in favor of the defendant, who argued convincingly that his ancestor, though a slave, had been adopted by his owner's family and that he had been appointed to succeed the last family head. The court rejected the plaintiff's claim that their predecessor had chosen him to succeed to the headship, on the grounds that "under customary law no person had the right to appoint his successor before his death."[20]

As in other African societies, claims on people have long been regarded as a form of wealth in Asante, and people often devote a significant part of their material and financial resources to nurturing and augmenting social ties and claims on others. Expenditures on marriage gifts, funerals, education, and the maintenance of dependents (including, in the past, slaves, pawns, and subjects) may be said to represent, *inter alia*, investments in wealth-in-people.[21] But the link between material resources and social relationships is not a one-way street. Claims on people (many of which are established, reaffirmed, or strengthened through transfers of goods or money) also help to define, maintain, and protect claims on material resources. Throughout Asante, family ties create and legitimate claims on land and other forms of material wealth, as well as vice versa. In addition to the inheritance of proprietary claims—which turns, as we shall see, on questions of matrilineal descent as well as individual bequest—family relationships are also associated with various rights of access that stop short of complete or conditional proprietorship. Rights to cultivate particular pieces of family land, for example, are usually held by individuals, including some whose claims to family membership may derive from affinity, adoption, or even servitude rather than descent. Thus, a man who resides with or near his wife's kin enjoys a presumptive right to farm on land that belongs to her family.[22] People, and the relationships among them, are embedded in wealth, as well as wealth in people.

While family membership is widely recognized as a legitimate basis for making various kinds of claims on land and landed property in Asante, there is nothing automatic about the exercise of such claims, for descendant, affines, or adoptees. Access to family property[23] is just as subject to negotiation and contest among family members as, say, access to stool land is a matter of negotiation and dispute among stool subjects or citizens, elders, and chiefs. Relatives negotiate and often contest everything from farm boundaries within tracts of family land or the occupancy of individual rooms in a family house to family membership itself and associated claims to inclusion among the beneficiaries of a family estate. Claims to family membership and family property hinge, in turn, on questions of family history, much of it stored in people's memories rather than on paper.[24] Funerals are central events in Ghanaian social life, not only out of respect for history and the ancestors but also because, in coming together to honor the dead and share funeral expenses, people assert claims to family membership and the right to share in the enjoyment of family property.[25]

Inheritance tends to create family property. When a person dies, relatives gather to select an heir. The position of heir carries responsibilities, and kin of the deceased attempt to select someone who may be trusted to discharge them responsibly. In principle, an heir acts as a trustee, managing the estate of the deceased for the benefit of the family, rather than treating it as his or her individual property. The interests of the family rest, therefore, on choosing a person of good character to fulfill the duties of an heir. Kyeame Marfo (a resident of Asokore-Mampon) inherited from his maternal uncle property that included two houses in the Kwadaso section of Kumase and an oil palm farm.[26] During his uncle's last illness, rooms in both houses were rented out to raise money for treatment, and Kyeame Marfo was now using the rents to pay off his uncle's debts. Once the debts were settled, he planned to continue leasing out rooms, using the proceeds to renovate or enlarge the houses, or to help any member of the family who needed it. Kyeame Marfo used to visit his uncle frequently when he was alive, and his uncle "discussed everything" with him. When his uncle died, he explained, the family chose him as heir because he was close to his uncle, knew all about his affairs, and was considered to be a responsible person.[27]

Women also inherit property, often from other female relatives. Akua and her elder sister are first cousins to one of the senior chiefs of Asokore-

Mampon, and Akua is married to another.[28] Akua's sister was chosen to succeed their maternal aunt (the Akwamuhene's mother); if her sister dies, Akua will inherit their aunt's estate. When a person dies, she explained, a successor is chosen even if the deceased has no property to bequeath: the successor is still responsible for helping the children to perform the funeral and officiating in other family affairs, such as marriages or dispute settlement. In this case, Akua's aunt left a cocoa farm, which is no longer productive, and a house in Asokore-Mampon. Akua's sister shared the rooms among members of the family. Akua was given a room, but she already had a place to stay in her husband's house, so she gave the room to her sister. Some of the family members who were allocated rooms have chosen to rent them out to tenants.[29]

Providing for one's children is a subject of great importance in Ghana, and it often gives rise to intense debate. During the colonial period, European observers and officials worried about the "inherent conflict" between "the jural and moral claims and bonds *arising out of* marriage and fatherhood [and] those *imposed by* matrilineal kinship."[30] Among Asantes, conflict over matrilineal succession appears to have increased with the spread of cocoa growing. Cocoa farms take several years to establish, and men often relied on the labor of their wives and children to tend young cocoa trees and to grow food crops for household maintenance while they waited for the cocoa trees to mature. Though many women eventually acquired cocoa farms of their own, it was often difficult for them to mobilize unpaid family labor to work on their farms, and they were still expected to contribute to household consumption and even to work on their husbands' mature cocoa farms. In time, family members began to expect compensation for working on relatives' tree crop farms, and some women argued that the labor they and their children had invested in their husbands' farms entitled them to a share of the farms as well.[31]

During the colonial period, the courts generally upheld the claims of matrilineal heirs, unless the deceased had left a written will that specified otherwise. Since independence, successive national governments have favored some form of statutory protection for the rights of wives to inherit from their husbands and children from their fathers—with ambiguous results. PNDC Law 111, enacted by Rawlings' military regime in 1985, stipulates that if a person dies intestate, the bulk of his or her estate must go to the surviving spouse and offspring.[32] The law applies only to self-acquired property, however: any property a decedent inherited during his/her lifetime is considered family property and hence exempt from the law's provisions. It is also subject to ongoing interpretation, not only in cases heard by the courts but also in the informal moots that provide many people with an inexpensive alternative to the formal judicial process. In arbitrating one family dispute, the Asokore-Mamponhene warned a man that his plan to bequeath a plot of land to two of his six children would probably cause trouble after he died, because under PNDC Law 111 "a man cannot disinherit his children."[33]

Ambiguity and tension over the meaning of inheritance and "family property" are also reflected in daily practice. It is common for Asantes to use the terms "children" and "parents" in a classificatory sense, to refer to siblings' children or parents' siblings, as well as their own biological offspring and genitors. Thus, Akua spoke of her elder sister as the heir of "our mother" and her sister' daughters as "my children." For many people, inheritance is clearly an important source of access to farmland and/or housing. Half of my informants in Kenyase and 80 percent of my informants in Asokore-Mampon were living in family houses, and most of those who were currently engaged in farming were doing so on family land. But people were also concerned to provide for their children. Half a dozen of my informants in Asokore-Mampon were living with their siblings, having turned their own houses over to their children, and several others were in the process of building a second house "for the children."

In Kenyase, a third of the people I interviewed said that they or their families owned more than one house in the town. "Family" may have multiple meanings, depending on what is at stake. Kofi Poku said that his family owns four houses in Kenyase, each built by a different individual. The house in which Kofi Poku was living had been built in 1954 by his uncle who worked as a driver. When the uncle died, in 1977, the family chose his senior brother to succeed him. The brother, who owns a cocoa farm at Tepa, is head of the whole family but heir only to the driver, whose house he manages as family property. If another family member were to die, Kofi Poku explained, the family head would organize the selection of an heir, but the successor would be chosen from within the decedent's own house— not from one of the family's other houses.

Some of my informants had made wills, or given verbal instructions, bequeathing self-acquired property to their spouse(s) and children. George Manuh, recently retired after twenty years as a technician with the Ghana Broadcasting Corporation (GBC), had acquired a plot in Asokore-Mampon in the mid-1970s and built a house where he lived with his wife and four children. He likes it in Asokore-Mampon, he explained, and plans to stay. In 1993, he invested the first installment of his GBC pension in cement, which he sold from a shop across the road from his house. He had also built a house in his home town, near Ejisu, which will become family property in the long run. "My brother helped me to become what I am," he explained, adding that should he die first, his personal house at home will go to his brother. George Manuh had made a will, bequeathing the house in

Asokore-Mampon to his wife and children. "If I die tomorrow, there won't be any problem for her."

Wills may be contested, of course, by either the family or the spouse and children of the deceased. In Asokore-Mampon, Kyeame Marfo intended to leave his house to his wife and children: he had not made a will but had "planned it all in his head." Since he had no siblings, he was confident that things would go as he intended. When siblings survive, however, even written wills may not suffice to protect a man's children. If siblings (or other matrilineal relatives) can prove that they contributed to building or acquiring the property in question, the courts may rule that it is family property and therefore exempt from the provisions of the will.[34] And PNDC Law 111 offers scant protection to anyone who cannot afford to hire a lawyer. Agnes Mim's late husband had worked for the Highway Department in Tamale, earning enough so that his wife was able to stay in the house and look after their children. During his lifetime, he built a comfortable cement-block house on the main road in Asokore-Mampon and even acquired a car, but when he died, "the family took it all." Agnes's sons were given two rooms in their father's house, but she had to move to a mud-walled house with no access to the road, which belonged to her maternal kin. Directly opposite Agnes's residence, a widow and her three children were sharing a tiny room with her mother, who had come from Bodomase to look after the children so her daughter could hawk a few provisions around neighboring villages.[35] The daughter's husband was a native of Asokore-Mampon and they had lived with his family, but after he died, she quarreled with his relatives and they turned her out. The husband left his wife a cocoa farm, but his family took it away, and she and her mother had no money to litigate for it.[36]

In its first decade, then, PNDC Law 111 appears to have made only modest inroads into the practice of matrilineal inheritance or the evolution of personal into family property over time.[37] At the close of the twentieth century, property rights in Asante remain subject to ongoing negotiations, within families as well as among them, and individuals' fortunes continue to depend on their relations with kin and affines, as well as their own efforts in the marketplace. Created (or destroyed) through people's interactions, family relations cannot be taken for granted. If matrilineal succession continues to cast a wide net in contemporary Ghana, it is no guarantee of safety—for the poor or the well-to-do.

MAKING WAY FOR DEVELOPMENT

As land values rise on the suburban frontier, local chiefs stand to profit handsomely from the conversion of farmland and bush to building plots—

as long as they remain on the stool. This depends not only on their ability to realize the gains from rising land value but also on what they do with the money after they get it. Like their colonial predecessors, governments in postcolonial Ghana have been eager to channel stool land revenues into the public coffer. The 1992 Constitution stipulates, for example, that 55 percent of the revenue accruing from stool lands be turned over to the district assembly[38]—a body of elected and appointed representatives of local communities, whose primary responsibility is to mobilize resources "necessary for the overall development of the district."[39] The rest is divided between the chief and the stool elders, but the law is mostly silent on their obligation to use it in the public interest. Indeed, since the "prices" that chiefs receive for allocated plots are not matters of public record, it is difficult to tell how far stools actually comply with the requirement that the greater part of the money realized from land allocations be turned over to the district assembly.

Such constraints as chiefs do face on their fiscal autonomy come not from the state but from the citizenry. As in the colonial period, a chief who makes too many enemies may come under pressure to step down. Such pressures can be resisted, of course, and often are: chieftaincy disputes tend to be long, rancorous, and very expensive.[40] Those who wish to retain their seats without incurring such costs take care not to antagonize powerful subordinates, and they pay at least rhetorical attention to the welfare of their constituents. Some chiefs do much more than that—working actively to promote development in the areas under their jurisdiction and mediating on behalf of their constituents with outside organizations and the state.

The fact remains, however, that the extent of chiefs' obligations to the public has never been clearly defined. Ironically, by restricting their formal authority to matters of chiefly succession and protocol, and making their role in local government informal and voluntary, the Ghanaian state has reactivated some of the debates over chiefly accountability that colonial officials worked so hard to resolve. The desks of Ghanaian bureaucrats may no longer be cluttered with the complaints over stool debts and chiefly misconduct that taxed the patience and understanding of their colonial predecessors, but they are still struggling to capture rents and contain conflicts that arise from chiefs' control of stool lands. Excluded *de jure* from electoral politics and formal administration in postcolonial Ghana, chiefs are extensively involved *de facto* in both.

Most of the building plots in Asokore-Mampon and Kenyase were allocated by three men: Nana Boakye Danquah, Asokore-Mamponhene from 1944 to 1986; his successor Nana Boakye Ansah Debrah; and Kenyasehene Nana Owusu Agyeman III, who first occupied the stool from 1946 to 1952 and returned to it twenty-seven years later, in time to preside over the suburban land rush of the 1980s. All three found their tenure in office financially rewarding, and all have faced criticism, from citizens, stool elders, and the state, over their handling of land allocation and the resulting revenues. Though their skills and strategies have varied, each man has struggled to balance personal ambition and the public interest, to seek rents, promote development, and navigate its ambiguities and contradictions. Their stories open localized but revealing windows on to the complex mosaic of rent-seeking and local politics through which "state-society relations" are defined and mediated in contemporary Ghana.

Asokore-Mampon: Nana Boakye Danquah

In 1944 or 1945, Asokore-Mamponhene Nana Kwame Owusu was destooled[41] and Boakye Danquah was summoned home from Tachimantia, where he was working as a carpenter, to contest for the stool.[42] Boakye Danquah was not educated, however, and the elders passed him over in favor of a literate kinsman. But the new chief's reign was brief: stricken with illness, he "lived forty days" and died on the stool without having accomplished anything of lasting significance. Boakye Danquah succeeded him and, except for a brief hiatus during the turbulent "NLM days" of the mid-1950s, remained on the stool for forty years.

By all accounts, Nana Boakye Danquah took an active interest in the affairs of the stool and its subjects. Unlike his predecessors who, according to one of the late chief's protégés, "did nothing," Nana Boakye Danquah added drums, jewels, kente cloth, and an umbrella to the stool regalia in order "to raise the status of the chieftaincy."[43] He was also attuned to the changing structure of economic opportunities in mid-twentieth-century Ghana and sought to exploit them for the benefits of his constituents as well as for himself. Drawing on his contacts in Tachimantia, he acquired land and planted cocoa in Brong-Ahafo, traveling back and forth between his farm and his chiefly responsibilities in Asokore-Mampon.[44] Following his lead, a number of his subjects established cocoa farms of their own at Tachimantia, Tepa, and Mim. Though uneducated, Nana Boakye Danquah understood the importance of schooling as a key to opportunity in modern Ghana, and he is credited with having brought the first secondary school to Asokore-Mampon. Opened in 1957 as the Sadler Baptist Academy, the school was staffed by American missionaries until 1964, when the state took it over and it was renamed Kumasi Academy.[45]

Nana Boakye Danquah mobilized spiritual as well as temporal resources to safeguard and advance the welfare of his stool. According to Reverend Samuel Asante, the late chief was a Christian who also used witchcraft to protect himself. The present Asokore-Mamponhene related, with some amusement, that when the government acquired a piece of Asokore-Mampon stool land to extend the Kumase Airport, Nana Boakye Danquah enlisted the prayers of Muslim clerics in Kumase Zongo to aid him in his negotiations with the state. He also encouraged spiritual practitioners to settle in the village. Samuel Asante, who was born in Mampon and raised as a Catholic, attended school in Cape Coast. "During the reign of Dr. Kwame Nkrumah," he worked for the Ghana National Trading Corporation (GNTC) as a storekeeper, but in 1969, he was baptized by the Holy Spirit and left GNTC to evangelize. When he came to Asokore-Mampon, in 1975, Nana Boakye Danquah invited him to come and live in his house.[46] At that time, Reverend Asante recalled, most of the town was pagan, but gradually people came to the Gospel. In 1993, Samuel Asante was still living in the late chief's house, healing the afflicted through prayer and remembering his late patron with evident affection.

Another of Chief Boakye Danquah's protégés, Komfo Abena Anim, was born in Nsuta and, like Reverend Asante, brought up Catholic.[47] In her youth, she trained as a seamstress, but she had to give up her trade when she was seized by spirits who "made her head rasta" and caused her to turn her cutlass against her own arms and legs instead of the weeds in her farm. Her parents sent her to a priest in Brong-Ahafo who cured her and taught her how to use herbal medicine and invoke the gods to cure others. After seven years, she returned to Nsuta, healing people there and in Kumase. Later, Nana Boakye Danquah brought her to Asokore-Mampon and she stayed there. Komfo Abena used to prophesy in public, but the Christians didn't believe her, so she stopped. She continues to treat people who are sick, however, and also helps them find work and travel safely. Many of her clients are Christians: even spiritualist preachers come to her for power to develop their churches. "What the Christian God can do, my gods can do also." Her house in Asokore-Mampon was built by her daughter, who works in Germany; it contains a shrine, where the priestess stores her ritual paraphernalia, and a small garage, where she keeps a white Mercedes Benz, also provided by her daughter. Secure in the care of her gods and her family, Komfo Abena is a respected member of the village elite.

If the citizens of Asokore-Mampon took Boakye Danquah's religious eclecticism in their stride, they were less complacent towards his dealings in land. According to the present Asokore-Mamponhene, when the Town and Country Planning Department prepared a layout for Asokore-Mampon in the late 1970s,[48] his illiterate predecessor did not immediately grasp its significance. Nana Boakye Danquah must have caught on quickly, however: by 1986, when Nana Debrah succeeded to the stool, 85 percent of the building plots in Asokore-Mampong had already been allocated.[49] The late chief deployed his powers of land allocation for patronage as well as profit— giving away plots to local allies and supporters, while selling others at hefty prices to well-heeled "strangers." The subchiefs and linguists whom I interviewed had each received at least one plot free of charge. Kyeame Marfo, for example, had received three plots as gifts from the chief: he resold two of them, one for ₵120,000 and one for ₵800,000, and built a house for himself and his family on the third. At the time of my research, the Benkumhene was building a second house "for the children," adjacent to the one he lived in. Both houses stood on plots that he had received from the late chief.

Other citizens were not so well favored. In the later years of his reign, some recalled, people turned against Nana Boakye Danquah "because of jealousy—he was selling building plots to strangers."[50] Matters came to a head in 1986. A year or two earlier, Nana Boakye Danquah had been asked by the Asantehene to preside over the arbitration of a land dispute. In the course of the proceedings, Nana Boakye Danquah accepted a present from one of the disputants and then made the mistake of ruling in favor of the other. The disappointed contestant went public, and the chief was convicted of accepting a bribe. Hoping to put the scandal behind them, the stool elders paid his fine, but the chief's critics were not prepared to let matters rest and brought their complaint before the Kumase Traditional Council. At first it appeared that the chief had no case to answer: the elders of the Asokore-Mampon stool refused to appear and, as the Asantehene's senior linguist pointedly reminded the council, while "youngmen" could *report* a chief's conduct to Otumfuo, according to custom, only stool elders could prefer charges. Duly summoned to give the council their side of the story, the elders sidestepped the issue of bribery, dwelling instead on the temerity of the "youths" who not only refused to help pay the chief's fine but also summoned people to a public meeting in Asokore-Mampon to reiterate their view that the town should not be held liable for the chief's misdemeanor. With a general admonition that "it is wrong for the CDR [Committee for the Defence of the Revolution] to beat gongon without the authority of the chief," the Asantehene sent everyone home to think things over. Three weeks later, Nana Boakye Danquah abdicated the stool—not, he insisted, as a concession to the dissatisfied "youths" but in deference to the custom that a convicted criminal may not occupy an Asante stool.[51]

Kenyase: Barima Owusu Agyeman

As the Asantehene's admonition to the CDR illustrates, the idioms of custom are often brought to bear in conflicts of quite modern origin. When

Flt. Lt. J. J. Rawlings took power in Ghana, for the second time, on December 31, 1981, he and his associates launched an enthusiastic campaign to stamp out corruption and profiteering at all levels of society and the state. Recalled by sceptical contemporaries as "hurry-up boys," the activists in Rawlings' regime were as impatient with indirection as with entrenched privilege, and they sought to cut quickly through accumulated layers of bureaucratic inertia, judicial delay, and the archaic edifice of chiefly privilege. Some of their methods were brutal and have been deservedly condemned,[52] but they also made serious, if sometimes ill-conceived, efforts to promote economic recovery and create a network of grassroots organizations through which ordinary citizens could participate in the work of national governance and development.[53]

Committees for the Defence of the Revolution (CDRs, also known as "unit committees") were created by the Provisional National Defence Council (PNDC) to promote development through local initiative and self-help. Originally designated People's or Workers' Defence Committees, they were charged in the early years of the Rawlings "revolution" with exposing illegal activity, such as bribery and hoarding, and mobilizing the people in support of the revolution. Some zealous cadres interpreted their mandate broadly, attacking market women as well as corrupt officials, or circumventing the law's delay by dispensing quick, sometimes summary, justice in local disputes—actions that were not universally popular.[54] In 1987, the committees were renamed CDRs and encouraged to focus primarily on local development needs. L.B.A. Bediako, who represented Kenyase in the Kwabre District Assembly in 1993, had served as secretary to the local CDR in the mid-1980s. "In those days," he recalled, CDRs were part of the government and "worked very well." Recast as nongovernmental organizations (NGOs) under the 1992 Constitution, their position was much debated, sometimes hotly, as I discovered during one of my first visits to Kenyase.

I had gone to meet the Kenyasehene, to learn something about his career and the history of the stool, and to explain my interest in conducting a series of interviews with residents of the town. When I arrived, the chief explained that he had called a public meeting that morning to discuss matters of community business and suggested that I come along "to meet the people" and explain my project—a plan to which I readily agreed. By 11:00 AM, a small crowd had gathered in an open area in front of the Methodist church, on the main road through town, and the chief, three or four elders and linguists, and several other men seated themselves on a row of wooden chairs facing the crowd. Conversation was somewhat hampered by the roar of large gravel trucks, which drove through the village every few minutes, en route between Kumase and a nearby quarry, but the chief's linguists coped handily, using a battery-powered megaphone to relay his words to the crowd. Later, members of the audience also used the megaphone to address the chief.

Dispensing quickly with my introduction and a few routine announcements, the chief turned to the main business of the meeting. Reminding his audience that Kenyase was in the midst of an ongoing campaign to raise money for town improvements, Barima Owusu announced that he was appointing an interim committee to carry on with the work of development until the National Assembly had completed the task of creating a new local government structure to replace the old CDRs.[55] The assembled townspeople listened quietly to the chief's announcements, but when he read out the names of those appointed to the new interim committee, the meeting came to life. For over an hour, one citizen after another stepped forward to denounce the chief, the elders, the district assembly, the regional minister, the "CDRfoɔ," the "committeefoɔ," and anyone else who had been involved, one way or another, in efforts to "mobilize" the townspeople for "development." A few speakers defended the town's would-be developers, but the majority were critical, some angrily so. When the chief finally took the floor, he spoke for a long time, begging people to cool down and promising to take their words to heart. His linguists repeated everything he said, also at length, and the meeting dispersed. Visibly exhausted, the chief walked home, accompanied by his elders, in silence. When we reached his door and I asked permission to leave (a matter of routine politeness at the end of any visit), his only comment was, "Well, that's democracy."

My subsequent visits to Kenyase were uneventful, and I was able to piece together more of the story from conversations with a number of people, including several who had been criticized at the town meeting. One point on which everyone agreed was that local economic opportunities were few and far between. Kenyase used to be a productive farming area, I was told, but the soil was worn out by frequent cultivation with inadequate inputs.[56] A few people grew maize, tomatoes, and/or oil palm for sale, but others only planted cassava, and the majority of my informants did no farming at all. With few locally generated sources of income and meager financial support from the government,[57] development in Kenyase depended on "self-help."

In recent years, the chief, the elders, and the CDR had appealed repeatedly to the townspeople to contribute money and "communal labor" for improvements in the town's infrastructure. Many did, but the results were often disappointing. Money was collected for electric poles in 1989, but the amount raised was not enough to cover the full cost of bringing electricity to the town, and the project languished. It was finally completed, in May 1993, when with the help of their recently elected member of Parliament, Kenyase's leaders persuaded the government to step in. Buoyed by that success, the chief and the committee had launched a new drive, in August, to raise money for the projected water supply. They collected ₵1,700,000, but this fell far short of the amount they needed to raise before the Ghana Water and Sewerage Corporation would kick in with matching funds to cover the cost of a pipeline from Kumase. Anxious that the money should not lie idle, the committee proposed that it be spent on street lights, but the chief insisted that it was for water. After much debate, it was decided, anticlimactically, to hire a sanitation firm to pump out the public latrine.

Such delays and disappointments left many citizens doubtful about the benefits of "self-help," and its advocates looking for scapegoats. "Tikya" Konadu, who had been active in the CDR since 1988, when he was posted to Kenyase's primary school from his home town of Ofinso, was one of those whose appointment to the interim committee provoked the loudest complaints. He admitted that people were fed up with inaction—"the old committee didn't do anything, so its members should not serve on the new one"—but insisted that Kenyasefoɔ opposed *him* because "I am not from their town." The chief (who bowed to public opinion after the open meeting and withdrew his nominations for the interim committee) thought differently. Neither the CDR nor the town development committee that preceded it had ever given a full account of how they spent the money collected for development projects, he explained, and people did not want the new interim committee to include those who had "disappointed them" in the past. Bediako, the assemblyman, also criticized the chief, for acting "too quickly" and appointing the new interim committee without consulting anyone.

A longtime supporter of the Rawlings "revolution," Assemblyman Bediako[58] spoke warmly of its aims and accomplishments. If communities expected to develop, he declared, they had to take some initiative. "If you help yourselves, government will see and help too, but if you just sit down, they won't help at all." Members of the old town development committees were lethargic: "they would just say 'I am on the committee,' and fold their arms." But the CDRs really worked with the people. And, unlike other chiefs "who fought the CDRs," Nana Owusu had cooperated with them to help develop the town. Under the new Constitution, however, the CDRs were history and nothing had been created to take their place: "Parliament has to do it." Nana should have waited for Parliament, instead of trying "to dictate" to the people. Though Ben supported the chief's plans for development, he refused to serve on the interim committee. "It was an honor [to be appointed], but that is not the way you do it. That is not democracy."

As I talked to more people, it became clear that tensions in Kenyase had arisen not only from misunderstandings over development projects but also from resentment over land allocation. One morning my assistant and I were approached by a man who said he wanted to talk with us. Introducing himself as a former footballer, who had played with the famed Asante Kotoko team and travelled four times to Abidjan, the man said he was now "a leader of the opposition" against the Kenyasehene. The chief, he complained, was "spoiling the town." Nana had sold a lot of land, but instead of bringing development to Kenyase, "he has eaten the money." Opanin cited personal experience to support his accusations: not only had the chief sold *his* land without his consent, but when he tried "as a native of Kenyase" to apply for more, Nana told the elders not to give him any. In truth, he added darkly, the chief was not a royal at all but an upstart who had "bought" the stool and deserved to be overthrown.

When I mentioned Opanin's complaint to other Kenyasefoɔ, some suggested that politics had more to do with it than land. Some members of the royal family wanted to sit on the stool themselves, one man explained, adding that Opanin had been a subchief but refused to serve his superior, so Nana Owusu had him removed from office. But concerns about land went beyond the grievances of disgruntled royals. Kofi Poku had completed Form 4 by the time he left school, in 1958, to earn his living. For thirty years, he ran his own radio repair shop in Kumase, but he lost it in 1990, when his landlady took away his room. He returned to Kenyase and began farming "a little" on a site about a mile from town. His forefathers had farmed there, he explained, and "anyone in the family may do so." But the future was uncertain. If the town continued to expand, the chief could sell the land for building, and his family would have no place to farm. When the chief sells your land, Kofi Poku explained, he gives you "a small amount" and the buyer *may* compensate you for your crops. After that, you are on your own.

Kofi Poku's story was confirmed, independently, by both the chief and the assemblyman. If a plot is allocated for building, Nana Owusu told me, anyone who is farming there may continue to do so until the leaseholder is ready to build. If he is in a hurry, he may pay compensation for the crops; otherwise, he will wait until they are harvested. But the farmer has no alternative: "I have made the people understand that they must stop cultivating to allow building." The chief implied that this was not really a problem. People in Kenyase can't survive on what they grow anyway, he explained: "they feed at Central Market." Assemblyman Bediako was more forthright. "Well, that is the problem. . . . Under our system, nobody but the chief" has the right to sell land, and people resent it. In fairness, he added, Barima Owusu had used some of the money from land sales to build a workshop for the junior secondary school and "to encourage the workers" on the electricity project. "But it's not on record. That's the way our system works." The Kenyasehene, he repeated, was not like some chiefs, who pocket *all* the money from land sales and do nothing for the town. "But he could give us more."

Asokore-Mampon: Nana Boakye-Ansah Debrah

In 1993, Asokore-Mamponhene Nana Boakye-Ansah Debrah was making a concerted effort to do more. When the elders chose him to succeed Nana Boakye Danquah, Nana Debrah was living in Canada where he had been since 1972. He had earned a degree in architecture at Ryerson Polytechnic in Toronto and later worked for York University as an architect and designer. He succeeded to the stool in 1986, but did not move back to Ghana until the early 1990s, after he had built a house in Dichemso, an upper-middle-class neighborhood in Kumase, and "established himself in business." An energetic and articulate man in his early forties, Nana Debrah's ambitions reached beyond Asokore-Mampon. When I met him in 1993, he had already attained prominence in the Kumase Traditional Council and was gaining a reputation among city and national officials as an "enlightened" chief. In 1994, he was elected presiding member of the Kumase Metropolitan Assembly.[59]

Thanks to his predecessor's efforts, there was not much land left in Asokore-Mampon for Nana Debrah to allocate, and he had to build his personal fortune from other sources[60]—a circumstance that may have shielded him from some of the opprobrium directed toward Nana Boakye Danquah and Barima Owusu Agyeman. As a chief, Nana Debrah cast himself as a modernizer who respected tradition. He was chosen to head projects for the Kumase Traditional Council that required some managerial skill,[61] and he sometimes presided over council meetings when the Asantehene was not available. He had also taken steps to modernize aspects of his own stool administration—such as compiling a computerized database of building plots in Asokore-Mampon.[62] He was chosen for the stool, in part, because of his education and experience abroad, but he admitted that at the time of his accession, he "knew nothing about Asante custom" and had to learn—by reading published authorities, such as Rattray, Danquah, and Busia, and questioning his stool and family elders.

Like Barima Owusu in Kenyase, Nana Debrah was keenly interested in bringing improvements to Asokore-Mampon, and well aware that to do so required not only money and local initiative but also the ability to negotiate effectively with the government. Soon after his accession, Nana Debrah began to lobby for improvements to the unpaved, badly eroded road that linked the town with Kumase. It took repeated visits to Accra as well as Kumase before the Kumase Metropolitan Authority gave out a contract on the road, and the project soon bogged down in disputes over money and shoddy workmanship.[63]

While negotiations over the road to Kumase were still underway in late 1993, Nana Debrah became involved in another struggle—this time to block a government-initiated plan to zone the southern portion of Asokore-Mampon stool land for light industrial development. "Even though we would benefit from it," he explained, the noise, congestion, and pollution would be a permanent detriment to the village.[64] Invited to speak at the inauguration of the Green Forum, a new environmental NGO, in September 1993, Nana Debrah delivered a spirited attack on the environmental irresponsibility of Kumase's carpenters—the first local industry slated for relocation to Asokore-Mampon.

The chief's concerns about pollution were no doubt well founded, but he was also interested in testing the state's resolve on matters of land appropriation.[65] Under Ghanaian law, the government could acquire stool land unilaterally—"you may read about it in the newspaper"—and the chief admitted that he did not know anyone who had challenged such acquisitions successfully. But he was willing to try. If "the carpenters" could not be stopped in the name of environmental protection, perhaps the stool could re-claim other land, which the government had acquired in the past but failed to develop according to plan.[66] At the very least, he argued, the stool deserved some credit for cooperation with government requests. Over time, the chief pointed out, Asokore-Mampon had "given" quite a lot of land to the government—for the airport, the Crop Research Institute, the new railway station, and now the carpenters. "If government won't help us with the road, we'll find a way not to give them any more land."

"DID HE WALK?" LAND, GODS, AND
HISTORY ON THE SUBURBAN FRONTIER

If ordinary people resented the opportunities for rent-taking that chiefs enjoyed under indirect rule, they also counted on their "traditional" rulers to defend stool lands against challenges from rival chiefs. Land litigation often drained stools' resources, taxed their subjects, and, if successful, stood to benefit the chief and elders more than the community, but a chief who did not "fight for" stool land courted accusations of incompetence, or worse.[67] Such expectations did not disappear after independence: chiefs continue to play a key, if ambiguous, role in the construction of tenure security at the close of the twentieth century.

As we have seen in previous chapters, stool land disputes often turn on historical precedents, which are as subject to debate and reinterpretation at the end of the twentieth century as they were at its beginning. Begun in the library and in consultations with his elders, Nana Debrah's education in matters of Asante custom continued in the courts.

In 1988, the Asokore-Mampon stool (represented at the time by the queen mother) won a case against one of its own subordinate chiefs by convincing the circuit court judge that the subchief's account of "traditional history" had too many inconsistencies to sustain his claim for title to the disputed land. In the course of his testimony, the subchief had argued, variously, that his ancestress first arrived in Asokore-Mampon in about 1700, between 1781 and 1797, and between 1874 and 1883, and that, in giving her land, the Asokore-Mamponhene had acted both in his own right and as agent for the Asantehene. Since these claims could not all be true, the judge refused to accept any of them and rejected the subchief's claim to title. Having lived on the land for a long time, however, the subchief was "entitled to [continued] possession and enjoyment" of it.[68] This decision was upheld on appeal and, in 1992, Justice Rose Owusu of the Kumase High Court rejected the plaintiff's request to reopen the case on the grounds that "possession" might be interpreted as a claim to title.[69]

In 1993–94, I had the opportunity to observe (in part) Justice Owusu's handling of another land dispute, which also turned on conflicting interpretations of "traditional history" and its significance for contemporary claims on property. This case involved conflicting claims to land at Duase, another community on Kumase's suburban frontier, located about four miles east of Kumase on the road to Kenyase. I first heard of the Duase case while I was attending sessions of the high court to observe the way land cases were presented there. In 1993, there were actually two cases before the court concerning land at Duase: one had been running for two years, the other for ten. I followed their progress, intermittently, during the court's 1993–94 session, and I also interviewed some of the litigants and witnesses in both.[70] In July 1996, during a brief visit to Ghana, I learned that Justice Rose Owusu had given judgment in one of the Duase cases, but that her judgment had been overturned on appeal and the case had gone to the Supreme Court. Unfortunately, I was unable to obtain a copy of the high court judgment, and the limited evidence I was able to collect does not allow me to construct a full account of the dispute. I cite excerpts from it here, not to assess the merits of the litigants' claims or the judges' rulings, but to illustrate the way in which historical accounts proliferate and authority is contested, as a land dispute moves from one judicial venue to another.

In 1975, a businessman named Kakari Mensah built a small knitting factory at Duase on land allocated to him by the *odikro* (village head) of the community. Some time later, when Rawlings was in power, Mensah Domfeh (Kakari Mensah's cousin) reportedly uprooted some cassava belonging to one Madam Yaa Mensah, on the grounds that it had been planted on his land without permission.[71] The police were called and arrested Mensah Domfeh; on further investigation, they discovered "a series of land cases involving so many people at Duase."[72] After some discussion, the complainants agreed to withdraw their cases from court and submit the whole matter to the Regional Office for arbitration. Kwadasin wrote a report, and the regional secretary read it out to the assembled disputants, asking if anyone objected to its conclusions. At the time, Kwadasin later testified, no one did.

The sequence of events that followed is not entirely clear. To the dismay of the original complainants, Kwadasin's report apparently concluded that Mensah Domfeh had acted within his rights.[73] In 1983, one of his antagonists, Mfrefuohene Nana Agyepon, decided to seek redress in court. Arguing that Kwadasin's hearing (at which no witnesses were called and no one was represented by counsel) was only a nonbinding arbitration, he sued Mensah Domfeh for title to his (the Mfrefuohene's) portion of Duase land.[74] Others turned to the Kumase Traditional Council, where the case quickly bogged down in uncertainties over the council's jurisdiction.[75] Despairing of action by the council, Nana Gyambibi Owusu Afriye and Kwabena Poku filed a separate suit against Mensah Domfeh in 1991, claiming title to "their" respective portions of Duase land.[76]

In both suits, Mensah Domfeh's defense rested on a claim that his ancestor, Opoku Gyan, had been settled at Duase, together with the "fetish" Tano Kwabena, by Osei Tutu, to guard the eastern frontier of the fledgling Asante state. Testifying on Mensah Domfeh's behalf, Kakari Mensah told the court that Opoku Gyan came to Duase from Suntreso, where he had settled after the first Dormaa war, and that no one else was living in Duase at the time.[77] The plaintiffs in both cases challenged this story on several grounds. All asserted that Tano Kwabena was brought to Duase not by Osei Tutu but by his successor, Asantehene Opoku Ware I; that the god had been captured at Takyiman (not Dormaa); that their own ancestors were already living at Duase when he came; and that Mensah Domfeh was *odikro* of the Kusease section of Duase only, not of Duase as a whole.[78]

Nana Gyambibi and Kwabena Poku both claimed to own land at Duase as descendants of *aheneyere*—wives of the king.[79] Kwabena Poku told the court that his ancestress, Adwoa Tuapim, had come from Denkyira "with a thousand followers" and settled at Manso Apopom, during the time of Asantehene Opoku Ware I. She later married the Asantehene and requested that her husband find land for her that was closer to the capital. The Asantehene appealed to Nana Oti Akram of Duase, who agreed to give land to the king's wife.[80] Nana Owusu Afriyie's ancestress, Adwoa Buta, was also from Denkyira. When she married Opoku Ware I, she was living at Dadesua, near the road to Lake Bosumtwi. Dadesua is separated from Kumase by the River Oda and, when it overflowed, she was unable to visit her husband. Accordingly, the king obtained land for her from Mfrefuohene Oti Akram at Duase. Because Adwoa Buta was the Asantehene's wife, Nana Owusu declared, the land belongs to her descendants in pereptuity: Oti Akram's people cannot claim it back.[81]

Further perspectives on the Duase case were provided by Buokromhene Nana Owusu Bempah, an avid student of Asante history and a gifted raconteur, who shares a boundary with landholders at Duase. Nana Bempah had testified in court on behalf of the plaintiffs and readily consented to my request for an interview. In a cogent and vivid narrative lasting more than an hour, he advanced two main arguments about the historical and "customary" merits of the case: to wit, that the claimants' forebears "all passed through Buokrom" on their way to Duase, and that the defendants' claim that the Asantehene had given land at Duase to Tano Kwabena was inherently implausible.

Buokrom, the chief declared, was the first stool to settle at Kumase, before Tafo, Amakom, Ohwim, or Kaase. Together, "the five aboriginal settlements" joined in resisting Osei Tutu's initial attempts to assert his authority over all of Asante. "We fought the Asantehene seven times, but eventually we were overpowered." To escape execution after his defeat, the Buokromhene "made a truce" with the king through marriage. Later, one of his nephews was raised to the status of Dadiesoabohene and "the war died a natural death." Although Buokrom lost the war, the Asantes were unable to dislodge the Buokrom people from a hillside east of Kumase, and they decided to remain there after the truce. Subsequent settlers had to pass through Buokrom in order to reach the unoccupied lands to the east, so the Buokromhene knew the order in which they came. The Mfrefuohene was the first to settle at Duase (Oti Akram had been there but was "pushed away"). He was followed, in order, by Adwoa Tuapim, the Aberade stool, and Tano Kwabena. Today, the chief explained, Buokrom shares a boundary with the first three, but not with Tano Kwabena who came last.[82]

The Buokromhene's second argument—that the Asantehene could not have given land to Tano Kwabena—also hinged on the story of a journey. "How did Tano Kwabena get to Duase?" the chief demanded, rhetorically. "Did he *walk*?!" Of course not, he added, for my benefit: "he was carried," by his attendant Opoku Gyan. Having been captured at Takyiman, together with his shrine, Opoku Gyan decided "to fight with the Asantes" and was placed under the authority of the Nsumankwahene, the head of the *sumanfoɔ*, or priests, at Kumase. At first, he settled at Suntreso, but "he did not find peace there" and came to look for more land to farm on further east. Like any other settler, Tano Kwabena's caretaker was assigned land at Duase for his family and descendants "to feed on,"[83] but this did not mean that the Asantehene had given land outright to the god.

"When I gave evidence in court," Nana Bempah declared with a flourish, "I taught them the difference between a chief and an *odikro*!" An *odikro*, he explained, is subordinate to a chief, especially with respect to land: he cannot allocate land, or litigate for it, without permission (or today, a power of attorney) from the chief. If the Asantehene had really given land to Tano Kwabena at Duase, the land would belong to the Nsumankwahene,[84] and he would be defending it in court. At one time, the Nsumankwahene was involved in this case, but as of 1993, he had withdrawn and was "sitting back" because, according to Nana Bempah, he knew that the land did not belong to him.

Nana Bempah's argument—that since the Nsumankwahene had not claimed the land, his *odikro* could not do so either—suggested that Opoku Gyan had been made *odikro* in Duase, and his descendant Mensah Domfeh was listed as such in the second case filed against him in the High Court. The plaintiffs in both cases maintained, however, that Mensah Domfeh was *odikro* only for the Kusease section of Duase, not for Duase as a whole. Moreover his spokesman, Kakari Mensah, admitted under cross-examination that at one time, Nana Gyambibi had been the Odikro of Duase—though he denied that Nana Gyambibi had been forced out because of the land dispute.[85] Nana Gyambibi declared, however, that Duase had no chief: instead, occupants of the various stools got together when there was anything to decide. In 1964, however, when Duase's history was recorded for the Ashanti Stools History Project at Legon,[86] Nana Gyambibi Owusu Afriyie was listed as the fourteenth chief of the Duase stool. According to this account, Nana Buokromhene was correct in asserting that the "Duasehene" was subordinate to the Nsumankwahene. But it also stated that the Duase stool was created by Osei Tutu before the war with Denkyira, and that the first Duasehene, "Oko Gyan" (*sic*), walked before the Asantehene on the battlefield at Feyiase, carrying the "Fetish Tano."[87] In short, available accounts of Duase's "traditional history" are varied, to say the least.

As testimony accumulated before the court, Judge Owusu apparently reached the same conclusion. In November 1993, the lawyer for the plaintiff requested an adjournment before closing his case: he had subpoenaed the Asantehene to provide the court with an authoritative account of the relevant traditional history, but "he hasn't come." Judge Owusu replied tartly that they had already waited for Otumfuo in vain, and that she was closing the lawyer's case for him by rescinding the subpoena. Later, however, she changed her mind and decided to subpoena the Asantehene herself. Admonished in court by several lawyers not to base her decision on history books "written by foreigners," the judge retorted, "that's why I'm trying to get information from the palace."[88] In response to her summons, representatives from Manhyia appeared in court several times, but only to make excuses. In the end, Judge Owusu was obliged to decide the case without benefit of testimony from the palace. By withholding his testimony, the Asantehene helped to ensure the appeal that followed, since any litigant who was dissatisfied with the outcome of the case could claim that, without Otumfuo's testimony, the court's decision had been based on inaccurate historical information. When historical narratives figure centrally in disputes over property and power, as they do in Asante, an influential witness can shape the course of a dispute by remaining silent—particularly if the disputants know s/he is doing so.[89]

CONCLUSION

In chapter 3, we saw how, following the restoration of 1935, the Asantehenes' efforts to provide the Golden Stool with land led to new debates over the meaning of Osei Tutu's conquests and Komfo Anokye's constitutional charter. In Duase, the authority of the Asantehene came into play not through a direct claim of land for the Golden Stool but with respect to the interpretation of historical precedents relevant to other stools' claims thoughout Asante. In both these cases, as in many others, the position of the Golden Stool with respect to the interpretation of history, or the adjudication of a dispute, commands respect, but it is far from hegemonic. Both Prempeh II and Opoku Ware II have played influential roles in bringing history to bear on the affairs of the present—an endeavor in which they are joined both by experts and by many ordinary citizens. Taken together, their multiple invocations and ongoing debates over the lessons of the past have reinforced stools' power over land but circumscribed the ability of individual chiefs to dictate terms or control the outcome of disputes. The assertion and defense of claims on land remains an ongoing social process in Asante, in which the proliferation of precedents invites many to engage in the production of history, and security of tenure hinges on continued participation in debating the past, rather than bringing an end to the conversation.

NOTES

1. A typical older "storey house" is not only taller than many recently built residential structures, but the building surrounds a central paved courtyard and occupies most of the plot on which it is located, leaving little or no space for any kind of garden immediately adjacent to the house.

2. With the end of colonial rule, Ghanaians stopped referring to ordinary people as the "subjects" of this or that stool. Instead, the term "citizen" is used to designate all those who, by virtue of long-term residence and/or association with a particular stool, are entitled to claim access to portions of stool land, to dwell and "feed on," without paying money to the chief (except for token amounts of *aseda*) or obtaining formal leases. As with the matter of allegiance to a stool in colonial Asante, the question of who can legitimately claim "citizenship" with respect to stool lands in contemporary Ghana is a subject of considerable debate.

3. Ghana, *Population Census of Ghana. Special report on localities by local authorities, Ashanti Region* (Accra: Statistical Service, 1984). If one includes Anyinam (today, a section of Asokore-Mampon) and Kumasi Academy, the population of Asokore-Mampon in 1984 was close to 2,000.

4. Wilks, *Forests of gold*, 65. Wilks' principal sources are "The History of Ashanti Kings and the Whole Country Itself . . . ," prepared under the direction of Prempeh I during his exile in the Seychelles, and "Kenyase Stool History," recorded in 1964 for the Institute of African Studies (IAS) at the University of Ghana, Legon. According to the present Kenyasehene, the village was founded by migrants from Kokofu before the time of Osei Tutu. Interview with Kenyasehene Nana Owusu Agyeman III, 9/29/93.

5. Interviews with Asokore-Mamponhene Nana Boakye Ansah Debrah and the elders of Asokore-Mampon, 8/13/93 and 8/22/93. See also IAS Stool Histories, No. 79 and 110; and interview with Kwamohene Nana Osei Amoako-Mensah II, 12/8/93.

6. Interview with Nana Debrah, 8/13/93. There are several different accounts of both the number and the names of the original constituents of Asante. See Wilks, *Forests of gold*, 114; and the discussion of Eduaben's status in ch. 3, 88.

7. Interviews with Nana Debrah and the stool elders, 8/13/93, 8/22/93.

8. Wilks, *Forests of gold*, 337.

9. NAGA ADM 11/1/1906, District Commissioner's monthly report, Kumase, May 1926.

10. Interview with Nana Owusu Agyeman III, 9/29/93. Nana Owusu abdicated, under pressure, in 1952; he studied public administration in Ghana and in Britain and then worked in Accra until 1979, when he was reenstooled. "When you are chief," he explained, "people don't like what you're doing, but later they decide you were better than your successors."

11. Tabatabai, "Agricultural decline and access to food in Ghana," 721.

12. One man questioned me at length, after I had interviewed him, about the reception immigrants could expect in the U.S.—including the attitude of the police. He asked,

he explained, because he had children and grandchildren who would like to go abroad, and he wanted to know how to advise them.

13. I made no effort to carry out a formal sampling process in either community, but I did attempt to interview both men and women of different ages, as well as chiefs, community activists, and anyone else whom I was advised to contact by my informants. I am grateful to Ms. Agnes Obiri Yeboah for her able assistance, as an interpreter and a thoughtful interlocutor, in both Asokore-Mampon and Kenyase.

14. The break-up of OPEC in the early 1980s heralded an era of abundant supply and sagging prices on the world oil market, which, together with sustained misuse of resources by Nigeria's entrenched military ruling elite, helped undermine that country's once booming economy. In Côte d'Ivoire, sagging export prices and pressure from international donors to curtail government spending also helped bring on a recession. Several of my informants had returned to Ghana in the late 1980s, as opportunities revived there and dwindled abroad.

15. "Trotro" is the local name for the small passenger vans which, refitted inside to carry three or four times as many people as they were originally designed for, constitute the backbone of Ghana's local transportation system.

16. Interview with Madam Comfort Buama, 9/18/93.

17. Confirmed in the 1992 Constitution, such powers have been vested in the state since colonial times. See, e.g., N. A. Ollenu, *Principles of customary land law in Ghana* (London: Sweet & Maxwell, 1962); S.K.B. Asante, *Property law and social goals in Ghana, 1844–1966* (Accra: Ghana Universities Press, 1975); G. Woodman, *The development of customary land law in Ghana* (Cambridge: Cambridge University Press, 1966); Harvey, *Law and social change in Ghana.* Chiefs and lawyers with whom I discussed the question agreed that there was nothing a chief could do to prevent the state from taking over part of his/her stool land. When land or fixed assets are appropriated by the state, the owners are, however, entitled to compensation—a legal right that has proved a fertile source of disputes over title! See ch. 6.

18. In the literature on family relations in West Africa, "fostering" may refer to any situation in which an adult assumes some of the responsibilities of a parent toward another's child. See, e.g., E. Goody, *Parenthood and social reproduction: Fostering and occupational roles in West Africa* (Cambridge: Cambridge University Press, 1972); Bledsoe, "No success without struggle"; W. Soyinka, *Aké: The years of childhood* (New York: Random House, 1983).

19. In addition to long-standing debates among Africanist scholars over the relationship between slavery and kinship in precolonial Asante, there is considerable evidence that descendants of slaves (or people of servile status) could, in the absence of other heirs, succeed to their masters' property and position, and that claims deriving from such relationships have continued to figure in negotiations over inheritance and stool succession throughout the twentieth century. A. N. Klein, "Inequality"; Rattray, *Ashanti*, 43, and *Ashanti law*, 41; M. Priestley, *West African trade and coast society, a family study* (London: Oxford University Press, 1969). Citing recent cases from the *Ghana Law Review* and the Manhyia Record Office, as well as oral testimony and colonial court records, Akosua Perbi argues that both formal and traditional adjudicators throughout Ghana continue to consider evidence of slave descent in deciding cases of inheritance and stool succession. A. Perbi, "The legacy of slavery in contemporary Ghana" (n.d.).

20. *Ghana Law Reports Digest* (1989–90), no. 35, Edah v. Hussey, 74.

21. Miers and Kopytoff, eds., *Slavery in Africa*; Bledsoe, "No success without struggle"; Berry, *Fathers work for their sons* and *No condition is permanent*; Barber, "Money, self-realization and the person in Yoruba texts." In a stimulating recent contribution to this literature, Guyer has argued that insofar as people are valued for unique qualities—such as special skills, knowledge, or creativity—the augmentation of wealth-in-people in many African societies should be seen not as a process of accumulation, in which wealth is measured as the number of people under one's control, but rather as one of composition. Her point is well taken, but I think it is also important not to lose sight of the proprietary element in many social relationships, in Asante and elsewhere, which underlies the commensurability (and frequent exchange) of material and social resources. If, as I am arguing here, we conceive of property (in Asante and other African societies) as a social process, in which control is a matter of continual negotiation and maneuver, subject to ambiguity and multiple interpretations, it is still appropriate to speak of investment in social relationships as a form of accumulation. Explicated in this way, the "accumulation" of wealth-in-people may be seen as contributing to material, conceptual, and/or performative compositions, which also constitute part of the wealth of African societies—just as the accumulation of musical skills contributes to the work of a composer. Guyer, "Wealth in people and self-realization in equatorial Africa"; Guyer and S. Eno Belinga, "Wealth-in-people as wealth-in-knowledge: Accumulation and composition in equatorial Africa," *Journal of African History* 36 (1995): 91–120.

22. C. Okali, *Cocoa and kinship in Ghana: The matrilineal Akan* (London: Routledge, 1983). Fifteen percent of the sixty farmers whom I interviewed in Kenyase, Asokore-Mampon, and Kumawu said they were farming on land that belonged to their spouses' families. See ch. 5, 154.

23. All individuals are members of families, but not all property is family property. Self-acquired land or other assets are held, in law and practice, to belong to the individual who acquired them. There is, however, a tendency for individual property to become family property through inheritance, which persists in Ghana today, despite recent legislative efforts to curtail matrilineal inheritance. Okali, *Cocoa and kinship*; G. Mikell, *Cocoa and chaos in Ghana* (New York: Paragon Press, 1995). See below, 112–13.

24. See ch. 5, 145–50.

25. Arhin, "The economic implications of transformations in Akan funeral rites" *Africa*; Dei, "The economics of death and funeral celebration in a Ghanaian Akan community"; Gilbert, "The sudden death of a millionaire: conversion and consensus in a Ghanaian kingdom." See ch. 5, 148–49.

26. Interview with Kyeame Kwaku Marfo, 9/25/93.

27. Conversations with Kyeame Marfo and others reveal little about the actual management of family property but do describe clearly what people expect from the person entrusted with this task.

28. Akua's cousin, a successful timber contractor who was building a second house in Asokore-Mampon in 1993, is Akwamuhene of Asokore-Mampon. According to the present Asokore-Mamponhene, his predecessor created the stool for Nana Appau because he was "a good person who was helping the town." Nana Appau has maintained close ties with his numerous offspring, encouraging those whose mothers live elsewhere to reside with him or other relatives in Asokore-Mampon. One of his daughters

explained with pride that her father had limited the number of children he had by each wife and taken "full responsibility" for all of them. She compared his sixteen children by seven women favorably with the family of a neighbor who had died recently, leaving thirteen wives and forty-six children.

29. It is common for an heir to allocate individual rooms in a family house to specific members of the family—a process that may give rise to disputes over which family members are entitled to receive rooms, or who is a legitimate family member. Mary Owusu, another resident of Asokore-Mampon, contributed money to help her brother build his house (in the 1950s) so that she would have rooms there for herself and her children. As a young woman, she followed her husband to Agogo, where he worked as a carpenter, but she maintained a farm of her own in Asokore-Mampon and eventually returned there to live. In 1993, she had six rooms in her brother's house, which she shared with some of her children (she had borne fourteen) and grandchildren.

30. M. Fortes, "Kinship and marriage among the Ashanti," in C. D. Forde & A. R. Radcliffe-Brown, eds., *African systems of kinship and marriage* (London: Oxford University Press, 1950), 283. My italics. Compare Rattray, *Ashanti law*, ch. 4.

31. See, e.g., Okali, *Cocoa and kinship*; Mikell, *Cocoa and chaos.*

32. Under PNDC Law 111 of 1985, if a person dies intestate, the spouse and children inherit the chattels and one house belonging to the deceased. Together they also receive three quarters of the remainder of the estate. If the deceased is survived by a spouse but no children, s/he receives half of the remainder.

33. Interview with Nana Debrah, 9/29/93. What the law actually says is that if a person dies intestate, the family may not disinherit his/her children or spouse(s).

34. As the Supreme Court put it, in an inheritance dispute in Berekum, "once a family property, always a family property. . . . " *Ghana Law Reports Digest* (1989–90), no. 64, In re Krah (deceased). See also *Ghana Law Reports Digest* (1987–88), nos. 63, 67.

35. The room was so small that the furniture—a bed, a dresser, three chairs and a low table—nearly filled it: adults had to squeeze to get in. An anteroom about three feet deep served as a kitchen. When the widow's in-laws turned her out, she tried to rent a room from one of the subordinate chiefs in Asokore-Mampon. A prosperous timber contractor, the chief declined to rent out rooms in his own house but agreed to add a room on to his family house to accommodate the widow and her children. Bodomase, of which we shall hear more in ch. 6, is about 2 km from Kumawu.

36. Interview with Fosuhemaa (the widow's mother), 11/7/93.

37. Compare Mikell, *Cocoa and chaos.*

38. Net of administrative costs, for which 10 percent of the price is allocated to the Lands Commission. Ghana, *Constitution of the Republic of Ghana* (1992), article 267.

39. Ibid., article 245.

40. My incredulity that busy lawyers could find it worthwhile to sit on the Kumase Traditional Council—which meets every Monday and Thursday, in sessions that may run for several hours in the middle of the day—was considerably reduced when one such member of the council explained to me that there is far more money to be made from representing a client in a chieftaincy dispute than from most land disputes, even when the latter drag on for many years.

41. By some accounts, Asokore-Mamponhene Nana Kwame Owusu was framed, by (unnamed) enemies who tricked him into purchasing an unlicensed gun and then tipped off the police. By law, an individual who has been convicted of a crime is not eligible to occupy a stool. Like other rules, this one is sometimes honored in the breach. See ch. 6, 167–72.

42. When a stool falls vacant, the elders (subordinate chiefs, including the queen mother) meet to select a successor. Eligible candidates vie for the support of the "kingmakers"—mobilizing supporters to attest to their qualifications (an eligible candidate must be a member of the royal family, but character is also important) and demonstrating what they can do for the stool by judicious displays and/or distributions of personal wealth. When I pressed for further details, one informant replied in mild exasperation, "It's just like an election campaign in America."

43. Interview with Rev. Samuel Asante, 9/4/93.

44. Compare Ohemaa Serwah Amponsa who, in the 1990s, commuted between Kumawu and Toronto, managing the affairs of her stool in the former, her household in the latter, and her business interests in both. See ch. 5, 141.

45. Interview with Ms. Beatrice Bonsu, Acting Headmistress, 8/28/93.

46. Interview with Rev. Asante, 9/4/93.

47. I interviewed Madam Komfo Abena, at the suggestion of the Asokore-Mamponhene and other stool elders, on 9/18/93.

48. State oversight of land allocation at the local level begins with the layout—a map prepared by the Department of Town and Country Planning, which demarcates allocable plots in a given community, provides the legal definition of the property described in the lease, and serves as the starting point for negotiations between a prospective leaseholder and the stool, the Lands Commission and the Asantehene's Lands Office. A layout is not, of course, superimposed on an empty landscape: to the extent that existing patterns of land use are displaced when plots are allocated, the layout becomes a potential instrument of dispossession. In practice, layouts are subject to a variety of negotiations, both within and outside the Town and Country Planning Department. Since chiefs are rarely prepared to incur the opprobrium that would arise if people were displaced from their homes, the relationship between a layout and the actual arrangement of buildings in a settlement may be slight. This was certainly the case in the center of Asokore-Mampon; even on its outskirts, the actual placement of plots and buildings suggested that, in some cases, further negotiations had taken place between the preparation of the layout and the actual allocation of the land.

49. Based on data kindly supplied by Nana Debrah. Mr. Sarpong, Head of the Regional Lands Commission in Kumase, who owns a house in Asokore-Mampon, confirmed that by the time Nana Debrah was installed as chief, there was little stool land left for him to allocate. See below, 123.

50. Interviews with Rev. S. Asante, Assemblyman Forkuor, and Nana Debrah.

51. My account of Nana Boakye Danquah's abdication is based on interviews and minutes of the meetings at which the Kumase Traditional Council discussed the case. MRO, Kumase Traditional Council Record Book, 1985–86. Informants sympathetic to Nana Boakye Danquah added that Otumfuo had privately urged the chief to step down, after forty years on the stool, "because of his good reputation." Nana Boakye Danquah died in 1987.

52. Blaming "middlemen" for shortages and soaring prices of staple foodstuffs and other essential consumer goods, agents of Rawlings' regime harassed market women in particular. G. Clark, "Price control of local foodstuffs in Kumasi, Ghana, 1979," in Clark, ed., *Traders versus the state* (Boulder, CO: Westview, 1985). After the end of press censorship in 1992, opposition newspapers fulminated at length against human rights abuses in the early years of Rawlings' rule, notably the execution, in 1982, of three judges and a senior military officer who had spoken out against the government. A junior officer was tried and convicted in the case, but it is widely believed that he acted on orders from very senior government officials. The report of an official investigation, carried out in 1983 but never made public, was published in *The Statesman* in 1993.

53. See, e.g., F. Drah, "Civil society and the transition to pluralist democracy," in K. Ninsin and F. Drah, eds., *Political parties and democracy in Ghana's Fourth Republic* (Accra: Woeli, 1993), 101; Nugent, *Big men, small boys and politics in Ghana;* P. Anyang' Nyong'o, ed., *Popular struggles for democracy in Africa* (London: Zed, 1987); D. Rothchild, ed., *Ghana: The political economy of recovery* (Boulder, CO: Lynne Rienner, 1991).

54. See, e.g., Clark, *Traders versus the state*; Nugent, *Big men*, 45, 76–77.

55. The 1992 Constitution abolished the CDRs but left it to the National Assembly to decide what to replace them with after the transition to civilian rule. The assembly, which took office at the beginning of 1993, was still deliberating at the time of my research. Matters were not clarified, in the interim, by the government's announcement that the CDRs should reconstitute themselves, on a voluntary basis, as NGOs.

56. Not because people were ignorant of the benefits of fertilizer or pest control measures, but because they could not afford them.

57. Governments everywhere are limited in their ability to mobilize resources, Nana Owusu explained philosophically, "because people wouldn't be happy to be bored with more taxes."

58. L.B.A. Bediako ("most people call me Ben") attended Kumase Polytechnic, then worked as a clerk and an accountant, first for the bishop of Kumase and later for the United Trading Company (UTC). When Rawlings started his "revolution," Ben joined the Workers' Defence Committee (WDC) at UTC. The WDCs, he explained, mobilized workers to ferret out illegal activity, such as hoarding and price gouging, and report it to the government. They also reported people's reactions to new laws and "advised the government on policy planning." In 1986, he left UTC, started an oil palm farm in Kenyase, and "began my political work" as secretary to the local CDR. Later, he moved to the district secretariat and, in 1988, was elected to represent Kenyase in the Kwabre District Assembly.

59. *The Pioneer*, 5/23/94 and 5/24/94.

60. On plots he could allocate, Nana Debrah began by laying the foundation of a house, an investment that greatly increased its value. Toward the end of 1993, a customer based in Germany sent him a Mercedes Benz to pay for a plot-with-foundation, thus enabling the chief to catch up with the priestess. See above, 117. At about the same time, he built a second story on his house in Dichemso, to provide space for a telecommunications center.

61. He had, for example, compiled a roster of the chiefs in the Kumase Traditional Council to be used in collecting contributions for improvements to the palace, and he

had helped to organize the reception following a durbar held in honor of Britain's Prince Edward, on 30 October 1993.

62. See n. 48.

63. The road was completed in 1994.

64. Interviews with Nana Debrah, 8/13/93, 8/29/93.

65. Apparently the chief's concern for the quality of Asokore-Mampon's environment did not stand in the way of all development. Toward the end of 1993, while negotiations over the direct road to Kumase were still underway, a new unpaved road was suddenly opened up, connecting Asokore-Mampon to the main Kumase-Accra road at a spot near a projected railway depot, slated to be built in the near future. Almost immediately, heavy lorries began to rumble through the previously quiet center of the village.

66. Interview with Mr. Sarpong, 9/23/93.

67. See chs. 2 and 6.

68. Circuit Court, Kumase, Nana Boakye Ahenkan v. Nana Kwabena Yeboah and Nana Serwa Die Owuo, Judgment, 9/13/88.

69. KHC, Suit No. LS 1003/90, Nana Boakye Ahenkan and others v. Nana Boakye Ansah Debrah and others, Ruling, 11/17/92.

70. The defendant (in both cases) and his spokesman were unwilling to discuss the cases while they were pending before the court. The plaintiffs displayed no such reluctance, and I also spoke with some of their witnesses. The high court sits from 1 October to the end of July. I tried to attend court whenever the Duase cases were scheduled during the 1993–94 session, except from mid-January to the beginning of June, when I was in the U.S.

71. One informant said that crops were uprooted in 1976; others mentioned 1982. Kakari Mensah stated in court that Mensah Domfeh is "the son of my mother's uncle." KHC 115/83, Nana Yaw Adibey v. Opanin Mensah Domfeh, 12/2/93.

72. B. G. Kwadasin, Chief Superintendant of Police, Accra, testifying in Kumase High Court, 12/2/93. In 1982–83, Kwadasin said, he was an assistant superintendant of police in Kumase, and chairman of the PNDC Information Center, located in the Ashanti Regional Office.

73. The contents of the report were not discussed in court; instead, Kwadasin's testimony was followed by a long argument over whether the court would accept a copy of the report as evidence, the original having been lost. My knowledge of its conclusions is based on conversations with several of the litigants and their witnesses.

74. KHC Suit No. LC 115/83, Nana Yaw Ajuben v. Opanin Mensah Domfeh. Sometime between 1983 and 1993, the original plaintiff, Nana Agyapon, had died and Nana Yaw Ajuben (also spelled Adibey) had taken his place. The Mfrefuohene is one of the numerous Gyaase stoolholders, or palace officials, in the Kumase Traditional Council. According to Nana Debrah's roster, there were eighty-one stools altogether in the six subdivisions of the Gyaase *fekuo*.

75. MRO, Kumase Traditional Council Record Book, 4/21/86, 5/5/86.

76. KHC Suit No. LS 983/91, Nana Gyambibi Owusu Afriyie and Nana Kwabena Poku v. Mensah Domfeh, Odikro of Duase.

77. KHC Suit No. LC 115/83, 11/18/93.

78. Ibid.; also KHC Suit No. LS 983/91, 12/1/93; and interviews with Nana Owusu Afriyie, 11/20/93, Nana Kwabena Poku, 12/4/93, and Opoku Agyeman, 11/20/93 and 7/7/94.

79. See chapter 3, 71.

80. KHC Suit No. LS 983/91, 12/1/93.

81. Interview with Nana Owusu Afriyie, 11/20/93. Nana Owusu occupies the Aberade stool, which Opoku Ware I created for his son by Adwoa Buta. Nana Owusu introduced himself as the youngest child of Prempeh I, born after Prempeh returned from the Seychelles in 1924. He attended a commercial secondary school in Kumase and worked for many years as a secretary and later an administrator for the government and the University of Ghana. In 1975, he was transferred to the University of Science and Technology in Kumase, where he helped set up the university hospital. He retired in 1992.

82. The Buokromhene's narrative suggests an explanation for a narrative device that I encountered frequently in the course of fieldwork. In describing how their ancestor(s) had arrived at their present abode, informants not only identified their place of origin but also listed all the places where their forebears had sojourned en route. In Kumawu, where I collected the largest number of such narratives, one informant named as many as nine places, consulting a handwritten diary to be sure his list was accurate. The Buokromhene's story suggests that the importance of such ancestral itineraries rests, in part, on the possibility that people who live in those places today may be able to confirm that so-and-so's ancestor passed through there, at such-and-such a time, thus lending weight to the historical basis of current claims to land and office.

83. See ch. 2, 51–53.

84. As chief of Asante *nsuman* (priests), the Nsumankwahene would have been Opoku Gyan's superior.

85. KHC LC 115/83, cross-examination of Kakari Mensah, 12/2/93. See also KHC LS 983/91, Kwabena Poku's testimony, 12/1/93, and interviews with Nana Kwabena Poku and Nana Owusu Afriyie.

86. Institute of African Studies, Legon, Ashanti Stool Histories No. 117, 3/5/64.

87. "The Duasehene swears to the Asantehene through the Nsumankwahene." He "cannot at present swear to the Asantehene in that he is a subordinate chief. . . . " IAS, Ashanti Stool Histories No. 117, 1.

88. KHC LC 115/83, 7/7/94.

89. See ch. 5, 147–49.

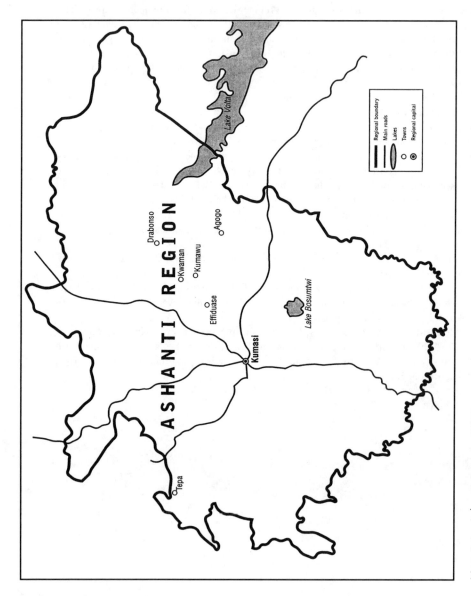

Map 5.1 Ashanti Region, 1989.
Source: Survey of Ghana.

5

MIGRANTS, TOMATOES, AND HISTORY: NEGOTIATING FAMILY, LAND, AND CITIZENSHIP IN KUMAWU

The preceding chapters have focused primarily on Kumase and the inter-locking debates over property, authority, and history through which people have asserted claims to increasingly valuable plots of land in the city and its immediate environs. For much of the twentieth century, Kumase has acted as a magnet, drawing people from the Asante countryside and from outside the region to work, trade, and build in the city. Yet without the countryside, the city would not have grown and prospered as it has. The wealth of Kumase—like that of Ghana—is drawn from the soil. Led by cocoa, timber, and gold—Ghana's principal exports—the products of Asante's forests, farms, and mines have fed the people and markets of the capital and provided the means for its construction. The regional economy rests on the interdependence of its rural and urban areas.

Kumase's economic links with towns and villages throughout the region have been created and sustained through continual movements of people and goods, and overlapping networks of kinship, allegiance, friendship, and faith. Family ties in Asante are extensive even by African standards since, in addition to the circles of kin and affines whom people speak of as family members, most Asantes belong to one of the giant matriclans, whose mem-bers were dispersed across the region before the time of Osei Tutu and may be found today in Ghanaian communities around the world.[1] Together with

shared traditions of origin, religious affiliations, stool allegiances, membership in trade associations or political parties, and so forth, family relationships promote ongoing communication and exchange among people who
may be scattered over great distances and are continually on the move.[2]

The economic and social interconnectedness of Asante is manifested in
many domains of social activity, including the process of making claims on
land. In this chapter and the next, I return to Kumawu—site of the chieftaincy disputes described in chapter 2—to illustrate changing patterns of
land claims and land use in a rural community, compare them with those in
Kumase, and explore the connections between them.

A modest-sized rural town,[3] Kumawu straddles the edge of the ecological transition zone between the forests of southern and central Asante
and the open savannahs of the Afram Plains. Established long before
Osei Tutu's rise to power in the late seventeenth century, Kumawu is an
old settlement—by some accounts one of the oldest in Asante. Tweneboa
Kodia, who fought and died helping Osei Tutu liberate Asante from
Denkyira's overrule, was the fourth, sixth, or seventh Kumawuhene, depending on one's source.[4] During the spreading turmoil of the 1870s
and 1880s, Kumawu's defenders were routed and its population scattered, but the town had regrouped, with the assistance of Ejisu and
Ofinso, by the time Agyeman Prempeh I was elected Asantehene in 1888.
Shortly thereafter, in an ill-judged bid to unify the community and consolidate his power, Kumawuhene Kwesi Krapa decided to "combine all
the stools at Kumawu into one."[5] Outraged, the chiefs of Kumawu threatened revolt, and the *omanhene* sought and obtained the Asantehene's
permission to execute the ringleaders. "At that time, there were no ex-
ecutioners (abrafoɔ) in Kumawu," so Barima Krapa sent for one from
the neighboring village of Timate, but the condemned chiefs ran away
before he arrived. Kwesi Krapa then threatened to burn the town, but
his mother stopped him: " 'What are you doing? You combined the stools
for peace! Also you did it without informing the elders first. So it's
your fault.' She told him to leave the stool, and he did."[6]

His successor, Kwame Afram, took office in 1896, as British troops were
occupying Kumase, and he wasted no time in establishing his credentials
with the new regime.[7] Subsequent occupants of the stool have followed his
lead, consistently supporting the government in power. For example, Barima
Otuo Akyeampon refused to endorse the Asante-based National Liberation
Movement in the mid-1950s, or criticize the Nkrumah regime, but abruptly
shifted his support from the Convention People's Party (CPP) to the military regime when Nkrumah was overthrown in February 1966. Asked to
explain his *volte face*, the chief replied "if you put a box there and call it
the government, I will support it."[8] True to form, Barima Asumadu Sakyi II

has been a consistent advocate for Rawlings' National Democratic Congress (NDC), although many Kumawufoɔ, including some of his own most loyal supporters, backed the opposition New Patriotic Party (NPP).[9]

The chief's loyalty to the government notwithstanding, Kumawu felt the full force of Ghana's economic decline in the 1970s and early 1980s, and the subsequent recovery was slow to trickle out to the countryside. Like many rural communities in Asante, Kumawu is a farming town with extensive links to the wider regional economy. Most residents farm, but they also engage in many other kinds of income-earning activities, often at some distance from Kumawu. During the cocoa boom of the 1950s and 1960s, many Kumawufoɔ joined the exodus of farmers from Asante seeking to establish new cocoa farms in the forests of the Central and Western Regions, while others left to pursue careers in trade, education, politics, or the civil service. One of Kumawu's well-known sons, Krobo Edusei, a prominent member of the CPP, was minister of finance during the First Republic. Another, B. A. Mensah, left Kumawu as a teenager and established himself in Accra, where he accumulated a substantial portfolio of business interests—including at one point a controlling interest in Rothman's, one of the largest distributors of tobacco products in Ghana.[10] Many Kumawufoɔ attended school in Kumase and remained there as adults, working as clerks, traders, or civil servants,[11] and informants in Kumawu frequently mentioned relatives who were living and working elsewhere in Ghana or abroad. The present Kumawuhene spends much of his time at his houses in Kumase and Accra, and his cousin, the queen mother, commutes from Toronto to carry out the duties of her office in Kumawu.

While some of the town's elite had clearly prospered, at the time of my fieldwork, for the majority of Kumawufoɔ, the gains from economic recovery and structural adjustment had been slim. In late 1993, the main road from Kumawu to Kumase was in poor condition; Kumawu's electricity was erratic; and water flowed through its outmoded system of pipes for an hour or two in the middle of the night, if at all. Nonetheless, many of the residents whom I spoke with in late 1993 and mid-1994 were cautiously optimistic.[12] Efforts to rehabilitate local cocoa farms through agricultural extension and government-sponsored loans had foundered on high costs, sagging prices, and bad debts,[13] but local farmers continued to cultivate foodcrops for home consumption and, as the economy recovered, for the market as well. By the early 1990s, the most conspicuous signs of agricultural recovery in Kumawu were the stacks of wooden crates, filled with tomatoes, which appeared at three- to four-month intervals alongside Kumawu's pathways and roadsides, awaiting transport to market in Kumase, Accra, Lomé, or Abidjan. Nearly every farmer whom I spoke to had tried growing tomatoes, and many had found them worthwhile. "Tomatoes built all these houses," one man exclaimed, gesturing toward a cluster of modest one- to three-room cement-plastered structures built by the members of a small Christian sect who had created their own settlement on the edge of town.[14]

TOMATOES AND TENANTS

Far from impeding agricultural adjustment, land tenure arrangements in Kumawu adapted quickly to the specific requirements of growing and marketing tomatoes. Most farmers plant tomatoes on plots of one hectare or less, often subdividing a single field into sections devoted to different crops.[15] Among the farmers I interviewed, most were cultivating more than one plot of land, though only a few had more than one field under tomatoes at any given time. It was common, however, to plant tomatoes two or three times during the year, and occasionally I met a farmer with as many as four fields under tomatoes at once. The preferred pattern of land use was to plant tomatoes on the same field for two to four cropping seasons of about three months each, then use the field for other crops or leave it in fallow, and use another plot for a new round of tomato cultivation.

Small-scale, short-term, and highly seasonal, tomato growing in Kumawu was also thoroughly commercialized. High yields were achieved through intensive use of chemical fertilizers and pesticides. Farmers reported spending anywhere from $45 to $80 or more per acre on fertilizers and pesticides for each crop of tomatoes, and they complained of the rising cost of these inputs. Most tomato growers also employed laborers, at $1.20–$1.50 for half a day's work, to prepare fields, harvest tomatoes, and headload crates to the nearest motorable road, and many used hired labor to help with planting, weeding, and spraying as well.

In 1993–94, farmers reported that the total cost of tomato cultivation ranged from $80 to $120 per acre for a single crop. How accurate these figures were is difficult to say. None of the farmers I interviewed kept close track of outlays on hired labor, although most did give a total figure for the amount "invested" in a particular field. In many cases, these figures may have represented sums that farmers had either borrowed or taken from savings to purchase chemicals and, perhaps, to pay laborers to prepare their fields for planting. If so, they probably understated the total cost of production, and reported returns of 100 percent on farmers' "investments" in tomato fields may have been exaggerated. Nonetheless, when market prices were favorable, it appears that farmers derived a modest profit from growing tomatoes. But the market was notoriously volatile, as I had occasion to witness in 1994.

Tomato buying, like tomato growing, is privately organized: government neither controls prices nor subsidizes marketing costs. During the harvest season, buyer;, most of whom are women,[16] travel daily from Kumase or Accra, in small, covered vans (panel trucks), which ply the roads around Kumawu from before dawn until 9:00 or 10:00 PM. Since tomatoes are perishable, they must be moved as quickly as possible, and buyers from Kumase make several trips to Kumawu in a day. Farmers bring their tomatoes to the nearest road, where they wait for the next buyer. Prices are negotiated on the spot: while farmers continually exchange information about local negotiations, buyers who travel to and from one or more of Ghana's large urban markets every day have better access to information about daily or even hourly changes in price, and farmers often feel themselves to be at a disadvantage in the negotiating process.

Perhaps their greatest disadvantage, however, is their own success as growers. When I settled in Kumawu, at the beginning of June 1994, farmers had not yet begun to harvest the spring crop, and the price of tomatoes stood at about $30 to $35 per box. By early July, when the harvest was in full swing, the roadside price had fallen to $1.50. At that price, farmers could not afford to hire laborers to pick their tomatoes and carry them to the nearest road—let alone recover any of the money they had spent on labor or chemicals earlier in the growing season—and many left their tomatoes to rot in the fields.

The collapse of farmgate prices in mid-1994 may have been exceptionally severe. In 1993, for example, farmers made modest profits at harvest time prices of $3–$6 per box. Even in a good season, however, growing tomatoes is a risky business. Economic liberalization may ease farmers' access to markets and stimulate increased output by attracting more buyers and sellers, but it also increases people's exposure to market fluctuations. In Kumawu, the steady growth of tomato production had clearly intensified competition and exacerbated seasonal fluctuations in price. Under the circumstances, farmers who wished to expand production often could not afford to do so: instead, they tried to cope with the risks of growing tomatoes by diversifying their crops and/or sources of income. Full-time farmers invariably grew other crops in addition to tomatoes, both for sale and for home consumption. Cassava, maize, and cocoyam were the most popular staples, but most farmers also planted some yam, beans, and other vegetables, and several women grew onions as a commercial crop. Many combined farming with other occupations: among the tomato growers I met in Kumawu were traders, artisans, civil servants, itinerant preachers, and a couple of aspiring musicians who, when they were lucky, might play at a club in Kumase at night, then catch an early morning "trotro" to tend their fields and take breakfast in Kumawu. All were well aware of the vagaries of the market, and they approached tomato cultivation as a kind of gamble—hoping to clear enough of a profit to make a long-deferred purchase or simply supplement their meager incomes from other sources; ready to move to other ventures and/or locations if they failed. For farmers seeking to augment their resources, or at least break even, mobility and diversification were facts of daily life.

Farmers frequently paid cash for access to land, as well as for labor and chemicals. About half the farmers I interviewed were growing tomatoes, as well as other crops, on "family" or inherited land, which, in principle, they used free of charge. The others had rented tomato fields, paying cash up front to use them for a few years or a few months at a time. Among the twenty-eight farmers I interviewed who were currently cultivating tomatoes, fifteen said they were using family land, fifteen were leasing one or more tomato plots, and two were sharecropping. A few farmers had arranged to lease plots for up to five years, but most were renting fields for a year, or a single cropping season of three or four months. Tomato tenants included local farmers as well as "strangers," and a few even said they were paying rent to their relatives.

While tomato growing had clearly served to commercialize short-term transactions in land use rights, it cannot be said to have created distinct classes of landlords and tenants in Kumawu. Unlike reported agricultural wages, which fell within a narrow, standardized band of rates, rents were individually negotiated and varied considerably from one farmer to another. Informants reported paying anywhere from $5 to $20 per acre to use a field for a year or a few months. Getting access to land for planting tomatoes was "not difficult," they said: "Lots of people want to lease out land to tomato farmers." Nor did farmers appear unduly burdened when landholders demanded to be paid cash in advance. Rental payments typically accounted for about 10 percent of a farmer's "investment" in tomato cultivation. Compared to the cost of chemicals and labor, land was cheap, and market fluctuations posed more of a threat to farmers' returns than did the demands of rapacious landlords.

Indeed, differences were sometimes more pronounced among tomato "landlords" or "tenants" than between them. As we have seen, growing tomatoes is too risky to encourage specialization: farmers treated them as a kind of speculative investment rather than a source of livelihood and took care to hedge their bets by diversifying their crops and sources of income. Tomato "landlords" were also a heterogeneous group.[17] The majority were women, whose fortunes varied widely. My informants ranged from the queen mother—whose transcontinental lifestyle, seventeen-bedroom house, and multiple business interests set her apart from most women in the town—to Akua Afram, also a member of Kumawu's sprawling royal family, whose crumbling mud-walled dwelling could be entered only by climbing over a pile of loose rock to reach a room that had become a verandah when its outer wall collapsed. Indeed, some of the poorer women appeared to be landlords only in name. I spoke with a few young men who said that they had paid cash to rent land from a "grandmother" or an aunt. When I interviewed them separately, however, the older women complained that "the children" had never paid them any money, and that they (the women) felt powerless to insist.[18]

In short, landholding is a mixed bag in Kumawu: neither "landlords" nor "tenants" can be said to constitute a "class" of people who have gained or lost from recent agricultural developments to the same degree. In part this reflects the fact that land ownership in the rural areas of contemporary Asante is no less subject to multiple, overlapping, and frequently contested claims than it is in Kumase, or was in the colonial period. While the money to be made from tomato leases is modest—compared, say, to cocoa tribute in the colonial era, or the "rents" generated by urban construction or government land acquisition today[19]—the spread of tomato cultivation has given rise to competition among land claimants, reactivating debate over who exercises what kinds of authority over particular tracts of rural land, and how their claims to land reflect on their relations with one another. Many tomato "landlords" were not chiefs or even family heads but women and men of modest means attempting to supplement their meager resources by subletting their rights to use a portion of family land. As people negotiate claims to farmland, they also negotiate claims to kinship and citizenship: their debates reflect the links between property and social relationships in Asante and illuminate the dynamic qualities of both.

FAMILY SECRETS

Since colonial times, the courts have held that while allodial rights to land belong to the stool, families' rights of usufruct are secure from arbitrary intervention.[20] Individuals may and often do purchase long-term leaseholds, which they secure by planting trees or putting up buildings. In the past, individually acquired property has often been transformed into family property through inheritance—a process that continues today, despite recent statutory changes intended to limit the practice of matrilineal succession.[21] In principle, any individual is entitled to use some portion of his or her family's land, but people's abilities to exercise such claims vary a good deal in practice and are often subject to dispute. Disputed claims may turn on conflicting accounts not only of individuals' histories of land use, field boundaries, or contributions to land improvements but also their status within the family, or even their claims to family membership itself.

Family membership is not, in other words, a jural fact, given in advance of social practice, which guarantees a person's access to property or income. In practice, relatives may wield very different degrees of influence over land and other assets; like "tomato landlords" or tenants, members of the same family often command very different levels of income and wealth. Admitting somewhat sheepishly that he did not know some of his poorer relatives, a friend mused that families in Asante are "one people," yet divided. "If you look from a distance, you see the forest, but up close you see that each tree is different." Like relations of property, family ties are enacted in the course of people's daily lives, and they are subject to negotiation, renewal, and dispute.

Families have established long-term rights to land in Kumawu in a variety of ways, and family members may request the use of one or more parcels of land from the family head (or elders), or from a parent or sibling who has already received his/her own allocation. Transfers of land rights among relatives are usually described as "gifts" and acknowledged with small return gifts of drinks or money, known as *aseda*, or "thanks." Paid in the presence of witnesses, *aseda* serves not only to confirm the gift but also to create a living archive, in the form of witnesses' recollections, which may be drawn upon at any time to defend the rights of the recipient against rival claims. Disputes over boundaries between family members' plots occur often but rarely reach the courts: they are usually resolved by family elders or, failing that, by elders of the stool. As the queen mother (a frequent arbiter of boundary disputes, especially among women) pointed out, intrafamily boundaries are rarely marked. "If your farm lies next to a stream, good for you!" In most cases, however, individuals' claims stand or fall with the recollections, and reputations, of their witnesses.[22]

As we saw in chapter 4, many intrafamily transfers occur through inheritance, which tends to follow matrilineal lines of descent, unless the decedent made other provisions while alive. In the twentieth century, it has become common for individuals to bequeath self-acquired property by means of written wills. Such bequests may be challenged by the matrilineal family, however, often on the grounds that property specified in the will was not self-acquired but already belonged to the family. If such a claim can be sustained, it implies that the deceased person was not entitled to give or bequeath the property in question and the will is, therefore, not valid.[23] Claims of this sort have multiplied since the passage of PNDC Law 111, which mandates that when a person dies intestate, the major part of the estate should go to the deceased's spouse(s) and children, rather than the matrilineal kin.[24] Since the law applies only to self-acquired property, however, matrilineal heirs have sought to protect their claims by arguing that particular properties were, in fact, acquired or built with the help of other family members. A number of land cases brought before the courts after 1985 involved inheritance disputes in which family members claimed, often successfully, that the deceased's estate was family property and thus exempt from PNDC Law 111.[25]

Claims to family property turn on accounts of family history. In Kumawu and throughout Asante, claims are based on past transactions, including not only formal leases and recent exchanges and gifts but also agreements made and battles fought long ago. Since, in principle, families' rights are subordinate to those of the stool, any historical event that served to define a family's relations to the stool may be adduced to support, or question, their claims to portions of stool land. With few exceptions, my inquiries about family history elicited stories of ancestors who had migrated to Kumawu from other parts of Asante—in several cases, before the founding of the Asante state—and had been allocated land by the chief or another earlier settler for themselves, their families, and followers "to eat upon."[26] Some also claimed to control hunting or fishing rights in more distant portions of the territory controlled, or claimed, by the Kumawu stool. In most cases, family history and family land were closely interrelated.

In Kumawu and elsewhere, people frequently referred to family history as "our secrets." Since assertions of secrecy were usually followed by a detailed account of the speaker's forebears and their exploits, they were apparently not meant to withhold information, from me or anyone else. Rather, I would argue, they served to remind the audience of power—both the speaker's power to shape the historical narrative and the power of history to shape negotiations over claims to property and influence. As a friend in Kumawu put it, when I pressed for an explanation, family history is a secret "because it can affect you."[27]

The metaphor of secrecy, applied to family history, points to the value of history in the social economy of Asante in the twentieth century. Unlike the commodities (or "goods") of neoclassical economics, history derives its value not from scarcity but from practice. The production of history in Asante is a performative as well as an archival process. To "affect" people—to protect or enhance their claims to property or office—history must be heard and seen: its value depends on having an audience. The statement that history is a secret reminds listeners that the speaker has the power to impart information, as well as to withhold it.[28] The ensuing recitation is thus presented as a gift, which both establishes a claim on the auditors' good will and implies an obligation to reciprocate. Like the payment of *aseda* to one who bestows a gift, or offerings to the ancestors at the *adae*,[29] the telling of history creates social relationships—ties of shared knowledge and obligation, which may be called on in the future to substantiate historically grounded claims.

By offering their recollections, or proposing their own interpretations, witnesses in turn become historians, contributing to the proliferation, as well as the preservation, of knowledge about the past.

The proliferation of historical accounts both reflects and reinforces the malleability of family membership and status, and the boundaries between one family and another. Claims to family membership are likely to be asserted, and challenged, at moments of succession to property and/or office. Casting doubt on a rival's ancestry is a common tactic in chieftaincy contests. Family membership is also on display, and it may be subject to challenge, in salient public settings—notably, funerals, where attendance, gifts, contributions, and participation in specific rituals both reflect and help to constitute the actor's relationship to the deceased. As Rattray pointed out in the 1920s, participation in funeral rites and gift giving implies "that a certain relationship between the deceased and the person who took a particular part in certain rites must have existed," and was accepted as evidence thereof in the colonial courts.[30] The cost and composition of funeral gifts and ceremonies have changed over time, but their centrality to defining and affirming social relationships has not. Writing of his own parents' funerals, in 1989 and 1991, Kwame Arhin described how "cloths, drinks and [bank]notes" and other gifts were "borne in containers on the heads of well dressed young women . . . while the orator among them recites the names of the owners of the exhibits, their quantity and quality, and the reasons for the show."[31] "Those who share the funeral debt," he added, "have rights in the estate of the deceased."[32]

Michelle Gilbert described similar practices in her account of the funeral of a wealthy man in Akuapem, at which his maternal and paternal relatives "competed for the glory of claiming him as a member."[33] In this case, the deceased man's mother came from Abiriw, a Guan town where descent is reckoned patrilineally, and his father came from Akuropon, an Akan community whose inhabitants follow matrilineal rules of succession; jurally, their son could not inherit from either. During his lifetime, he had worked to overcome this anomaly by investing, materially and ritually, in both communities; after his death, both sides invoked his achievements in claiming rights of burial and succession. The question of his family status was debated throughout the funeral: "it was only when the elder brother was named as successor that Abiriw people formally *knew* that Kofi Barima came from" their town. In this case, knowledge of family ties was as much a result as a condition of social practice.[34]

Because funerals are usually well attended, they provide opportunities for people to know their own kin as well as those of the deceased. A friend in Kumawu commented that some men father so many children that their offspring don't know all their brothers and sisters and run the risk of committing incest without knowing it. "That's one reason for attending funerals—the whole family comes and one can see" who is who. Sometimes, a funeral may lead to embarrassing discoveries. As Arhin pointed out, funeral gifts may have multiple meanings. *Awisiado*, a "necklace that men and women publicly put round the necks of their spouses who are performing funeral rites for their parents," is meant as a gesture of consolation. However, "[i]f there is only one wife, the show may be directed at actual or supposed girl friends."[35]

During a funeral, or at subsequent family meetings to choose a successor, questions may also arise as to whether certain family members are descended from slaves. According to customary law, on a slave's death, his/her property reverted to the master, and persons of slave ancestry could inherit family property only if there were no surviving freeborn kin available to do so.[36] Although slavery was legally abolished by the colonial state, the courts have continued to debate the relevance of slave ancestry for people's claims to family membership and property.[37]

In most cases, of course, the details of family history are debated *in camera*, so it is difficult to say how often individuals are actually barred from succession because of rumors of slave descent. By definition, however, the choice of an heir is a matter of family politics—a point that is sometimes made quite explicit. Following the recent funeral of a Kumawu royal, I was told, the family passed over the deceased's eldest nephew as successor, in favor of a younger man who worked as an engineer in Kumase. According to my informants, such behavior was normal. "When a successor is chosen," one man explained, "the family elders have to go into his background, consider his character." "It's like George Bush," his uncle chimed in: when he ran for reelection as president of the U.S., people criticized him and he wasn't chosen. In both cases, they agreed, the outcome probably depended as much on "underground work," as on the candidate's credentials.[38]

Like individuals' claims to family membership or status, family boundaries are also subject to reinterpretation and revision. Kumawu's royals—those eligible by descent to sit on the stool—belong to the Aduana clan,[39] but not all Aduanas in Kumawu are royals. The royals themselves are divided into three branches—Odumase, Anininya, and Ankase—each of which has supplied candidates for the stool at various times in the past. Among recent Kumawuhenes, Kwesi Krapa (ca. 1873–1896), Kwame Afram (1896–1916, 1925–43), Otuo Akyeampon (1952–73) and Asumadu Sakyi (1973–present) were Ankases; Kwabena Kodua (1922–25) and Tweneboa Kodua IV, a.k.a. "Nana Seth" (1944–52), were Anininyas. Informants gave varied accounts of the origins of each branch and the order of precedence among them. According to Nana Dua, the

Odumases settled in Kumawu before either of the other royal families. Their behavior led to a war, in which the Odumases and some of the earliest settlers were defeated, thereby losing any future claim to the stool, which passed to the descendants of their conqueror, Aduofoworo Ahye. Other sources suggest that several of the earliest *amanhene* were Odumases, and that this branch of the royal lineage was excluded from the stool because of an act of cowardice in battle. Members of the Ankase family traced their descent from Aduofoworo Ahye but gave different accounts of how he became chief. A son of the late Kwame Afram opined that the Ankases only claimed Aduofoworo Ahye as their ancestor because of his conquests; really, he insisted, there was no connection.[40] Details of family history have been challenged, or revised, in the context of stool succession contests. The Odumases fielded a candidate for the stool in 1973, for example, despite their "prohibition," and, as we have seen, Kweku Boaten (1916–20) acquired a royal geneaology *after* he was installed as chief and lost it again when he was destooled.[41]

The apparent fluidity of family memberships and boundaries does not mean that family relationships are unimportant in Asante, or that their significance has dwindled in recent times. On the contrary, *because* kinship and family ties figure so centrally in people's lives, they are subject to continued scrutiny and discussion. Knowledge of family history is carefully guarded, proudly displayed, and earnestly debated—especially at moments of succession, when the past is at a premium and its custodians have much at stake. Like property relations, family ties are continually in the making—as people reaffirm and reinterpret their connections with one another through daily interaction and debate—and the road between them is a two-way street.

"WE'RE FROM KUMAWU"

In addition to family, clan, region and nation, Asantes attach considerable symbolic and practical importance to their communities of origin. "Kumawufoɔ ni yen," people say: "we are from Kumawu."[42] At any given time, of course, there may be people residing in a community who are not "from" there. Such people are referred to, generically, as "strangers" (*ahoho*),[43] those of local provenance as "citizens." In other words, among English speakers at least, the term "citizen" may refer not only to Ghanaian nationality, but also to membership in a local community.

Like membership in a family, "citizenship" is historically contingent. It is often spoken of in terms of descent: a person's origins are those of his/her ancestors. But citizenship is not simply an amalgam of family relationships, a social boundary separating local or indigenous kin groups from those of "strangers." Differences of citizenship may exist within families as well as between them. If spouses come from different towns, they may be considered strangers in each others' families and communities. If, as in the Akuapem funeral described above, a man from a matrilineal family marries a woman whose people happen to be patrilineal, according to customary law, their children are social descendants of neither.[44] More insidiously, a person who is rumored to be of slave ancestry may be denied privileges routinely accorded to family members—treated, in effect, as a stranger by his or her own kin.[45] Like boundaries between fields, the boundary between citizens and strangers is enmeshed in family history and equally subject to contestation and change.

When I asked about family history, people usually began by recounting how their forebears first came to Kumawu. They specified the ancestor(s)' time of arrival—sometimes as a specific date, more often by naming the founders of families who preceded or followed them—thus placing their family in a common chronological ordering of migration and settlement. Informants usually named the place where their ancestor(s) had originated and described the route that they followed from there to Kumawu, noting the places where they had stopped along the way and the length of time they stayed at each. People also described early encounters between their forebears and the families who preceded them, sometimes drawing explicit connections between these events and the family's position in Kumawu today.

Oheneba Okyere Agyei-Diatuo, for example, traced his descent from a queen mother of Kontonase. (As his title implies, Oheneba's father was a member of the royal family of Kumawu.) Consulting a handwritten diary to be sure of the details, he explained that his ancestors, members of the Oyoko clan, scattered from Kontonase in the time of Asantehene Opoku Ware I (ca. 1720–50) because of a war. His own branch of the family journeyed through Akwapim to a place near Krakye; there, his grandmother[46] was married to the Kumawuhene, who brought her to Kumawu and thence to Bodomase, in 1742. When she and her people arrived in Bodomase, they found that other Oyoko people were already living there, having been brought from Takyiman by Opoku Ware I, following a war. The land at Bodomase, Oheneba explained, is "for" the first Oyoko settlers from Takyiman; his own people are "under" them on the land.[47]

In Oheneba Okyere's account, claims to family land and office were carefully circumscribed by stories of precedence and descent. As the son of a royal father, he could speak of the royal family's history but was not eligible for the stool; as descendants of the Oyokos who arrived in Bodomase in 1742, his family's rights to land were subordinate to those of the clansmen who preceded them. In other accounts, a family's place in the contemporary social order was not so closely calibrated to their order of arrival. According to Nana Dua Awere II, his ancestors were the first people to settle at Kumawu—their origins so remote in time that they had become lost to remembered history. "Even the Asantehene cannot say where we came from." They stayed at Apemso, behind the present site of Tweneboa Kodia Secondary School. When others (including the royal family) arrived, he added, "I received them." Later, however, a war broke out, following a quarrel over borrowed funeral regalia, and "we were defeated. That is why we are not on the stool."[48]

Another family head, Nana Obiri Yeboah, also did not specify his ancestors' community of origin; instead he stated that they had descended from the sky and established themselves at Dadease, the quarter of Kumawu where his house now stands. Later, unable to throw off the oppressive rule of their powerful neighbor Ataala Firam,[49] they followed the advice of a priest and sent to their "relatives" (that is, fellow members of the Aduana clan) in Assuminya for help. Together, the Aduanas defeated Ataala Firam, and the newcomers settled down at Kumawu, under their leader Adufoworo Ahye. Later, the Aduanas at Kumawu sat down together and made a covenant, agreeing that "we are all one people." When he felt his own death approaching, Nana Obiri Yeboah I called his relative from Assuminiya to take over the stool.[50]

On the face of it, Nana Dua Awere and Nana Obiri Yeboah gave conflicting accounts, each claiming that his ancestors were the original inhabitants of Kumawu.[51] In many respects, however, their narratives paralleled rather than contradicted each other. Neither chief named his ancestors' place of origin; both stated that they arrived before the royal family but had later lost or relinquished the stool. Moreover, each man identified the specific location in Kumawu where his ancestors settled, using place names that are recognized today. Together with the assertion that their forebears reached Kumawu before those of the royal family, these details implied that they had not received permission from anyone to settle on the land.

Following the convention that one does not speak of another's history, neither man referred, of course, to the other's story of first settlement.[52] By speaking only of his own family's history, each man asserted a claim to first settlement without challenging the other's and implied (again without directly confronting contrary claims) that his family's authority over its land was not "under" anyone else's.[53] In contrast, Oheneba Okyere's careful account of his family's subordinate position with respect to land corresponded with customary rules of the sort that Oheneba's royal relatives routinely invoked to justify the stool's claims to authority. Together, these narratives help to show how historical accounts proliferate, and how proliferation keeps alive multiple claims to property and authority.

If everyone in Kumawu claims to have come originally from somewhere else, what distinguishes "citizens" from "strangers"? The answer, unsurprisingly, is that it depends on whom one asks. This was vividly illustrated in my conversations with several residents of the zongo—a residential quarter of Kumawu established around the turn of the century by immigrants from the savannah.[54] According to the present Serikin, the zongo was founded by his maternal grandfather, who came from Togo "when Kwame Afram was on the stool."[55] Gradually he was joined by migrants from northern Ghana, Benin, Nigeria, and Burkina Faso, as well as Togo. Today, the inhabitants of the Kumawu zongo speak a variety of different languages and represent many nationalities and ethnic groups. Most are Muslim—easily distinguishable from the Asantes in Kumawu by their dress, their prayer beads, and their habit of congregating around the zongo and its mosques. Most Kumawufoɔ refer to zongo residents as "strangers" or "northerners," but when I asked zongo residents where they came from, they replied "we're from Kumawu."[56]

Criteria for determining "foreign" origin in Asante changed under the combined influence of cocoa and colonial rule. In the eighteenth and nineteenth centuries, according to McCaskie, the state distinguished, jurally and in practice, between Asante citizens and non-Asante strangers.[57] In the colonial era, as we have seen, British officials sought to anchor colonial rule on customary foundations by vesting land rights and some forms of administrative and judicial authority in the stools. To make indirect rule work, they insisted that every Asante acknowledge allegiance to a stool, and they encouraged chiefs to separate the rights and obligations of stool subjects from those of "strangers." Under indirect rule, then, the term "stranger" came to mean not only a person of non-Asante origin but also any Asante who was subject to another stool than the one in question.[58] Since chiefly jurisdictions remained hotly contested throughout the colonial period, the line between subject and stranger was drawn in shifting sands. [59]

After independence, chiefs were stripped of their judicial and administrative powers, and allegiance to a stool lost all statutory force vis-à-vis people's civic rights and responsibilities. Legally, stool "subjects" were replaced by citizens of Ghana. In practice, however, local loyalties and identities remained important, subsumed under the new rubric of national citizenship rather than superseded by it, and subject to ongoing contestation and debate.[60]

The multiple and contested meanings of citizenship in contemporary Asante are rooted in ongoing debates over the relationship between past

and present claims to land.[61] The Kumawu Traditional Council continues to insist on its right to collect tribute from "strangers"—an important source of tension in current struggles over rights to land in the
Afram Plains.[62] To date, the council has not claimed the right to lease
out land for tomato cultivation, but there is some evidence that individual chiefs may be starting to do so.[63] Strangers are not necessarily
disadvantaged, however, in terms of access to land. As we will see in
the next chapter, the Kumawuhene has actively encouraged recent migrants from northern Ghana to settle on disputed territory in the Afram
Plains and use it in the name of the stool.[64] How long they remain
"strangers," and in whose eyes, remains to be seen.

The ambiguities of citizenship were also reflected in the experiences of
two Afro-European families with long-standing ties to Kumawu. Alice
Aduana Norris was born in Kumawu, the daughter of Captain A. W. Norris,
district commissioner at Juaso from 1911 to 1916,[65] and a niece of Kwame
Afram.[66] She was educated at Cape Coast and later taught domestic science. Married three times, twice to Europeans and once to a Ghanaian,
"Auntie" Norris raised eight children—"all colors"—including one adopted
son. In 1994, her two sons by her first husband were living in Kumawu:
one, a former agricultural extension officer, had retired from the civil service; the other had recently returned to Ghana, after twenty years' residence in Germany, with a Ph.D. in animal science, and settled in Bodomase.
He was reportedly popular in the town, and friends speculated that might
stand for election to the National Assembly in 1996. As a royal, he was
also eligible to contest for the stool, but it was unlikely he would be chosen, I was told, because "people do not think that a 'red' [i.e., fair-skinned]
man should sit" on a paramount stool.

The other Afro-European family in Kumawu was founded by a British
schoolteacher named Allan Cole, who emigrated to Ghana in the early 1960s.
He married a woman from Kumawu and, though posted to schools in other
parts of Asante for much of his career, treated Kumawu as his home. Cole
acquired a plot of land not far from the palace, where he maintained a
small farm and began to put up a house. Eventually, he was named headmaster of Tweneboa Kodia Secondary School (TKSS) in Kumawu, a post
from which he retired in 1992. In 1994, two of his children were living in
Kumase; the third worked as the librarian at TKSS.

Like the Ghanaian millionaire whose funeral was described by Michelle
Gilbert, Cole had worked to overcome his lack of inherited family and
community in Ghana by establishing a place for himself in his adopted
town. Instead of wealth, which he did not have, he put his educational
skills to work for the traditional council, combing the National Archives
and other repositories for documentary evidence on the history of Kumawu

and its boundaries, for the stool to use in land disputes with its neighbors. He also accumulated a good deal of historical knowledge by word of mouth. Eventually, Cole was made a chief and took a seat on the Kumawu Traditional Council, with the stool name of Nana Osei Bediako Firaw. His knowledge of Asante history, particularly in reference to land matters, was well-known, and he was frequently called upon to testify or advise on stool land matters outside of Kumawu as well as within it.[67]

Like other long-term residents, Cole's status as a member of the community was subject to multiple interpretations. He described himself as a naturalized Ghanaian and appeared committed to spend the rest of his life there; yet some in Kumawu called him a foreigner and opined that he would eventually return to Britain. Loyalty to the stool did not prevent him from taking independent political positions—he supported the NPP, for example, rather than the ruling NDC—but this did not earn him the trust of NPP supporters in Kumawu who were at odds with the chief. In short, like other long-term residents of foreign origin, Nana Cole was both citizen and stranger in Kumawu.

CONCLUSION

Commercial tomato growing in Kumawu is a story of adjustment—an innovation in cropping patterns and cultivation methods that brought modest gains to some farmers, losses to others, as Ghana gradually emerged from economic collapse in the late 1980s and early 1990s. Constrained by a volatile market and their own limited resources, farmers did not specialize in tomatoes or cultivate them on a large scale, but they kept their income sources diversified and their options open. In 1994, farmers were actively considering alternative new crops, such as citronella, and/or reverting to staples, such as maize or cassava, with steadier markets. Kumawufo devised new institutional arrangements, such as tomato tenancies, to accommodate the needs of tomato growers, but these did not transform relations between landholders and land users, any more than tomatoes made local farmers wealthy, and will not necessarily become permanent features of the local economic landscape.

The significance of the tomato story lies less in its "success" than in its ephemerality. The apparent ease with which Kumawufɔ adapted farming practices and institutional arrangements to the requirements of commercial tomato growing reflects the flexibility of economic and social relations that allow people to experiment and improvise, without risking their access to resources or future opportunities. Contrary to recent literature, which argues that sustainable development will not take place unless rights to valuable resources are "clearly defined, complete, enforced and transferable,"[68] assets and relationships in Kumawu appear to be flexible and resilient because they are *not* clearly defined, or completely and unambiguously transferable. Multiple, overlapping claims on land, and the proliferation of historical precedents on which they turn, allow—indeed require—that people participate in ongoing negotiations over who "owns" what, on what terms, and what it means for the division of labor and the distribution of opportunity and wealth. Understanding the nature of property relations and their significance for economic and social change means asking how such negotiations proceed and how people participate in them.

In previous chapters, I have argued that throughout the colonial period and after independence, Asantes debated claims on land and office in terms of historical precedent. In making claims on property, people continually invoked and reinterpreted relations of authority, as well as property rights *per se*, and debated the relevance of historical precedents for both. In the course of these debates, accounts of the past proliferated, insuring that many people would continue to take part in (re)producing them. History in this context is both an archive of documents and memories and an ongoing drama, enacted as well as read, which takes its meaning from the audience as well as the performer(s), and from the engagement between them.

The importance of historical performance was illustrated for me, in Kumawu,[69] when I asked Nana Obiri Yeboah to tell me about his family history. On the appointed day, Nana assembled the elders of his stool and began by pouring libations and offering prayers to his ancestors. After recounting in vivid detail the story of his forebears' descent from the sky, he offered to show me his family shrine, located in the bush on the spot where his ancestors alighted at Kumawu. Together with the family elders and a small troop of children, my assistant and I followed him to the shrine. Here Nana again offered libations and prayers, courteously including a prayer for the success of my studies in Ghana and my safe return home. Our way to the shrine led past the village of Nana's tenants, the Gyedifo , as they returned from their farms at the end of the day. As we passed, they exchanged greetings with the chief and witnessed our procession to and from a key icon of his ancestral rights in Kumawu.

In the present chapter, I have explored several kinds of social performance—conversations, ceremonies, contests—in which people affirm and reinterpret relations of kinship and citizenship, as well as claims on land, and debate their historical antecedents. My aim is not to assess the "impact" of such peformances on development or democracy, or to tease out their significance as indicators of norms and networks that structure social behavior and determine its outcomes. Relations of property, family, and citizenship are not "social capital"—commodified attributes or institutions to be packaged, priced, and put to work in the service of economic and political progress. To portray them in this way not only risks conflating cause and effect (do networks create trust or reflect it?) but also ignores a mass of cross-cultural evidence that the most intimate social relationships are often the most conflict-ridden.[70] The point is not to separate harmonious networks from hostile ones but to recognize the tension between trust and suspicion that permeates all social relationships and try to understand its dynamic power and potential. Like boundaries between fields, families, and citizens and strangers, relations of property, family, and community in Kumawu are continually in the making—enacted, renewed, and redefined through numerous daily dramas of assertion, contestation, and debate. Such debates have not produced certainty or consensus, nor have they foreclosed dissent. As we shall see in the next chapter, when we turn to the history of Kumawu's battles for the Afram Plains, the conversations continue.

NOTES

1. J. M. Sarbah, *Fanti customary laws*, 3rd ed. (London, Frank Cass, 1968); Rattray, *Ashanti*.

2. Spatial mobility and dispersion operate at all levels of social interaction in Asante. It is common, for example, for spouses to reside in different houses, and children to move from one relative's household to another from an early age.

3. According to the most recent Ghanaian census, the population of Kumawu was 8,409 in 1983. The town appeared to be more than twice that size in 1993–94, but whether it had grown that much in a decade, or the official count in 1983 was too low, is unknown.

4. Reindorf names Kumawu as one of the five founding members of the Asante union; Rattray gives a different list, which excludes Kumawu. C. C. Reindorf, *History of the Gold Coast and Asante* (Basel: Missionsbuchshandlung, 1895), 53; Rattray, *Ashanti law*, 235. Kinglists were provided by Tufohene Oheneba Okyere Agyei-Diatuo, 6/16/94, and Barima Tweneboa Kodua IV, 7/1/94, and they may also be found in Rattray, *Ashanti law*, 234, NAGK 29, Kobina Kodia, Omanhene of Kumawu—election of, 1922, and NAGK 34, Enquiry into the constitution of the Kumawu stool, 11/25/24–12/4/24. The last-mentioned source recounts the story, still popular in Kumawu, that when Komfo Anokye predicted that a chief must die to ensure Asante's victory over Denkyira, Tweneboa Kodia volunteered to sacrifice himself and died on the field of battle. In gratitude, Komfo Anokye decreed that Kumawu royals could not be executed. McCaskie, *State and society*, 396–97.

5. This account is based on interviews with Panin Yao Mensah, 7/11/94, 7/14/94, and 7/16/94.

6. Interview with Panin Yao Mensah, 7/14/94.

7. Tordoff lists Kumawu as one of the first *aman* to sign a separate treaty with the British in 1896. Tordoff, *Ashanti*, 83.

8. I heard this story from Allan Cole, in one of many conversations at his house in Kumawu. See below, 154–55. Kumawu's history of loyalty—from Tweneboa Kodia's sacrifice in Asante's war against Denkyira to Kumawu's refusal to support the NLM—was detailed in 1957 by the Kumawu State Council, in a petition requesting a separate regional assembly and house of chiefs for Asante-Akyem. Kumawu State Council Papers, 8/14/57.

9. Barima Asumadu Sakyi's turbulent reign is discussed in detail in the following chapter.

10. Interview with B. A. Mensah, 1/10/94. An outspoken opponent of Rawlings' regime, B. A. Mensah was charged with tax fraud, and his passport and many of his assets, including Rothman's, were confiscated by the government. He was not reduced to poverty however: in 1994, he maintained an imposing residence near the airport in Accra, plus a country estate, which occupies a commanding position on Kumawu's southern escarpment. He kindly allowed me to stay in the guesthouse of his establishment in Kumawu, while I carried out fieldwork in June and July 1994.

11. Interviews with M. Adu-Gyamfi, Nana D. C. Boadae, E. A. Frimpong, Yaw Amponsah, and Barima Asumadu Sakyi, among others.

12. With some justification. Work on the Kumase road was underway by mid-1994, and it was completed as far as Kumawu by the end of the year. When I returned for a brief visit in 1996, the journey from Kumase took barely an hour—about half the time required to make the trip in 1993–94.

13. According to the managing director, the Kumawuman Rural Bank had stopped making loans to cocoa farmers because of the ease with which they evaded repayment. Berry, "Tomatoes, land and hearsay."

14. Interview with the sect's "Chairman," Opoku Mensah, 6/14/94. Popularly referred to as the Gyedifoɔ ("Believers"), most of Chairman Mensah's followers were not strangers, but Kumawufoɔ who had broken with fellow congregants in Kumawu's Savior Church. To live "without interference," they decided to separate from the rest of Kumawu, creating their own "town" (*kurom*) on the outskirts of Kumawu, where they practiced a distinctively communal way of life. See below, 156.

15. I interviewed a total of thirty-one farmers in Kumawu, twenty-four of whom were growing tomatoes at the time. About half the interviews were conducted in farmers' fields. In several of the fields I visited, farmers had planted one part of the field in tomatoes, another part in food crops such as maize, cocoyam, beans, or cassava. Tomatoes were grown in sole stands, rather than interplanted with other crops, although farmers often followed a few tomato crops by planting maize, beans, or cassava, in order to take advantage of fertilizer residues remaining on the tomato fields.

16. The history of how women came to dominate regional trade in foodstuffs in Asante is given in Clark, *Onions*.

17. My small, unsystematically collected list includes informants who identified themselves as tomato landlords as well as those named by farmers who were renting in tomato fields. In six cases, I sought out and interviewed individuals who had been identified as landlords by their tenants. All six confirmed that they had rented out fields to tomato growers and discussed some of the risks as well as the benefits of tomato leases for landholders.

18. Interviews with A. Pokuaa, 7/2/94; A. Afram, 7/2/94; Nana Afua Komaa and Komfo Yaa Badu, 7/3/94.

19. The repercussions of government land acquisitions in the Afram Plains on political contestation and the circulation of wealth in Kumawu are discussed in ch. 6.

20. N. A. Ollenu and G. R. Woodman, eds., *Ollenu's principles of customary law.* 2nd ed. (Birmingham, England: CAL Press, 1985).

21. Viz., PNDC Law 111 (1985), which seeks to attenuate the system of matrilineal inheritance by assigning the lion's share of the estate of anyone who dies intestate to his/her spouse and children. Since the law's provisions are limited to individually acquired property, its impact has been more gradual than might at first seem likely. Moreover, both wills and intestate estates are subject to frequent contestation, both in and out of court, which often helps to keep inherited property "in the family."

22. Interview with Maame Abena Mfoum, 12/23/93. When a neighbor tried to take her land, on the grounds that it belonged to his mother, Maame Abena took him to the magistrate's court. She won the case, she explained, because she could "describe the boundaries, and call witnesses" to support her claim, whereas her antagonist could do neither. Compare S. F. Moore, *Social facts and fabrications: Customary law on Mt. Kilimanjaro, 1890–1980* (Cambridge: Cambridge University Press, 1986).

23. A detailed account of one such case is given in S. Miescher, "Of documents and litigants: Disputes on inheritance in Abetifi—a town of colonial Ghana," *Journal of Legal Pluralism* 39 (1997): 81–118.

24. PNDC Law 111. See also G. Mikell, "The state, the courts and 'value': Caught between matrilineages in Ghana," in Guyer, ed. *Money matters.* Ties between fathers and sons are not unimportant, of course. In precolonial times, succession to certain offices followed the male line of descent, and royal marriages were sometimes arranged so that successors to the Golden Stool were grandsons of former Asantehenes, as well as descendants of the mother or sister of their immediate predecessor. Wilks, *Asante,* 329–30 McCaskie, *State and society,* 61–62, 81. Sons followed their fathers in certain occupations, and groups of male kin might be summoned for public labor. Lewin, *Asante,* 208. I am grateful to an anonymous reviewer for drawing my attention to this point.

25. Based on a review of unpublished cases on file at the Council on Law Reporting, Accra.

26. Rattray, *Ashanti law,* 354–5. See also ch. 2.

27. In the same vein, Murphy has argued that by limiting young people's access to secret knowledge, Kpelle elders reinforce the value of such knowledge as property and a source of power. W. Murphy, "Secret knowledge as property and power in Kpelle society: Elders versus youth," *Africa* 50, no. 2 (1980): 193–207.

28. Compare the Asantehene's refusal to testify in Kumase High Court, Suit No. LC 115/83, described in ch. 4.

29. See introduction, xxviii–xxix.

30. Rattray, *Religion and art,* 153.

31. Arhin, "The economic implications of transformations in Akan funeral rites," 316. Arhin illustrates his argument with details from the funerals he performed for his parents in 1989 and 1991.

32. Ibid., 317. See also Dei, "The economics of death," 49–62.

33. Gilbert, "The sudden death of a millionaire," 291.

34. A point made in a different context by L. Bohannon, "A geneaological charter?" *Africa* 22, no. 4 (1952): 301–15.

35. Arhin, 316.

36. Sarbah, *Fanti customary laws*. See also Rattray, *Ashanti*, 43.

37. Perbi, "The legacy of slavery." See also ch. 4, n. 18.

38. Conversation with M. Adu Gyamfi and Pastor Opoku, 6/22/94.

39. All Asantes belong, in principle, to one of several dispersed matriclans, which, together, comprise the Asante people. Following earlier observers, Rattray considered matriclans the original structural units of Akan society, but Wilks has argued that they were probably formed between the fifteenth and seventeenth centuries, as Akan peoples expanded into the forests and tranformed their principal mode of livelihood from foraging to forest agriculture. As the regional economy became increasingly commercialized and diversified, from the late nineteenth century, he adds, the economic importance of the matriclans declined and their number dwindled from twelve to seven. Wilks, *Forests of gold*, 79 and ch. 2.

40. Interviews with Oheneba Okyere Agyei-Diatuo, 6/16/94; Nana Dua Awere II, 6/18/94; Panin Yao Mensah, 7/14/94. Rattray lists Aduofoworo Ahye as the founder of the royal dynasty. Rattray, *Ashanti law*, 235.

41. See ch. 2.

42. Literally, "we are Kumawu people."

43. In Twi, the term *ahoho* may also be translated as "visitors" or "guests"—terms that in English carry a stronger connotation that the outsider is welcome than does "stranger." What degree of welcome is accorded to particular *ahoho* must be inferred from the context.

44. Gilbert, "The sudden death of a millionaire," 301.

45. Before the colonial era, if a man married his slave, their children belonged to his family, but the stigma of having had a slave mother could follow them and their descendants for generations. To speak publicly of a person's slave ancestry was legally proscribed by the Asante state and is considered socially offensive today. Although slavery was legally abolished under colonial rule and, under Ghanaian law, cannot be used to disqualify a person from succession, allegations of slave ancestry continue to shadow claims to family membership and may weigh against individuals' hopes of sharing in family property or compromise the authority they are able to exercise vis-à-vis their kin. Compare Perbi, "The legacy of slavery." On slavery and social origins in precolonial Asante, see Arhin, "Rank and class"; Klein, "Inequality in Asante"; McCaskie, *State and society*, 88ff; Wilks, *Forests of gold*, 223, 244.

46. I.e., a matrilineal ancestress, not necessarily his own mother's mother.

47. Interview with Oheneba Okyere Agyei-Diatuo, at his house in Bodomase, 6/16/94.

48. Interview with Nana Dua Awere II, 6/18/94.

49. The history of Kumawu's wars with Ataala Firam, a powerful chief based in the Afram Plains, has figured centrally in the stool's territorial claims since the mid-nineteenth century. See below, ch. 6.

50. Interview with Nana Obiri Yeboah II, 6/30/94.

51. Others confirmed that both families were already living in Kumawu when the royals arrived. Interviews with Panin Yao Mensah, 7/14/94; Aduanahemaa Afua Komaa, 6/24/94.

52. Neither was, of course, present when I interviewed the other. While there was no overt prohibition on people being present when another family's history was being

discussed, families who were at odds tended to avoid one another's company. My research assistant, a member of the royal family, was astonished when, at my insistence, we successfully elicited narratives of family history from some of the stool's most inveterate opponents.

53. On occasion, informants imparted information, usually of a scandalous or unflattering nature, about another family's history, but asked me not to write it down. Explaining that he could speak only about his own family, one informant warned that people would tell me things favorable to themselves, but "it's not necessarily true." In some cases, however, informants were quite open about their own forebears' transgressions!

54. The term "zongo" is used throughout Ghana to denote urban residential quarters populated by "strangers" of predominantly "northern" origin. See, e.g., Schildkrout, *People of the zongo*.

55. Interview with Mohammed Sanni Abubakr, 6/22/94.

56. Interviews with Serikin Abubakr; Mohammed Ibrahim, 12/11/93; Mohammed Salis, 12/11/93.

57. McCaskie, *State and society*, 88–90.

58. See ch. 1.

59. Compare Rathbone's stimulating discussion of contested citizenship in Akyem Abuakwa. During the interwar period, Rathbone argues, Okyenhene Ofori Atta's efforts to court the loyalty of his subjects by fostering their sense of a common identity foundered, in part, on their resentment of his increasing demands on their pocketbooks. "Ordinary Akyemfo, however they were defined, might feel patriotic about the kingdom and proud of its past, but this sentiment was not necessarily on all fours with accepting the increasingly invasive paramountcy of their king." R. Rathbone, "Defining Akyemfo: The construction of citizenship in Akyem Abuakwa, Ghana, 1700–1939," *Africa* 66, no. 4 (1996): 506–25.

60. Mamdani argues that the legacy of indirect rule in postcolonial Africa has often been a continuation of "participation without representation. . . . Participatory forms [of governance] that stress the autonomy of a bounded group . . . can justify and uphold the most undemocratic forms of central power." Mamdani, *Citizen and subject*, 298–99. If group boundaries are permeable or ambiguous, the line between participation and representation may also be less rigid. It is precisely such "gray areas" of practice (and conceptualization) that merit further study, if we seek to understand the daily realities of political life.

61. Compare Rathbone, "Defining Akyemfo," 513ff.

62. See ch. 6.

63. For example, in 1993, the queen mother claimed that a tract of land at Abotonso (a village just south of Kumawu), where a number of farmers had leased tomato fields from a Kumawu resident, belonged to her stool. In 1993, I heard that the matter was under dispute. Six months later, the dispute had been resolved: the lessor, I was told, had relinquished his claims when it was explained to him that "the land is for the queen mother."

64. In areas where most of the tenant farmers were strangers, tenants could not mount credible claims to land ownership (because of who they were) and landlords, therefore, did not oppose the sale of cocoa trees. Where the majority of tenants belonged to local families, however, landowners resisted outright buying and selling of

established cocoa trees, for fear that buyers of trees might also claim to own the land they stood on. Compare S. Berry, *Cocoa, custom and socio-economic change in rural western Nigeria* (Oxford: Clarendon Press, 1975), 112–13.

65. See ch. 2.

66. This account is drawn from several conversations with Auntie Norris in June and July 1994.

67. On at least one occasion, the ambiguities of Cole's "citizenship" gave rise to a courtroom debate over whether or not his knowledge of Asante history qualified as "traditional." See ch. 6, 174–76.

68. World Bank, *Towards environmentally sustainable development.*

69. Other examples are discussed in ch. 4, 127–29.

70. Efforts to measure social capital in terms of underlying attitudes and behaviors, and assess their impact on institutional performance, have often led, not surprisingly, to inconclusive results. For a recent example, see J. Widner with A. Mundt, "Researching social capital in Africa," *Africa* 68, no. 1 (1998): 1–24. Widner and Mundt use survey data on attitudes and expectations to measure both "social capital" and "institutional performance."

6

BATTLES FOR
THE AFRAM PLAINS

Throughout Asante, as we have seen, most of the land held or claimed by individuals and families is vested, by custom and the Constitution of Ghana, in the stools. Chiefs keep a close watch on local land transactions and disputes to make sure that, in exercising their claims to individual or family land, residents do not usurp the stool's prerogatives of land allocation, especially to strangers. Since the early days of colonial rule, they have also worked assiduously to define and assert the boundaries of their stool lands and defend them from erosion or encroachment by other stools. In Kumawu, the stool was actively engaged in extending and defending its territory long before the British took power over Asante, and its occupants have continued to do so ever since. Their claims have not been modest: extending from villages west and south of Kumawu town, such as Wonoo and Woraso, to the shores of Lake Volta, the Kumawu stool's claims include a substantial slice of the Afram Plains (see Map 5.1).

OF CONSERVATION AND COMPENSATION

In September 1971, the government of Ghana acquired two adjacent tracts of land, known as Digya and Kogyae, for a national park and a nature reserve. Digya-Kogyae is located on the Afram Plains—a vast wedge of open savannah that dips south from the plains of northern Ghana, dividing the rainforest belt that blankets the coast on either side of it, to touch the Atlantic at Accra. At an early date, the Afram Plains caught the attention of colonial authorities as a potential "breadbasket" for the Gold Coast Colony and beyond, but the cost of opening up the area for commercial farming and ranching exceeded their resources. Officials made some attempt to persuade local chiefs to reroute trade through the area and take up "improved" livestock raising as an example to others but, without motorable roads or reliable access to water, these efforts came to little,[1] and the plains remained sparsely populated and relatively isolated from the cocoa- and urban-centered commerce of the colonial economy. In 1972, construction was completed on the huge Akosombo Dam across the Volta River, flooding a large slice of the Afram Plains, displacing many of its residents, and laying the groundwork for renewed official interest in the open lands to the west of Lake Volta.

With interest in the plains increasing, news of the government's impending acquisition spread quickly. In March 1974, before formal notice of the acquisition had been published, a claim for compensation was filed on behalf of the Kumawu stool. The lawyer who submitted the claim acted "on the instructions" of the late Kumawuhene, Barima Otuo Akyeampon, who had died the year before.[2] Seven months later, the stool's claim was effectively superseded when three members of the Kumawu Traditional Council, declaring themselves to be "freehold owners" of the land at Digya-Kogyae, filed separate individual claims for compensation.[3] Similar claims were made soon afterwards by individual subjects of the stools of Agogo and Kwaman.

According to the high court judge who presided over the subsequent trial, lawyers involved in the case pointed out to the chief lands officer that a dispute between the stools of Kumawu, Agogo, and Kwaman (over the land in question) was then pending before the Stool Lands Boundaries Settlement Commission, and that claims for compensation could not properly be settled before the question of ownership was resolved.[4] The chief lands officer appears not to have been unduly concerned at this news, but "a more discerning Principal Secretary of the Ministry of Lands" ordered the lands officer "to suspend payments to any of the claimants until the Stool Lands Boundaries Commissioner has settled the matter beyond all dispute."[5]

Goaded by the prospect that compensation might be delayed indefinitely, the three stools got together and arrived at a resolution of their differences. Reaching deep into the past, they invoked a time toward the end of the seventeenth century, when the stools of Kumawu, Kwaman, and Agogo joined forces in a war against the Dwan people who were occupying the Afram Plains on their eastern flank. Together, the three Asante stools defeated the Dwans, drove them and their chief Ataala Firam across the Volta River, and remained on the conquered land "as brothers." On the basis of this historical account, the stools declared themselves co-owners of the land at Digya-Kogyae, and they promised to divide the compensation money amicably among themselves. This exemplary display of chiefly cooperation was promptly rewarded. Written notice of the stools' agreement was filed with the Ministry of Lands on December 15. The following day, a check was issued by the Ministry of Finance and handed to a lawyer who represented the Kumawuhene. Further payments in mid-January brought the total to ₡1,500,000—Kumawu's one-third share of the overall compensation package of ₡4,500,000.[6]

At the time these transactions occurred, the Kumawuhene was a comparative newcomer on the stool. The death of Barima Otuo Akyeampon in 1973 was followed by a brief but tumultuous struggle over the choice of a successor.[7] Barely two weeks after the old chief's demise, the kingmakers settled on William Kore, a man in his early thirties with a university degree and a few years' professional experience with the Town and Country Planning Department.[8] Their decision was made under intense pressure from some of the town's most prominent businessmen and professionals, who were convinced that Kore's education outweighed his comparative youth and inexperience in qualifying him for the job. Promising that an educated chief would bring "development" to the town, Kore's backers persuaded a majority of the kingmakers to vote for him, rather than for any of his rivals, who were all senior to Kore but lacked his "modern" accomplishments.[9] Taking the stool name of Asumadu Sakyi II, after a hero of the early Asante wars, the new Kumawuhene was sworn in on March 26, 1973.[10]

Two years later, after the Digya-Kogyae compensation claims had been processed "with what might, for all time, stand as unprecedented promptitude and alacrity in the annals of the Civil Service of this country,"[11] the young Kumawuhene paid a visit to Accra. Accounts of what he did there vary. The high court did not mention this episode in its ruling, stating only that the first instalment of the compensation money was handed over to a lawyer, one Appiah Menkah.[12] Prominent backers of Kore's candidacy for the stool later complained that their protégé collected the money himself but—in a flagrant breach of political etiquette—did not tell them why he had come to Accra or that he was returning to Kumawu with a large amount of cash in the boot of his car.[13] It is, however, a matter of public record that on Dec. 26, when the town was awash with holiday cheer, members of the traditional council were directed to make their way to Bodomase, a village about 5 km from Kumawu town, to hear some news. Upon arrival, they were invited, one at a time, into a sawmill owned by Siankwahene Nana Adu Gyamfi and given payments that ranged from ₡1,000 to ₡4,000 apiece.[14]

Each of the recipients was sworn to secrecy, but word got out—spread, it is said, by one of the beneficiaries who, being literate, noticed that some of those listed on the chief's roster of payees had received more money than he. As news of the share-out percolated through Kumawu, the anger of elders who found themselves on the low end of the receiving line in Bodomase was soon exceeded by that of the majority of their fellow citizens, who had received nothing at all. But public grumbling turned to clamorous outrage when the size of the original payment came to light[15] and Kumawufoɔ realized that the entire share-out at Bodomase amounted to only 8 percent of the total compensation package of ₡1.5 million.[16] What had happened to the rest of the money?

Early in April, at a press conference in Kumase, the chief admitted that he and his elders had received part of the compensation money at Bodomase, but he insisted that most of it had been used to pay lawyers and surveyors' fees or deposited in the stool's account. However, the sums that he mentioned still fell short of ₡1.5 million. In July, five exasperated citizens[17] filed suit "for themselves and on behalf of the Oman of Kumawu" against the three "landowners" who had filed individual claims for compensation.[18] The land belonged to the stool, they argued, and hence to the entire *oman* (that is, the body politic under the authority of the paramount stool)—*not* to individual elders as "freehold" property! Charging that the three subchiefs' claims were fraudulent, the plaintiffs demanded that they make restitution for the full amount of the compensation to the stool. When the plaintiffs were subsequently challenged in court (on the grounds that only chiefs and elders could take legal action on behalf of the stool), their lawyer argued that the subchiefs and elders had so compromised themselves, by participating in the share-out at Bodomase, that the citizens had no recourse but to take matters into their own hands.[19]

Initially the defendants reiterated their claims to "freehold ownership" of land in the plains, but Nana Agyei and Nana Adu Boaten later changed their pleas, declaring that they had been duped into fixing their thumbprints to documents whose contents they could not read. They had no idea, they said, that claims of ₡429,000 and ₡600,600 had been filed in their names, and they had received nothing more than the ₡4,000 handed to each of them at Bodomase. Nana Adu Gyamfi admitted that he had lied about his "ownership" of stool land and had helped to distribute some of the compensation money at Bodomase, but denied any wrongdoing. In a statement the court found "rather disturbing," he explained that "in accordance with the customary oath of allegiance loyalty and obedience which he [the second defendant] swore to the Kumawuhene when he [the second defendant] was duly installed as a [sub]chief he acted on the instructions of the Kumawuhene as his overlord."[20] At the request of all three defendants, the court then ordered that the chief be joined to the suit as a codefendant "in his personal capacity as William Kore."[21]

The trial judge found for the plaintiffs and ordered the four defendants to repay to the stool's account whatever part of the compensation money they had received. When they failed to comply with the court's order, they were arrested. Adu Gyamfi was released the next day, but the other two chiefs spent two months in prison, and the Kumawuhene was incarcerated twice for a total of one and a half years.[22] In 1981, the high court's ruling was overturned on appeal—on the grounds that the plaintiffs had not been legally entitled to sue and that the state's acquisition of the land had never been properly effected in the first place. The plaintiffs appealed to the Supreme Court, which restored the trial court's judgment and ordered that the ₵1.5 million be deposited in the stool's account. By this time, seventeen years after the compensation was paid out, its official exchange value had dropped from about $1,300,000 to $3,750, and the Kumawuhene complied promptly with the court's order.

Thanks to the publicity that surrounded the trial and the chief's incarceration, Kumawu was propelled once again into the forefront of national debates over custom and chiefly accountability. Like Kwame Afram's mishandling of the War Fund in 1915, Asumadu Sakyi's attempt to pocket the compensation money for Digya-Kogyae touched off a furor in Kumawu, which escalated into a campaign to destool the chief. Unlike his predecessor, however, Asumadu Sakyi was never actually removed from the stool. Instead, the chieftaincy case dragged on for years, amid hints of scandal and intrigue. As the years wore on, some of the chief's opponents "got tired," renewed their oaths of allegiance, and returned to the traditional council. Others died or succumbed to the infirmities of age. But the town remained deeply divided, and bitter memories lingered.

In addition to dividing the citizenry of Kumawu, the destoolment case against Asumadu Sakyi continued to intersect in the following years with ongoing disputes over Kumawu's boundaries and the stool's rights over land. Throughout his tenure in office, battles over the stool have infused and been inspired by the stool's battles over the Afram Plains. Like the chieftaincy disputes of the late 1910s and early 1920s, Digya-Kogyae touched on two long-standing bones of contention in Kumawu—boundaries and chiefly accountability—drawing together two separate but related processes of contestation, with implications for the constitution and exercise of chiefly authority, as well as for the stool's rights over land. If these struggles have earned Kumawu a reputation for exceptional contentiousness, they speak nonetheless to much broader questions of property, development, and the place of the chief in modern Ghana.[23]

THE ABORTIVE CAMPAIGN TO
DESTOOL BARIMA ASUMADU SAKYI[24]

Like the personal and financial peccadilloes of his predecessor, Kwame Afram,[25] Asumadu Sakyi's clumsy attempt to "keep the compensation money in Kumawu"[26] by diverting it to his own and Adu Gyamfi's pockets raised questions not only about his personal qualifications for the chieftaincy, but also about the long-standing issue of chiefly accountability. By the late 1970s, the constitutional status of chiefs in Ghana had changed fundamentally from its pivotal, if ambiguous, position under indirect rule. Under Nkrumah's regime, chiefs were removed from their former roles in the judicial system and in local administration, and their authority over land was sharply curtailed.[27] The Constitution of 1969 restored stools' authority to allocate land rights and receive revenue from land users, but it continued to limit their judicial and administrative roles to the realm of chieftaincy affairs. Under the Constitution of 1992, chiefs are expressly debarred from participating in party politics or standing for elected office.

The disposition of revenue from stool lands has also been subject to statutory regulation. After struggling for decades with the perennial problem of stool debts, the colonial administration reversed its initial insistence that under customary law the chief was indistinguishable from the stool, and it drew a firm line between a chief's personal property and income and that of the stool.[28] This principle has been maintained under Ghana's successive constitutions. Stools are required by statute not only to keep accounts but also to turn over the lion's share of their revenues to various agencies of local government. (By filing claims for compensation in the names of individual "landowners" in the area of Digya-Kogyae, the stools of Kumawu, Agogo, and Kwaman were evidently attempting to bypass this rule.) Throughout the several changes of national regime and accompanying reorganizations of local government that have marked Ghana's history as an independent nation, the state has sought to draw clear boundaries around the scope of chiefly jurisdiction and place strict limits on chiefs' ability to exercise fiscal or political authority independently of the state.

According to some observers, these efforts have been only partially successful. Early optimism over the extent to which Nkrumah's "revolution" had swept away the whole anachronistic structure of chiefly power has faded.[29] Historians and political commentators of many persuasions have commented extensively on the pervasiveness of clientilism and corruption in postcolonial Ghanaian politics, and the complicity of "traditional authorities" in both taking advantage of and reproducing informal networks of rent-seeking and influence peddling.[30] As friends in Kumawu expressed it, if a transaction requires official participation, it will need a dose of "vitamin M" to survive.

Such arguments echo prevailing themes in recent literature on African politics. In the storm of criticism that has been directed at African govern-

ments since the first wave of military coups and one-party states brought
down early postcolonial experiments with multiparty politics, many have
argued that Africa's "failed states" are deeply imbued with traditional attitudes and practices. Rooted in traditional institutions in which power is
vested in persons rather than the law, Africa's "neopatrimonial" regimes are
said to founder on their own stubborn resistance to modernity.[31]

Others see clientilism, corruption, and outright repression as consequences of colonial rule, rather than evidence of its ephemerality. Far
from preserving ancient institutions, indirect rule, it is argued, created
new ones in the name of "custom, which were often more rigid and
authoritarian than those that preceded them."[32] Recently, Mahmood
Mamdani has taken this argument to a new level of generality and sophistication. South Africa's dismal history of apartheid was not, he argues, an exception to the mainstream of recent African history but "the
generic form of the colonial state."[33] Chiefs and customary law played a
pivotal role under colonial rule, as instruments of state domination, creating a form of power that Mamdani calls "decentralized despotism."
"No nationalist government was content to reproduce the colonial legacy
uncritically,"[34] but "the main tendency of . . . reform was not towards
the democratization of the legal system inherited from colonialism, but
towards its deracialization."[35] In the decades since independence, he concludes, Africa has not suffered from "the structural defects of a historically organized civil society" but rather experienced "the crystallization
of a different form of power" in which "fused power, administrative
justice, and extra-economic coercion [are] all legitimized as customary."[36]

On one level, the career of Barima Asumadu Sakyi reads like a textbook
case in support of Mamdani's argument. Having appropriated over a million cedis of his constituents' money, the chief not only managed to delay
paying the money back until its purchasing power had dwindled to insig-
nificance but also fended off concerted popular efforts to remove him from
the stool for more than fifteen years. From what I was able to learn in a
few months of fieldwork, the chief's longevity in office cannot be readily
attributed to the chastening effects of his early disgrace over Digya-Kogyae.
Stories of his personal extravagance circulated freely, among his allies as
well as his opponents, along with tales of the bold maneuvers by which he
had attempted to postpone or influence the outcome of the destoolment
case and frequent assertions that his active support of Rawlings and the
NDC had helped secure his seat on the stool. Sources close to the palace
added that the stool's accounts were kept mostly in the chief's head, and it
was widely believed that much of the cost of the stool's litigation and the
palace establishment was borne, ultimately, by the townspeople—especially
those considered "strangers" on Kumawu land.

More generally, it could be argued that the frequency and length of
land and chieftaincy disputes serve to entrench chiefly power in Asante
and enhance chiefs' ability to seek (and find) rent. Whether disputes are
prolonged deliberately, as many Kumawufoɔ believe, so that lawyers
and adjudicators can "take money" from the contestants, they certainly
do take time. The case against William Kore and his coconspirators, for
example, made fairly rapid progress through the high court,[37] but the
appeal process was not completed until December 1991.[38] The
destoolment case took even longer.

When destoolment charges against Barima Asumadu Sakyi were first
brought before the Regional House of Chiefs, in 1976, they were rejected
on the grounds that the petitioners were not kingmakers and hence had no
capacity, under customary law, to take action against a paramount chief.[39]
After persuading several senior members of the Kumawu Traditional Council to join them, the chiefs' opponents petitioned a second time, but they
were told that they could not "graft a living branch onto a dead tree"[40] and
rebuffed again. Eventually the Regional House of Chiefs agreed to hear the
case, but the judicial panel appointed for that purpose was disbanded on the
eve of announcing its findings, amid widespread rumors that the panelists
had been bribed by the Kumawuhene's opponents. A second panel was convened, but it too was blocked from issuing a ruling—this time by the original petitioners, who wanted to know "why the first panel's findings had
been set aside?"[41] It was left to the Supreme Court to untangle the proce-
dural deadlock, and the case was still pending at the time of my last visit to
Kumawu in 1996.

In the meantime, surviving members of the original group of "malcontents" lodged two new complaints against the Kumawuhene with the Regional House of Chiefs. In one, they argued that even though Asumadu
Sakyi had finally paid back the Digya-Kogyae compensation money, the
fact that he had been to gaol was sufficient to disqualify him from occupying the stool. In a separate action, the chief's opponents charged that Barima
Asumadu Sakyi and seventeen other members of the traditional council had
never been properly enstooled in the first place, because some of the elders
had not been present at their installation ceremonies. Shielded by a protec-
tive screen of pending litigation, in 1996 the chief's position appeared likely
to remain secure for some time.[42]

Like the wave of destoolment cases that swept Asante in the wake of
colonial "conquest," those of the late twentieth century reflect a local
political dynamic of shifting coalitions and antagonisms, rather than clear
structural divisions. In Kumawu, the chief's supporters and opponents
were not neatly divided along lines of class or even party affiliation.
The businessmen and professionals who led the campaign to put Kore

on the stool in 1973 were among the first to turn against him in the Digya-Kogyae case. Throughout the ensuing struggles, the chief could count graduates and illiterates, successful traders and ordinary farmers, elders and "youngmen" among his supporters—and among his opponents. Families were divided over the question of loyalty to the stool. The Ankobiahene and Amaniehene supported the chief although most of their relatives did not, and some members of the royal family were sympathetic to the opposition. The traditional council was also split, and several of its members changed their minds during the course of the Digya-Kogyae trial and appeal.

When party politics resumed in 1992, after a decade of military rule, the chief and many of his allies declared their support for the NDC, while the majority of his opponents backed the Asante-based NPP. But local antagonisms did not always translate into electoral politics. In 1992, Amaniehene Nana Dua Awere was elected to represent the Etia ward (center of opposition to the Kumawuhene) in the Sekyere District Assembly, although he "remained loyal" to the chief. Party alignments were reshuffled again during the second round of parliamentary and presidential elections in 1996. In Kumawu, as in Ghana more generally, political divisions are both deep and malleable. Alliances cross lines—between rich and poor, between "modern" and "traditional" authority, between citizens, kinsmen, and strangers—and individuals renegotiate their positions in multiple, sometimes unexpected ways.

There has, however, been considerable continuity over time in the circumstances which lead citizens to try to unseat a chief. In 1975, as in 1915, Kumawufoɔ turned rebellious when the chief failed, or refused, to be held accountable for stool property. Indeed, in confirming the high court's decision that the plaintiffs were entitled, on behalf of the *oman*, to the compensation that government had paid for Digya-Kogyae, the Supreme Court set something of a precedent on the issue of chiefly accountability. Specifically, it has been suggested that the court's ruling on the Digya-Kogyae appeal overturned an important precedent, first enunciated by John Mensah Sarbah, that a family head (and, by extension, a chief) cannot be held accountable for losses in the family's (or stool's) assets.[43] Mensah Sarbah's dictum was overturned, with respect to family heads, in 1985.[44] Following the Supreme Court's ruling that the Digya-Kogyae plaintiffs were legally entitled to recover the compensation money on behalf of the stool, many Ghanaians argued that the court had "overturned Mensah Sarbah" for chiefs as well.[45]

Yet Asumadu Sakyi's success in retaining his stool, despite the fact that his conduct was labelled fraudulent by the courts, suggests that Digya-Kogyae may have done less to reduce the scope of chiefly power than this assessment implies. It is arguable that the central issue in the case was not whether Asumadu Sakyi had misbehaved, or even whether his conduct disqualified him from holding traditional office, but what kind of power he exercised as a traditional ruler—in practice as well as in principle? Do stool lands operate, in Ghana, as one-way channels of rent-seeking, or do they provide arenas in which authority may be exercised but also held to account? In seeking to understand the wider implications of the chieftaincy dispute, we come back to the ongoing battle between the stools of Kumawu, Kwaman, and Agogo over a major portion of the Afram Plains.

"WAR BY ANY OTHER MEANS"

Kumawu's agreement with Kwaman and Agogo, that they owned the land at Digya-Kogyae jointly, proved as ephemeral as it was expedient. Twenty-five years earlier, Kumawu had become involved in a boundary dispute between Kwaman and another stool, Beposo. In 1950, Beposo accused subjects of Kwaman of trespassing on Beposo stool land. When Kwaman countered that the land in question belonged to them, Beposo replied that this could not be—Beposo's boundary was with Kumawu, not Kwaman.[46] Although Kumawu was not, initially, a party to the case, Beposo's argument suggested that the court's decision could affect Kumawu's claims to the "vast land" stretching from Beposo to the Volta River. To protect its own interests, Kumawu joined the dispute on the side of Beposo. During the next twenty-five years, the Kumase Traditional Council made several attempts to arbitrate the dispute, without success, and in 1975, the case was transferred to the Stool Lands Boundaries Settlement Commission.

Like many of the cases discussed in earlier chapters, the dispute between Kumawu and its neighbors in the Afram Plains turns in part on the battles of the past.[47] Kumawu, Kwaman and Agogo all trace their claims to a war (or series of battles) that their precedessors fought against the Dwan chief Ataala Firam, toward the end of the seventeenth century.[48] The main point at issue in recent disputes is whether the Asante stools had joined forces against the Dwans as equals, driving Ataala Firam from the plains, and remaining on the conquered land "as brothers"?[49] In the Beposo boundary case, Kwaman insisted that they did. But Kumawu argued that it was they who led the fight against Ataala Firam: that Kwaman and Agogo assisted in the war after having placed themselves under Kumawu's protection, and that they later settled in the plains with Kumawu's permission.[50]

Both stools have told different stories on other occasions. In a dispute with the Dwanhene, in 1950, Kumawu argued that Kumawu and Agogo (but not Kwaman) had defeated Ataala Firam together, and that Kumawu had subsequently allowed Dwans to settle in the disputed area. But Agogo challenged this story—testifying that the three stools fought together until the Kumawuhene died, and that Agogo and Kwaman then finished the war alone.[51] Fifteen years earlier, having learned that Agogo had awarded a mining concession to an expatriate firm, Kumawu and Kwaman sued for a share of the royalties. Agogo, they argued, had no right to grant the concession without consulting them, because all three stools had conquered Ataala Firam together.[52] This, in turn, represented a departure from Kumawu's testimony in a previous case (in 1924), that Kwaman was subordinate to Kumawu because Kumawu once offered protection to Kwaman when Nsuta had taken to "chopping off Kwaman heads" for sacrificial purposes.[53] And so on. . . .

In addition to tales of ancient battles, Kwaman, Beposo, and Kumawu have also invoked colonial rulings to support their claims in the plains. When the "administrative" boundary was drawn between Asante and the Gold Coast Colony in 1906, a considerable number of Kwahus "discovered" that they were living in Asante.[54] When they complained, Chief Commissioner Fuller moved quickly to head off any intrusion into his own administrative domain by officials from the Gold Coast Colony. "I shall inform all settlers north of the Obosom," he wrote to Kwame Afram, "that they are in Ashanti territory and that they will have to obtain your permission to remain there."[55] Lest this sudden endorsement go to Kwame Afram's head, however, Fuller warned him not to push his luck by pressing claims to land south of the Obosom River (see Map 3.1). "The Kumawus are not numerous," he wrote, "but you are none-the-less left in possession of a vast territory, which you cannot properly look after for want of people. It does not therefore, behoove you to claim more land than has been granted you. . . . "[56]

Evidently neither side was prepared to abide by Fuller's pronouncements, for the following year he proposed that "the best solution of the problem was to declare all the land between the OBOSOM [*sic*] and Sene Rivers Government lands, thus to deprive Native Chiefs of nominal ownership of the land in dispute, while allowing their subjects to pay them tribute and follow their peaceful pursuits to their hearts' content."[57] Acting on Fuller's advice, the government acquired the disputed land for a game reserve and announced that henceforth "the claims of Kwahu and Kumawu cease to have any effect."[58] With a staff of eleven "political officers" for all Asante, however, he was in no position to enforce restrictions on activity inside the reserve.[59] People from both sides of the colonial boundary continued to hunt and farm across it, and tensions persisted between the chiefs of Kwahu and Kumawu over their respective areas of authority.[60]

If the game reserve proved to be a paper tiger, Agogo's mining concession was another matter. In this case, Kumawu and Kwaman invoked

the tradition of joint conquest and coequal ownership, but the court favored Agogo, arguing that in recent times the stools had "treated the
land around each state as the exclusive property of that state,"[61] and it
was too late to turn the clock back to 1700. In other words, by occupying and administering portions of the plains separately, the stools had
effectively divided ownership of the land as well. This ruling neither
ended disputes over ownership of the plains nor eliminated "traditional
history" as evidence, but it did help to shift the terms of subsequent
debate.

Since independence, the courts have frequently reiterated the principle
that, because history does not stand still, contemporary adjudicators should
give preference to evidence of recent practice in making their decisions. In
1993, for example, the Stool Lands Boundaries Appeal Tribunal argued that
when litigants present conflicting accounts of traditional evidence, the court
must base its decision on "recent facts [of] record."[62] But the court did not
repudiate traditional history: on the contrary. Both the commissioner and
the appeal tribunal commented at length on the admissibility of "traditional
evidence" in general, and on the status of such evidence in the case before
them. Their rulings are of interest not only because Kumawu was tangen-
tially involved in the case but also for the light they shed on the mutability,
and continued vitality, of "traditional evidence" in contemporary Ghanaian
legal and judicial practice.

The dispute in question involved the Pitikos, a group who had settled
near the Volta River long ago and were flooded out when the dam at
Akosombo was completed in 1972. They moved westward, into territory
controlled by the Kwahu stool of Abetifi, and later quarreled with Abetifi
over the land. Claiming distant kinship with Pitiko, Kumawu testified on
their behalf. If Pitiko had won the case, the effect would have been to
reactivate Kumawu's claim to land south of the Onwam River, which Chief
Commissioner Fuller had attempted to quash in 1907.

The controversial testimony in this case was provided by a witness from
Kumawu—Nana Osei Bediako Firaw, also known as Allan Cole. Born and
educated in Britain, Cole came to Ghana in 1960 and has lived there ever
since, employed as a secondary-school teacher and, later, headmaster until
he retired in 1992. Explaining to the commission that he was a member of
the Aduana family of Kumawu by adoption and had been installed as a
chief,[63] Cole testified at length about the history of the Pitiko stool, its
relationship to Kumawu, and its claims to the land under dispute. In ruling
for Abetifi, the commissioner discounted Cole's testimony—not because he
was not "competent and qualified" to give traditional evidence[64] (as Abetifi's
lawyer had argued), but because the evidence he gave was not traditional.
Pointing out that Cole had tendered "as many as (12) twelve documents to

show the various sources of his evidence," the commissioner argued that his testimony was not "handed down from generation to generation by the elders" but was "based on . . . his private and personal researches into materials other than his elders' information . . . " and was therefore not qualified "to be treated as traditional evidence and . . . admitted as an exception to the hearsay rule. . . . "[65]

Pitiko appealed, claiming among other things that "the Learned Commissioner misdirected himself by ignoring relevant evidence given by . . . the expatriate Nana Osei Bediako . . . as not qualifying to be treated as traditional evidence. . . . "[66] Although the appeal tribunal declined to overturn the commissioner's ruling, the presiding officer agreed with Pitiko's lawyer "that parts of [Cole's] evidence is [*sic*] traditional evidence," adding that "[i]t is the weight to be given to the evidence that needs consideration."[67]

The commissioners' debate over Cole's testimony offers a revealing glimpse into the dynamics of historical production in the context of contemporary struggles over property and authority. Like Judge Owusu Sekyere in Kumase, none of the participants in the Pitiko-Abetifi enquiry questioned the premise that traditional history is legitimate evidence—"permissible hearsay," which the courts must weigh as carefully as they would any other kind of evidence.[68] Instead, debate focused on questions of what constitutes valid traditional evidence and *who* is "competent and qualified" to provide it. To merit exemption from the hearsay rule, the Commissioner argued, evidence

> must be the history of the stool, its people and properties, as known to the stool elders and transmitted from generation to generation by them to the successive occupants of the stool on their installation. . . .
>
> I venture to say that it is the sacredness of its source and the solemn ceremony which accompanies its transmission by the elders to the new occupant of the stool that make such evidence so special and authentic as to warrant exception from the hearsay rule.[69]

For the commissioner, research based on documentary sources did not have these special qualities. For the appeal tribunal, however, "the mere fact that the word 'research' is used" was not sufficient grounds for rejecting Cole's testimony.[70] Taken together, their arguments suggest that the legitimacy of history as evidence turns not only on the history, identity, and status of the person(s) who provide it, but also on the technical, discursive, political, and spiritual processes through which their knowledge is acquired. Like individual agency[71] history's effect on present practice depends not only on the knowledge and skill of the historian but also on the social circumstances of its production, and on the processes of political and ritual legitimation that confer authority on both the producer and the product. As they adjudicate specific claims to land and office, Ghanaian courts demonstrate repeatedly that the production of socially relevant historical knowledge in general is a living process, in which the possibilities of participation as well as the qualities of the product are continually negotiated and reassessed.

DRABONSO

As I studied land and history in Kumawu, I encountered numerous references to Drabonso—a settlement about 20 km east of Kumawu, where battles over the plains have often been joined—and finally decided to pay a visit. From Kumawu to Drabonso is less than 25 km, but it seems much longer. Unlike Kumawu, which is well supplied with electricity and has had piped water for decades,[72] Drabonso has never had either. People light their way after dark with oil or kerosene lanterns and carry water in buckets from the river. In 1993, the roads between Kumawu and Kumase were much in need of repair (the work was well under way by mid-1994), but well traveled nonetheless. I never waited longer than half an hour in Kumawu for transport toward Kumase or to nearby settlements, such as Bodomase, which are readily accessible by paved or well graded roads. During harvest seasons, produce buyers' vans plied the roads through Kumawu from dawn until 9:00 or 10:00 PM,[73] and timber lorries and other heavy vehicles were not at all unusual. Toward Drabonso, however, the road was extremely rough. Drivers mindful of their vehicles might take two hours or more to make the trip, and most avoid it altogether. My assistant and I had to hire a private car, at a healthy price, to get there, and we were lucky to find a vehicle traveling back to Kumawu on the afternoon when we left.

Such limited accessibility might suggest that Drabonso is remote from the main currents of commerce and politics in Ghana. Several of the people I interviewed in Kumawu said they had land at Drabonso, but most complained that the place was "far," and that it was difficult both to use land there and to exercise effective control over tenants or squatters. Yet in two, admittedly brief, visits I had the impression that the population of Drabonso was substantial and growing, and that claims to land there, far from reflecting a state of benign disinterest, were the focus of palpable tension.

People have been living at Drabonso for a long time. During the eighteenth century, subjects or servants (*nkoa*)[74] of the Asantehene established several hunting camps in the Afram Plains, and some of them settled at Drabonso.[75] Soon after 1800, the king's hunters were joined by *nkoa* of the

Tafohene, who is said to have purchased them from Kumawu. During the reign of Asantehene Kwaku Dua Panin (1834–67), the Tafohene incurred a debt to the state and, in partial payment, surrendered his *nkoa* at Drabonso to the Asantehene, who transferred them to the recently created Manwere division (*fekuo*).[76] The Manwerehene brought additional settlers to Drabonso, including some who came originally from Kwahu.

After British offcers dismantled the Asante state and deported Prempeh I, the Manwere *fekuo* was disbanded, and its land and subjects parceled out to chiefs who were considered "loyal" to colonial rule. Twenty years later, the colonial state declined to recognize Manwerehene Kofi Nti's authority at Drabonso but, in 1935, his successor had better luck. With the support of the newly restored Asantehene Prempeh II, he persuaded the chief commissioner to reinstate Manwere's authority over his former subjects. The commissioner ruled, however, that the Manwerehene had no authority over other chiefs' subjects at Drabonso, and that the land belonged to Kumawu.[77]

Kwame Afram must have been gratified, if not entirely reassured, by this decision. Like other chiefs throughout Asante, he was well aware that Prempeh II, having been restored in 1935 to a stool without land, might soon start to look for some. Not content with Prempeh's public assurances to the contrary,[78] the Kumawuhene stepped up his efforts to secure Kumawu's authority over land in the plains by exercising it. He took every opportunity to levy fines on Manwere subjects at Drabonso, interfered with their efforts to cultivate, and, in 1938, imposed a tax on their cocoa, which was later extended to all non-Kumawu subjects. He also enlisted Kumawu elders in his efforts, assigning responsibility for allocating hunting and fishing rights or collecting tribute in different areas of the plains to particular subchiefs of Kumawu. The Kumawuhene's aggressive approach so alarmed the Kwamans that the Kwamanhene retaliated by claiming ownership of the land.[79]

With respect to land, Kwame Afram's successors have followed his example. From his accession in 1950 until his death in March 1973, Barima Otuo Akyeampon worked assiduously to defend and expand Kumawu's holdings in the Afram Plains. He assigned the task of collecting game and other forms of tribute at Drabonso to the Mponuahene of Kumawu, who later described himself as "caretaker" of Kumawu stool lands there.[80] In 1959, the Kumawuhene signed an agreement promising 10 percent of all future revenues from Kumawu's land in the Afram Plains to a solicitor, Forson Bandoh Mensah, if Kumawu won its case against Agogo.[81] Otuo Akyempon also pressed Kumawu's claims to land north of the Sene River and south of the Obosom—well beyond the large area under dispute between Kumawu, Agogo, and Kwaman—laying the ground in advance to claim compensa-

tion for land to be inundated by Lake Volta. Rival stools viewed these efforts with understandable alarm. When Kumawu sued the Dwanhene over
land north of the Sene River, Agogo testified on behalf of the Dwans.[82]

For Barima Asumadu Sakyi, smarting from the disgrace of Digya-
Kogyae, Kumawu's long-standing rivalry with Kwaman and Agogo presented an opportunity for political rehabilitation. In 1981, the Stool Lands
Boundaries Settlement Commission ruled that Beposo shared a boundary with Kumawu. Kwaman was thoroughly alarmed. Not only did they
stand to lose all claim to land revenue in the area, if the commissioner's
decision was upheld on appeal, but citizens of Kwaman who had lived
and farmed at Drabonso for decades might also find themselves reclas-
sified as "strangers" and obliged to pay tribute to Kumawu. Indeed the
comissioner acknowledged that Kwaman had grounds for concern. In
making his decision, he explained, he felt bound by Chief Commissioner
Fuller's ruling, in 1919, that Beposo's boundary was with Kumawu. But
he rejected Kumawu's claim that they had given permission for Kwaman
to settle on the plains:

> I am satisfied from the evidence generally that Kwamang and Kumawu
> together with Agogo fought and defeated one Ataala Fiam and took his
> lands. These three stools settled anywhere they pleased on the conquered
> land and the area they occupied became their exclusive possession. [Were
> it not for Fuller's judgment] I would have fixed the boundary between
> Beposo and Kwaman.[83]

Although the commissioner's decision dismayed Kwaman, his explanation
opened the door to an appeal that, if it succeeded, would not only save
Kwaman from the indignity of paying tribute to Kumawu but might also
turn the tables on Kumawu with respect to the land itself.

As Kwaman prepared to appeal, the contestants settled in for a long
siege. Barima Asumadu Sakyi may have miscalculated his subjects' gull-
ibility and his supporters' tolerance in the Digya-Kogyae case, but he
demonstrated considerable skill afterwards both in fending off his political adversaries and in strengthening Kumawu's position on the plains.
Like his principal predecessors,[84] the chief has pursued an active policy
of colonization—encouraging settlement, allocating hunting, fishing, and
farming rights, and delegating authority in particular localities to headmen who would agree to look after Kumawu's interests. He has also
gone a step further by undertaking to promote large-scale commercial
farming ventures in the plains.[85]

Many Kumawu families have land in the Afram Plains, most within "a
ten mile radius" of Kumawu.[86] Some, like the Kumi family, established

farms at Drabonso in Kwame Afram's time; others were given land there by the present chief, including the Norris/London branch of the royal family—descendants on the paternal side of District Commissioner A. W. Norris, whose efforts to defend his royal in-law against charges of misconduct in 1915 earned him a transfer to Ejura.[87] Some subchiefs control hunting and fishing rights in more distant areas—an arrangement that the stool has promoted in order to secure its borders. Under the colonial administration's policy of *de facto* indirect rule, such rights gained force when draped in claims of antiquity. As Norris wrote in 1918, with reference to a question of hunting tribute, government should not "alter an old arrangement of this sort—it will open up such a big question not only on the Afram Plains . . . but out Offinso way also. . . . "[88] In recent times, efforts to reclothe "old arrangements" in more modern garb have not always been successful. As two of the Digya-Kogyae defendants admitted in court, their claims to "freehold ownership" of portions of the game and wildlife reserve were based on nothing more than the hunting and fishing rights held by their ancestors.[89]

Although family rights in land are formally subordinate to those of the stool, they are not to be lightly overridden. Near Kumawu, as we saw in the previous chapter, families rent out portions of their land for cultivation, at going market rates, without seeking the chief's permission. The stool may acquire farmland to accommodate the growing demand for building plots, but if the land in question is already occupied by a local family, the family has a right to expect compensation. For example, when land along the road to Bodomase was allocated for building plots, the Kumi family received compensation in the form of several plots that the stool no longer controls.[90] Amaniehene Nana Dua Awere is still waiting for compensation for the portion of his family's land, which Barima Otuo Akyeampon gave as the site for Tweneboa Kodua Secondary School.[91] Similarly, when the Kumawu Traditional Council allocated 25,000 acres between the Onwam and Afram Rivers to KIFCOM, Kumawufoɔ who might be displaced by the firm's operations were promised part of the traditional council's 40 percent share of the profits.[92]

In addition to allocating hunting and fishing rights, subchiefs have sometimes acted as bailiffs for the Kumawu stool, collecting tribute and monitoring the activities of citizens, strangers, and the agents of rival stools at Drabonso and beyond. Nana Adu Gyamfi, the timber merchant and sawmill owner who filed a claim for individual compensation at Digya-Kogyae, had been promoted by Barima Otuo Akyempon to Siankwahene—a title one of his colleagues rendered as "one who blocks the road so that wayfarers may be robbed."[93] In 1994, Nsumankwahene Fordour was actively engaged in exercising the Kumawuhene's authority at Drabonso. When E. B. Sugri, the headman of an immigrant village at Drabonso, made the mistake of paying tribute to Kwaman, "this man [pointing to Nana Forduor] arrested me."[94]

Barima Asumadu Sakyi has also encouraged Kumawu citizens to take out formal leaseholds in the plains. Leases are expensive to process (among other things, they require that the land be surveyed), so the chief has appealed primarily to wealthy Kumawufoɔ. "Siankwahene Nana Adu Gyamfi was the first," he explained, adding that, by 1994, some twenty citizens had followed his example.[95] These acquisitions were not welcomed by everyone at Drabonso. Several residents who identified themselves as owing allegiance to other stools complained that individual chiefs from Kumawu had recently acquired large tracts of land and "sacked the people" who were farming there.[96]

CITIZENS AND STRANGERS AT DRABONSO

Kumawu's campaign to colonize the plains has not been limited to its own citizens. Throughout the twentieth century, successive Kumawuhenes have made strategic use of "strangers" as well as citizens to promote and defend the stool's interests, particularly with regard to land. When "northerners" established the Kumawu zongo, the stool allocated them land for farming and building and encouraged them to stay. Today, northerners are openly admired in Kumawu and at Drabonso for their skill at farming.[97] They also participate in local politics. The Serikin represents zongo residents in dealings with the Kumawu Traditional Council and, in 1992, the man elected to represent Kumawu's district in Parliament was "a Kotokoli," whose forebears came originally from Togo. And, as we have seen, residents of the zongo in Kumawu do not identify themselves as strangers.

Like other Kumawufoɔ, several of the men whom I interviewed in Kumawu zongo had land at Drabonso and complained about the difficulty of looking after it at a distance. Other immigrants from the north have settled directly on the plains, finding the savannah environment more familiar and congenial than it appears to many Asantes. Both Kwame Afram and Otuo Akyeampon cultivated ties with northern settlers, sometimes appointing Mossi or other strangers as village headmen, especially in remote border areas where Kumawufoɔ were reluctant to take up residence.[98] In Asumadu Sakyi's time, new immigration from the north has given the chief an opportunity to seek his own political rehabilitation by extending his network of clients and allies in the plains.

As economic conditions worsened in Ghana in the 1970s and early 1980s, increasing numbers of Ghanaians left home in search of economic opportunity, both in Ghana and abroad.[99] In 1983, economic decline combined with a severe drought to bring the Ghanaian economy to its lowest level in the postcolonial era. Bush fires destroyed large areas of timber and tree crops; many imported commodities simply disappeared from shops and markets; and locally grown staples were extremely scarce. To add to the misery, in February 1983, Nigeria abruptly expelled all undocumented aliens from the country, forcing more than a million Ghanaians to return home in the space of a few weeks.

During this period of dearth and upheaval, new settlers moved into the Afram Plains in search of land on which to farm and support themselves and their dependents. In contrast to longtime residents of Kumawu, for whom the plains were discouragingly remote, immigrants from the north were favorably impressed with the terrain. "The land is better here than in the north," I was told. One farmer estimated that he harvested as much from one acre of land at Drabonso as from three or four acres in Mamprussi.[100] The new arrivals broke ground, planted maize and cassava, and summoned their relatives and friends to join them. New villages were established in the vicinity of Drabonso, bearing the names of their founders' areas of origin—Mamprussi, Dagomba (a.k.a. Wirebonso)—and became new centers of agricultural colonization. In 1994, according to headman Mamadu al Ilasan, the population of Dagomba included Dagombas, Dagartis, Kusases, and Gurunshes. By 1994, the immigrants had exhausted available arable land around Drabonso and were expanding their farms "across the Afram River." Obtaining additional farmland there was not difficult, they said; their biggest problem was lack of transportation to convey their crops to market.

For the Kumawuhene, the immigrants' arrival was opportune. Beset by efforts to unseat him, and facing long and expensive legal battles over the stool's boundaries as well as his own misconduct, the chief moved swiftly to claim the immigrants as clients and tributaries of the stool. Land allocations to the new settlers were not surveyed or even closely demarcated. Early arrivals said they were simply shown "where they could farm" and left to do the same for relatives, friends, and even strangers who came to join them later on. After the KIFCOM venture went bankrupt, the Kumawuhene gave part of the land there to farmers from Dagomba. The immigrants were expected to pay annual tribute, in cash or in kind, but said that the amounts were not especially onerous and that the Kumawuhene accepted smaller amounts in difficult years.[101] Tribute brought revenue to the Kumawu stool, of course, but its primary importance was to provide annual acknowledgment (and hence legitimation) of Kumawu's claim to the land itself.

In addition to settling them on the land, Barima Asumadu Sakyi treated the headmen of Mamprussi and Dagomba as agents of the Kumawu stool. They were responsible for collecting tribute, on behalf of the stool, from their constituents and for settling disputes within their own communities. They were expected to inform the Kumawuhene of any infringements on his authority and, above all, to refuse demands for tribute from Kwaman or any other stool that might use such transactions to challenge Kumawu's authority over the land. Thus, E. B. Sugri was arrested (on the orders of Asumadu Sakyi's representative, the Nsumankwahene) when he made the mistake of placating Kwaman by giving in to that stool's demand for tribute. But no one objected when he and other farmers at Mamprussi arranged to rent fields from Kwaman or Drabonso farmers, when the Mamprussi fields were worn out or invaded by spear grass.[102] In short, the Kumawuhene has effectively incorporated the immigrants as clients of Kumawu. At Dagomba, farmers nodded when their headman explained that access to land at Drabonso would not be a problem "so long as the Kumawuhene is on the stool."[103]

In contrast to the situation at Mamprussi and Dagomba, Kumawu's relations with other Asantes at Drabonso appeared tense to the point of open hostility. My first visit to Drabonso was unannounced, and I expected to do no more than introduce myself and explore the possibility of coming back to discuss matters of history and land. However, the people whom I met on arrival began discussions on the spot. They introduced themselves as descendants of hunters who served the Asantehene and were sent to Drabonso long ago, when game became scarce around Kumase.[104] Hearing that Kumawu had "a vast land," the Asantehene asked the Kumawuhene for some for his hunters. "That is why we are here." Although their numbers have grown over time, the Kumase elders explained, they have not been allowed to expand beyond the area allocated "when Otumfuo first brought us here." They also complained that some of their land had been taken away and given to "northerners"—by the Kumawu stool at Mamprussi and Dagomba and by Kwaman at Mankessim—and that recently, two chiefs from Kumawu had acquired more of their land for large-scale farming. The Kumawu chiefs, they said, had surveyed the land, put up shelters, and "sacked" the people who were farming there, and one had begun to plant maize and cassava.[105]

Before we parted, I said that I planned to return to Drabonso in a few days, and they agreed to another meeting. When I arrived at the appointed time, however, none of my previous interlocutors was on hand. Gradually, a small crowd of onlookers assembled, curious to know my mission. After an hour or more, a few of the Kumase elders turned up, but their principal spokesman of the previous week was not with them and they declined to discuss any of the issues we had covered before. Without their colleagues, they explained, they lacked the authority to say anything; moreover, I must understand that history could not be discussed "in public." Thoroughly disappointed, I was obliged to settle for an impromptu seminar on the problems of farming at Drabonso. I learned much during the afternoon about the group farming scheme at KIFCOM, and about individual farmers' experiments with new crops and pesticides, but nothing about history or land.

About 8:30 that evening, as my assistant and I were chatting with fellow lodgers at the small Catholic hospital[106] in Drabonso, there was a knock at the gate and the Kumase elders filed in. They had come, they explained, under cover of night, because they did not want to discuss land matters in front of the people[107] who had been present in the morning—or even to have it known that they were giving us information. They then elaborated on their earlier outline of the history of their group at Drabonso; rehearsed their complaints about recent dispossessions; read excerpts from the report of a hearing, conducted by the colonial administration in 1935 on contested chiefly jurisdictions;[108] and gave a detailed description of the boundaries of the land they considered rightfully theirs at Drabonso.

The melodramatic flavor of this nighttime interview suggests something of the tension that surrounds matters of land and history at Drabonso.[109] Tension over Kumawu's dispute with Kwaman, in particular, was a subject of frequent discussion in Kumawu. In Drabonso, the few Kwamans whom I managed to speak with gave guarded replies or inquired suspiciously about my reasons for being there.

The stakes in Kumawu's dispute with Kwaman over the Beposo boundary are high. Not only are the contestants convinced that the courts' final ruling will determine which of the two stools controls a large slice of the Afram Plains as the area is opened up to commercial development, but the political ramifications of this case are also far-reaching. Behind the rather quaint and archaic story of how Otumfuo's hunters were settled at Drabonso and subsequently changed hands as the fortunes of particular Asante chiefs waxed and waned lies the ongoing saga of the Golden Stool's own search for land, whose widening ripples around metropolitan Kumase have been discussed in previous chapters. Both Beposo and Kwaman have seats on the Kumase Traditional Council, and the "Kumases" at Drabonso consider themselves subject to the Manwerehene at Kumase.[110] Kumawu, on the other hand, is a paramount stool, independent of the Kumase Traditional Council, and one of those whose land Prempeh II promised "not to interfere with" after the Confederacy was restored in 1935.[111] While no one knows precisely what the outcome of the Beposo boundary dispute portends for the Asantehene's future claims to land outside Kumase, the presence of descendants of Otumfuo's hunters at Drabonso points to a historic link whose precise significance as a precedent for contemporary claims is open to debate.

Like the history of Osei Tutu's conquests, stories of ancient battles in the Afram Plains have been invoked and reinterpreted more than once in recent times, in the context of shifting claims on land and authority, and debate can be renewed at any time. Should the Supreme Court finally decide the dispute over Beposo's boundary in Kwaman's favor, it would be a serious setback for Kumawu, but even a ruling in Kumawu's favor could lead to a backlash, not only from Kwamans who are living at Drabonso but also from Kumase. What will happen, I asked the Kumawuhene, if the Supreme Court finally rules for Kumawu? His response was immediate and unequivocal. "We'll have to sit down with the Kwamans and negotiate."

CONCLUSION

Stretching over three centuries, Kumawu's battles in the Afram Plains highlight many of the themes discussed throughout this study. The Digya-Kogyae case and the ensuing campaign to destool Barima Asumadu Sakyi illustrate, once again, the shifting, ambiguous lines of political interests and alliances in Asante. If the young Kumawuhene thought he could get away with pocketing compensation money for Digya-Kogyae by trading on the loyalty of his elite supporters and popular respect for the prerogatives of traditional authority, he miscalculated badly. The scandal split both "modern" and "traditional" elites in Kumawu, and the chief's subsequent maneuvers to recoup his political fortunes realigned but did not eliminate the resulting divisions. Like the long careers of Kwame Afram or Chief J. K. Frimpon in Kumase, Asumadu Sakyi's recovery from the disgrace of conviction and imprisonment illustrates, once again, that success in politics and in business is less a matter of separating private from public property, wealth from poverty, or civil society from the state than of playing both sides of the fence.

Or several fences. One reason for Kwame Afram's and Asumadu Sakyi's longevity in office seems to have been their ability to negotiate property and influence on many fronts—exploiting tensions within Kumawu families as well as between them, playing off citizens and strangers against rival stools as well as one another, cultivating ties to the national government in power and to the Golden Stool. At times the Kumawuhene's position appears to have been strengthened by the length and intensity of litigation aimed at undermining it, as Asumadu Sakyi's recent career suggests. Yet the dynamic of ongoing disputation provides a social medium in which officeholders are held to account as well as upheld in positions of influence. Once when I wondered why, if years of litigation never resolved the stool's claims to land in a definitive manner, the chief spent so much time and money in court, my interlocutor exclaimed, "but he daren't not fight!" As Kumawufoɔ explained to me repeatedly, it Kumawu were to lose land to another stool, citizens would accuse the chief of failing in his duty to protect their land.[112] If, on the other hand, Kumawu simply agreed to divide the land with Kwaman to avoid the costs of prolonged litigation, citizens feared that the Asantehene might use his authority over Kwaman, or the history of his ancestors' hunters at Drabonso, to "take over" the land. In the countryside, as in Kumase and its environs, the politically ambitious may protect themselves behind a web of contestation, but they ignore their constituents at their peril.

Multiple negotiations beget and thrive on multiple stories of victories, bargains, and betrayals in the past that may serve as precedents in the present. Multiple histories and contested interpretations serve to keep debate open and enable participation in ongoing negotiations over property, identity, and accountability. The discursive ambiguity surrounding the identity of today's residents of Kumawu zongo, for example, parallels the Asante prohibition against speaking openly of other people's origins, lest one be accused of falsifying their claims to citizenship.[113] It also reminds us of the importance of social networks as means of access to wealth and power, and of their fluidity and ephemerality. To function, even temporarily, as sources of legitimacy and access, social relationships must continually be replenished, just as history must continually be retold. To understand how wealth and power are produced and distributed in Asante, it is not enough to identify their producers or the rules that govern access and ownership, because precept and agency only take effect through movement and interaction. The history of Kumawu's battles in the Afram Plains is a story of ongoing debate and unresolved struggle. It is also the social medium in which property is transacted, authority is upheld and held to account, and the past lives, and is invented, in the present.

NOTES

1. NAGK 2, Afram Plains—development of, 1923–28.

2. Barima Otuo Akyeampon died on March 8, 1973, after an unbroken reign of over twenty years on the Kumawu stool. Said to have been a stern disciplinarian, he was appreciated by his subjects for bringing stability to the affairs of the town and for his reputed willingness to temper severity with dignity and grace. If he beat someone by day, an informant explained to me, he would go and apologize by night. After years of dissension under Kwame Afram and his successors, the townspeople were evidently content with Otuo Akyeampon's rule. He is the only Kumawuhene who "died on the stool"—i.e., who was not deposed—in the twentieth century.

3. KHC, Suit No. HC 245/76, Judgment; Gyamfi and another v. Owusu and others, *Ghana Law Reports*, 1981; Supreme Court, Accra, Civil Appeal No. 16/90.

4. The chief lands officer heads the Lands Commission, the government agency responsible for land administration throughout Ghana. The senior lands officer in Kumase heads the Ashanti Regional Division of the Lands Commission.

5. KHC 245/76, Judgment, 3.

6. Ibid., 3–4. A letter of protest from F. Bandoh Mensah, who claimed to represent the Kumawu stool, was apparently passed over by officials at the Lands Department and the Ministry of Lands and Mineral Resources. In his opinion in the ensuing trial, Justice Roger Korsah commented on the alacrity with which the Kumawu claimants' request was honored. "Such zealous attendance to duty is, to say the least, remarkable in our civil service and deserves nothing but the highest commendation, but in the face of the late Mr. Forson Bandoh-Mensah's letter of protest it appears to me that these claims for compensation were met with unseemly haste." Ibid., 5.

7. Since the young Kore had not yet built a house in Kumawu, he lodged with a supporter while he was contesting for the stool. According to Panin Yao Mensah, supporters of Kore's principal rival broke into the house at one point and also threatened Kore with bodily harm if he went to the Krontihene to take the oath of office. To protect him, Panin Mensah gave him a charm (which had belonged to Mensah's father, Kwame Afram) and appealed to his brother, Magistrate Daniel Boadae, to arrange for a police escort. Interview with Panin Yao Mensah, 7/11/94.

8. Interview with Barima Asumadu Sakyi II, 7/24/94.

9. In selecting a successor to a vacant stool, the stool elders function as a kind of "customary" electoral college, weighing the merits of rival candidates, and the strength of their supporters, before making a choice. In conversation, Asantes sometimes compared the "contest" for a stool to an electoral campaign in a system of multiparty democracy.

10. Interview with Nana Osei Kodua IV, Krontihene, 7/6/94. According to Allan Cole and Gyaasehene Nana Okyere Agyei, the Krontihene had been destooled "by his family." At the *akwasidae* in Kumawu that I attended on 1/2/94, the family was represented by the *obaapanin* (female elder). Like stools, Asante families usually have both a male and a female head.

11. *Ghana Law Reports*, 1981. Gyamfi and another v. Osusu and others, Justice Mensah Boisson's opinion.

12. KHC 245/76, Judgment.

13. I learned about this incident in conversations with B. A. Mensah, Yaw Amponsah, and Panin Yao Mensah. It was not clear from these accounts whether the chief's trip to Accra occurred in December, when the first instalment was paid, or in January, when the balance of the ₵1.5 million was disbursed. The substance of the story was confirmed by some of the chief's supporters.

14. KHC 245/76, Judgment, 9–12, and Proceedings, 557–709 passim; interviews with A. Cole, 12/22/93; E. A. Frimpong, 7/11/94.

15. First reported by Chris Asher in the *Palaver Tribune*, by April the story was known throughout Asante.

16. *Ghana Law Reports*, 1981, Gyamfi and another v. Owusu and others.

17. Since independence, the word "citizen" has replaced the colonial term "subject" as the common designation for people who profess allegiance to a particular stool. The

discursive ambiguity created by using the term "citizenship" to describe people's relationship to traditional rulers *and* to the Ghanaian nation is both symptom and source of the ongoing negotiations over authority, identity, and tradition (or history) that lie at the core of the Ghanaian political-economic process.

18. KHC 245/76, Judgment, 1. The self-proclaimed landowners, who became the original defendants in the suit, were Nana Kwabena Agyei, Kyidomhene, Nana Adu Gyamfi, Siankwahene, and Nana Kwadwo Adu Boateng, Gyaasehene—all of Kumawu.

19. KHC 245/76, Judgment, 20–21.

20. Ibid., 27–28. See also, KHC 245/76, Proceedings, 657–85.

21. KHC 245/76, Judgment. Since the plaintiffs had sued on behalf of the stool and the *oman*, if Kore were joined as codefendant in his capacity as Kumawuhene, he would be litigating against himself.

22. KHC 245/76, Proceedings, 577–94, 1020–21; interview with Nana Okyere Agyei, 7/13/94.

23. Just as Kwame Afram's destoolment, in 1916, reverberated through official colonial debates over Asante constitutionalism. To scholars of the late twentieth century, the argument of K. A. Busia's classic monograph, *The position of the chief in the modern political system of Ashanti*, may sound dated, but the question remains very much alive.

24. In collecting information on the stool dispute, as in all of my research in Kumawu, I benefited greatly from the ability and graciousness of my assistant, Michael Adu Gyamfi. A member of the royal family, Mike introduced me to many of the town's leading citizens, as well as its less affluent and influential ones, arranged and helped to conduct interviews, and offered many insightful comments as we worked. When, after several weeks of conversations with men and women who accepted or actively supported the chief's rule, I announced that it was time to interview members of the opposition, good manners prevented him from refusing to make the necessary arrangements, although as he later confessed, he thought it would be "impossible" and was agreeably surprised to discover that the chief's opponents were only waiting to be asked to tell their side of the story. No one whom we approached in Kumawu declined to discuss their views of the chief and the destoolment case, and Kumawufoɔ whom I contacted on my own in Kumase and Accra were equally helpful. While I am sure I have a great deal more to learn, I was at least able to consult people on both sides of the case and collect a substantial amount of quite varied information.

25. Kwame Afram was destooled in 1916 and reinstated in 1925, remaining in office for another eighteen years. In 1926 he was arrested and charged with having murdered a Gurunshi slave, as a gesture of welcome to the repatriated Prempeh I. According to his son, Panin Yao Mensah, the charges were true and many people testified to that effect, but the judge "put it all down to envy" and dismissed the charges. Official correspondence reveals that the administration was more worried about the implications for Prempeh I, who was said to have learned of the sacrifice but kept silent for fear of antagonizing the chiefs. "It looked as if all our plans for Prempeh were going to be blown sky high but providentially the Judge threw the case out for lack of evidence as the Police were unable to find the head and thus identify the body." Rhodes House, Oxford, Mss Afr S 593, Duncan Johnstone Papers, Notes on King Prempeh's return to the Gold Coast, 1924. Kwame Afram weathered another financial scandal in the early 1940s but was destooled again in 1944 after being accused of making himself a golden

stool—a privilege reserved to the Asantehene. He died in 1969. NAGK 987, Yaw Berku and others v. Omanhene Kwame Afram, 1931; interviews with Panin Yao Mensah, 7/11/94; Alice A. Norris, 12/29/93; Allan Cole, 11/12/93.

26. Both opponents and supporters of the chief later claimed that, had he not intervened, most of the Digya-Kogyae compensation money would have gone to Kumawu's long-standing rival Mampon. During the latter part of the colonial period, Kumawu was incorporated into the Mampon District and smarted under Mampon's domination of local government affairs. According to one informant, Barima Otuo Akyeampon initiated Kumawu's claim in order "to hijack the Digya-Kogyae money from Mampon." Interviews with Nana Kwabena Agyei, Kyidomhene, 7/9/94; A. Cole, 12/22/93, 7/9/94.

27. The reorganization of local administration, the judiciary, and chieftaincy affairs under Nkrumah's regime are described in detail in Harvey, *Law and social change*, especially ch. 2 and 207–12.

28. Ibid., 113–22. See also chapter 2, 38–43.

29. Harvey concluded (prematurely, as it turned out) that in "divorc[ing] the chief from the land," the law had "struck directly to the heart of the institution of chieftaincy itself," adding that "it is difficult to see how the chiefs can long remain a significant factor in the social, political or governmental life of the country." Harvey, *Law and social change*, 121–22.

30. See, e.g., Arhin, "Asante praise poems"; N. Chazan, *Anatomy of Ghanaian politics: Managing political recession, 1968–1982* (Boulder, CO: Westview, 1983); Herbst, *The politics of reform in Ghana*; Ninsin and Drah, eds., *Political parties*; Ocquaye, *Politics in Ghana 1972–1979*; P. Anyang' Nyong'o and E. Hansen, eds., *The African state in crisis* (Dakar: CODESRIA, 1989).

31. Bratton and van der Walle, "Neopatrimonial regimes and political transitions in Africa"; R. Sandbrook, *The politics of Africa's economic stagnation* (Cambridge: Cambridge University Press, 1985); T. Callaghy and J. Ravenhill, eds., *Hemmed in: Responses to Africa's economic decline* (New York: Columbia University Press, 1993).

32. Chanock, *Law, custom and social order*; T. O. Ranger, "The invention of tradition in colonial Africa," in E. Hobsbawm and T. O. Ranger, eds., *The invention of tradition* (Cambridge: Cambridge University Press, 1983); Crook, "Decolonization, the colonial state, and chieftaincy in the Gold Coast."

33. Mamdani, *Citizen and subject*, 8. Mamdani's portrayal of the bifurcated colonial polity based on a "state-enforced separation of the rural from the urban and of one ethnicity from another" represents only one strand in the story of contested authority and identity in colonial Asante, described in previous chapters.

34. Mamdani, *Citizen and subject*, 8.

35. Ibid., 136.

36. Ibid., 296.

37. Suit No. 245 was filed in the Kumase High Court in July 1976, and Justice Korsah read his decision on October 19, 1978. Compare land disputes cited in chs. 3 and 4 above.

38. Supreme Court, Accra, Civil Appeal 16/90.

39. The case was filed by the Mponuahene of Kumawu and the Odikro of Drabonso, who were also plaintiffs in the suit to recover the Digya-Kogyae compensation money for the *oman*. KHC 245/76, Proceedings, 1221–24.

40. Interview with A. Cole, 12/22/93.

41. Interview with Nana Osei Kodua IV, Krontihene, 7/6/94.

42. According to some observers, these new suits represented an attempt to fight fire with fire. Apprehensive that the Supreme Court might rule in the chief's favor, leaving them with an unmanageable bill for costs, the chief's opponents may have attempted to protect themselves against financial ruin in the first case by keeping open the issue of destoolment.

43. Sarbah, *Fanti customary laws*, 90. In other words, in accepting election to a stool or family headship, an individual does not assume unlimited personal liability for the value of the collective property of his/her constituents. Families or traditional councils may of course cite willful mismanagement of collectively held assets as potential grounds for removing a family head or chief from office.

44. PNDC Law 114.

45. Justice Wuaku was explicit on this point. Supreme Court, Accra, Civil Appeal 16/90, Judgment, 12–14.

46. Since both stools were members of the Kumase Traditional Council, the case went before the council and the Asantehene. Interview with A. Cole, 12/11/93.

47. Echoing a common locution, Allan Cole exclaimed that in Ghana today, litigation "is war by any other means! In the old days," he explained, "we would have gone across and burned Kwaman and that would have been the end of it." Nowadays, people turn to lawyers, rather than soldiers, to fight their battles over land. Interview, 12/11/93.

48. McCaskie places the war with Ataala Firam in the reign of Opoku Ware I (ca. 1720–50) but adds that the name "is often used eponymously of early rulers of the Kwawu-Afram plains area." McCaskie, *State and society*, 420, n. 222. The spelling of Ataala Firam also varies: I have followed the usual practice in court records, papers, etc., on Kumawu's recent cases.

49. Judgment has been given twice in this case—by the Stool Lands Boundaries Settlement Commission (SLBSC) in 1981, and the Stool Lands Boundaries Appeal Tribunal in 1994—both times in favor of Kumawu. Even while celebrating their second victory, Kumawufoɔ opined that Kwaman would appeal again and the case would "by all means go to the Supreme Court."

50. SLBSC No. 4/75, Judgment; Stool Lands Appeal No. 2/93, Arguments.

51. NAGK SCT 211/693–694, Nana Otuo Achampong I—Kumawuhene versus Nana Kwame Mensah—Dwanhene, 49ff. See also NAGK 1081, Juan Native Affairs, 1928–43. See also 177–78 below.

52. NAGK SCT 24/92, Concessions Record Book, Enquiry No. 246, Kumawu-Agogo Concession, 770.

53. NAGK SCT 24/6, Chief Commissioner's Court, Ashanti, 1928–29. The same story was told several years earlier, by Kumawuhene Kwabena Kodia. NAGK 465, Kumawu-Kwamang-Agogo Dispute, 1924–25. "Historical events the acquisition of Kumawu lands," 6/23/24.

54. See ch. 1, 12–15.

55. NAGA ADM 11/1/242, Papers re Kwahu-Kumawu-Agogo Land dispute, quoted in "Enquiry into Kwahu-Agogo dispute," 4/13/12.

56. NAGA ADM 11/1/242, CCA to Kumawuhene, 5/16/07.

57. NAGA ADM 11/1/242, CCA to CS, Accra. See also NAGA ADM 11/1160, Boundaries between the Gold Coast, Ashanti and the Northern Territories, 1905–06.

58. NAGA ADM 11/1/242, Secretary for Native Affairs to Commissioner Eastern Province, Akuse, 5/18/10.

59. Tordoff, *Ashanti*, 122, 126.

60. NAGA ADM 11/1/242, passim.

61. NAGK SCT 24/92, Concessions Record Book, Enquiry No. 246, Kumawu-Agogo Concession, 770. Kumawu appealed the decision, but the case was dismissed by the West African Court of Appeals in 1940.

62. SLBSC Enquiry No. 1/82, In the matter of the boundary dispute between Pitiko Stool and Abetifi Stool. Displaced by the waters of Lake Volta when the dam was completed at Akosombo in 1972, the Pitikos had moved westward into Abetifi territory, leading to conflict over the terms on which they settled. In the ensuing boundary dispute, Kumawu testified on Pitiko's behalf. If Pitiko had won the case, the effect would have been to reactivate Kumawu's claim to land south of the Onwam River, which Chief Commissioner Fuller had attempted to quash in 1907.

63. SLBSC Enquiry No. 1/82, Judgment, 7. I am grateful to Nana Cole for generously sharing with me his knowledge of land matters and history in Kumawu.

64. Specifically, the commissioner argued that, even if Cole's installation as a chief was improper (as claimed by Abetifi's lawyer), the fact that he had been "customarily enstooled as a chief *and told the history of the stool*" as part of the installation ceremonies meant that he was qualified to give traditional evidence. SLBSC Enquiry No. 1/82, Judgment, 8.

65. Ibid., 9, 11.

66. SLBSC Appeal No. 1/93, Ruling, 9.

67. Ibid., 4.

68. See introduction, xxvii.

69. SLBSC Enquiry No. 1/82, 12, quoted in Appeal No. 1/93, 3.

70. Appeal 1/93, 3.

71. See Introduction, xxiv–xxvi.

72. By the mid-1990s, Kumawu had long outgrown the capacity of its pumps and reservoirs. Water flowed irregularly from indoor taps and outside standpipes, especially on the hillsides which ring the town to the south. During the dry season, water is likely to come on for a few hours in the middle of the night, if at all.

73. See ch. 5, 143.

74. There is no exact equivalent in English of the Twi words *owura* (master) and *akoa* (subject), which together connote a relationship that includes elements of proprietorship and allegiance, as well as dominance and subordination. Klein, "Inequality," 166ff. Compare Rattray, *Ashanti law*, 34–35; McCaskie, *State and society*, 289.

75. T. C. McCaskie, "The history of the Manwere *nkoa* at Drobonso," *Asante Seminar* 6 (1976): 33.

76. The *fekuo*, a military and/or administrative division, was the primary organizational component of the Asante polity. McCaskie, "Office, land and subjects in the history of the Manwere *fekuo* of Kumase: An essay in the political economy of the Asante state," *Journal of African History* 21, no. 2 (1980): 190–91, and *State and society*, 281; Wilks, *Asante*, 454–65; Rattray, *Ashanti law*, ch. 10.

77. NAGK 8/73, Committee of Privileges, 1935–6, pp. 267–88; NAGK 856, Chief Kofi Nti—his subjects at Drabonsu, 1917–1921.

78. See ch. 3, 79.

79. McCaskie, "Manwere *nkoa*," 36.

80. KHC 245/76, Proceedings, 252–53; interview with Kumase elders at Drabonso, 7/18/94. According to some informants, the Mponua stool was created by Otuo Akyempon, but Ankobiahene Nana Boagye II (whose jurisdiction includes Drabonso) said the stool was created by Kwame Afram. Interview, 7/20/94. Offended that Asumadu Sakyi had not consulted him in the matter of compensation for Digya-Kogyae, Mponuahene Kwame Abranko joined in petitioning the Regional House of Chiefs to destool him. In 1976, he tried to collect compensation for Bomfobiri Forest Reserve, again on the grounds that Otuo Akyempon had appointed him "caretaker" of stool lands. KHC 245/76, 111ff.

81. Ibid., 111–12.

82. NAGK SCT 211/3–4, Barima Otuo Achampong I v. Nana Kwame Mensah Dwanhene, Asantehene's Native Court AI, Judgment, 10/30/52. Kumawu was also aggrieved over the colonial administration's decision to place Kumawu in the Mampon District and had been jockeying with Mampon over judicial and administrative authority in the plains since the 1930s. In the Dwan land dispute, Kumawu relied on the testimony of subchiefs in the plains who had supported the stool in its wrangling with Mampon, rather than calling on its "brother," Agogo. The strategy backfired when Agogo belied Kumawu's claims to historic "brotherhood" by testifying for the Dwans. NAGK 1081, Juan Native Affairs, 1928–1943. See also KHC 245/76, Proceedings, 252–53.

83. The case Fuller decided in 1919 began as a boundary dispute between Beposo and Kwaman before the Nsuta Native Court. The court gave judgment in favor of Kwaman but was overruled by the district commissioners of Juaso and Ejura. As the final court of appeal at the time, the chief commissioner endorsed the native court. "The decision of the Commissioners is reversed," he wrote, "and the boundary between Biposu and Kumawu shall be as follows. . . . " NAGK SCT 24/3, Chief Commissioner's Court, Ashanti, 1914–20, Biposuhene v. Kwamanghene, 5/15/19. In its subsequent dispute with Beposo and Kumawu, Kwaman argued that the word "Kumawu" in Fuller's ruling was a typographical error, and should have read "Kwaman," but the stool lands boundaries commissioner was not convinced. "We have often held in this Court in land matters, especially those originating from the former Native Courts, that the form of the writ is not to be stressed so long as the issue is clear. It is not improbable that although the dispute began as a boundary issue between Beposo and Kwamang, the issue which eventually emerged at the trial was between the Stool and Kumawu." SLBSC No. 4/75, Decision, 2.

84. Together, Kwame Afram, Otuo Akyempon, and Asumadu Sakyi occupied the Kumawu stool for eighty-five of the hundred years covered in this study.

85. Interview with Barima Asumadu Sakyi, 7/24/94; and see n. 70 above.

86. In discussing his strategy for guarding Kumawu's interests in the plains, the Kumawuhene drew a distinction between land within the "10 mile radius," where Kumawufo are numerous, and land beyond it, where it is difficult to persuade them to settle. Beyond the ten-mile radius, the chief relies more heavily on "strangers," especially people from the savannahs of northern Ghana and beyond, for whom the Afram Plains are a land of opportunity rather than isolation.

87. See ch. 2, 44. Interviews with Nana Boagye II, Ankobiahene, 7/20/94; Alice Aduana Norris, 12/29/93, 6/19/94.

88. NAGK 874, Claim of tribute from Nsuta subjects settling on Kumawu land, 1918.

89. KHC 245/76, Judgment, 21–22.

90. Interview with Nana Bogyae II, Ankobiahene, 7/20/94.

91. Interview with Nana Dua Awere II, 6/18/94.

92. Interview with Barima Asumadu Sakyi, 7/24/94. Unfortunately, as the chief acknowledged, the profits never materialized. See also J. C. London, "Investigation into the present state of production performance and the role of the Djallonke-sheep in small-farm-holdings in the Asante Region of Ghana" (Ph.D. diss., Technical University of Berlin, 1993); and ch. 5.

93. KHC 245/76, Proceedings, 577ff. Testimony of Kyidomhene Nana Kwabena Agyei.

94. Interview with E. B. Sugri, 7/15/94. He elaborated on the story when I interviewed him again, on 7/18, when Nana Forduor was not present. See below, 182.

95. Pointing out that the surveys and other documentation needed to support an application for leasehold are very expensive, Nana explained candidly that the stool could not afford them, and he has therefore endeavored to enlist citizens' private wealth in this patriotic endeavor. Interviews with Barima Asumadu Sakyi, 7/24/94, and Nana Dua Awere II, 6/18/94.

96. Interviews with Kumase elders and Kwamans at Drabonso, 7/18–19/94. See below, 182–83.

97. "They work like a machine!" exclaimed my research assistant, referring to "northerners" whom he had employed on his own farm.

98. Interview with Barima Asumadu Sakyi, 7/24/94. See also NAGK 1081, Juan Native Affairs.

99. Between 1974–75 and 1981, an estimated 2 million Ghanaians emigrated to Nigeria and Côte d'Ivoire. H. Tabatabai, "Agricultural decline," 718–19. See also G. Mikell, "Ghanaian females, rural economy and national stability," *African Studies Review* 29, no. 3 (1986); Loxley, *Ghana: Economic crisis and the long road to recovery*.

100. Interview with E. B. Sugri, 7/18/94.

101. Farmers at Mamprussi had been giving two bags of maize each as annual tribute to Kumawu but in 1993, the harvest was small and the entire community gave only eight bags. Farmers at Dagomba pooled their contributions: the usual total was thirty bags of maize and fifty tubers of yam per annum.

102. Interviews with E. B. Sugri, 7/15/94, 7/18/94.

103. Interview with Mamadu al Hasan and a group of farmers at Dagomba, 7/19/94.

104. On that occasion I spoke with the Krontihene of Drabonso and several relatives of their chief, Nana Boama Akyanko—a mechanic who lives at Suame, the center of auto repair in Kumase. There are several "chiefs" (*adikro*) at Drabonso, they explained, each presiding over a segment of the community. In addition to Nana Boama, the "Kumase Odikro," there is a Kumawu Odikro, a Kwaman Odikro, and an Nsuta headman. Relations among these constituencies, and their leaders, are conflicted, to say the least. Kumawu considers that the only *odikro* among them is the one representing the Kumawu stool: the others are merely "headmen." According to the Kumawu Ankobiahene, however, the successor to Kumawu Odikro Nana Owusu (a plaintiff in the Digya-Kogyae case, now deceased) has "*so* many problems to solve" before he can be properly enstooled. Available documentary sources on Drabonso history have been

carefully reviewed by McCaskie, "Manwere *nkoa*," who places the hunters' arrival there in the eighteenth century.

105. This story was confirmed, independently, by the chief in question. Interview with Nana Dua Awere, Amaniehene of Kumawu, 6/18/94. According to the Kumase elders at Drabonso, the Amaniehene's acquisition at Drabonso was about half a square mile, while the Nkosuahene had acquired nearly two square miles.

106. Built by a missionary priest with the help of a couple of lay brothers, the hospital was not actually functioning in 1994. The brothers were still trying to get their piped water system to work, and the priest had not yet managed to recruit a doctor. However, the compound had been built with several guest rooms, to accommodate visiting missionaries and future hospital staff, and the priest's assistants readily offered us lodging during our stay.

107. In particular, they objected to the presence of Kwamans and "CDRfo ." Formally reinvented as "NGOs" after the 1992 elections, the Committees for the Defence of the Revolution (CDR), first established during the radical phase of Rawlings' military rule, seemed to be functioning in uneasy limbo in 1994. Their presence on this occasion was cited, later, by the Kumase elders as one reason for their reluctance to speak openly—a sentiment that echoed the ambivalence towards "CDRfo " that I had observed in Kenyase. See ch. 4, 120.

108. NAGK 8/73, Committee of Privileges. Convened in 1935, to resolve outstanding disagreements over chiefly status and jurisdiction under the "restored" Asante Confederacy, the committee's hearings produced one more set of precedents, which have frequently been invoked in subsequent land claims.

109. It is only a suggestion. My visits to Drabonso were far too brief and impressionistic to provide a balanced, much less systematic account of the multiple interests at stake in contemporary struggles over land and authority there, or the ways different groups have pressed their claims at different points in time.

110. Interviews with Kumase elders at Drabonso; McCaskie, 1976, passim.

111. See ch. 3, 79.

112. See ch. 2, 50.

113. McCaskie, *State and society*, 99.

CONCLUSION

In a recent article, Gareth Austin questions the argument, developed by Ivor Wilks and others, that for much of the nineteenth century, the state exercised a virtual monopoly over wealth in Asante. With the gradual closing down of the Atlantic slave trade, he argues, trade and production shifted increasingly to gold, kola, and foodstuffs, creating expanded opportunities for small- as well as large-scale farmers and traders to accumulate modest amounts of wealth. The resulting proliferation of markets and assets undermined the state's ability to monopolize wealth through trade and monetary controls and taxation, and it led to a less concentrated pattern of accumulation and wealth. The diffusion of wealth was accompanied by a diffusion of political power: when Asantehene Mensa Bonsu raised taxes in the 1870s and early 1880's, commoners combined with chiefs to overthrow him. Austin adds, however, that opposition was directed against Mensa Bonsu and his policies, rather than against the monarchy *per se*. Far from remaining hostile to state power in general, some of Mensa Bonsu's leading opponents later threw their support behind Agyeman Prempeh, and sought chiefly office for themselves. Like the destoolment campaigns and trade boycotts of the cocoa era, protest in the late nineteenth century was directed against increased state appropriation of wealth, rather than against the state itself. "The 'rise of the commoners' did not mean the demise of the chiefs."[1]

Like the growth of "legitimate commerce" in the nineteenth century, the spread of cocoa growing in the twentieth created widespread opportunities for modest gains but also underwrote both the emergence of a class of well-to-do farmers and traders and the accumulation of chiefly wealth and influence. Studies in Asante and other parts of southern Ghana have shown that while a significant minority of growers held cocoa farms of twenty-five acres or more, the majority of farmers in the forest zone grew no cocoa at all.[2] The cases discussed in previous chapters indicate that the government's policy of recognizing and enforcing stool ownership of land played a major role both in fostering widespread but unequal participation in the gains from cocoa production and trade and in sustaining the influence of chieftaincy in Asante, not only under colonial rule but after independence as well.

The endless debates over chiefly succession, destoolment, and the management of stool revenues and property that pervaded colonial Asante and continued after independence attest both to the continued salience of chieftaincy as an institution and to its dynamism. The history of acquisition and contestation over land and office in twentieth-century Asante poses a challenge to theories that associate economic and political modernity or "development" with an increasingly sharp division between "public" and "private" spheres of authority and accumulation. The point is not only, as Austin and others have argued, that chiefs, commoners, bureaucrats, and politicians shared similar economic interests and political aspirations. The Asante case also challenges the idea that the separation of public and private property and authority are necessary conditions for sustained development and responsive or participatory government. The continued link, in law and practice, between land ownership and chiefly authority has helped to institutionalize chiefly rent-seeking in Asante, but it has also stimulated popular demand for chiefly accountability.

My argument is analogous to Jane Guyer's contention that in western Nigeria, the government's reluctance to raise revenue through direct taxation served, paradoxically, to undermine the state's accountability to its citizens.[3] "Representation without taxation," Guyer suggests, is a paper tiger: citizens who do not pay taxes have neither the means nor the incentive to hold official feet to the fire when government fails to provide basic services. Yoruba chiefs often work very hard to resolve local disputes and mobilize resources for community development projects, but they have neither the authority nor the wherewithal to deal forcefully or effectively with the state on behalf of their constituents. And ordinary citizens cannot pressure the state by withholding taxes until their concerns are addressed.

Chiefs in Asante are both more powerful and more controversial than their counterparts in western Nigeria—a difference that is directly related to their authority over land. Yoruba chiefs may acquire land as individuals or share in their families' properties, but there are no lands attached to chieftaincy titles.[4] In western Nigeria, therefore (unlike Asante), chieftaincy titles do not give those who hold them a presumptive claim to a share of the income generated by rising values of agricultural or urban land. Individual Yoruba chiefs may receive rent from personal or family property, but collectively they do not constitute a rentier class.[5]

In Asante, as we have seen, the colonial administration's interpretation of customary law with respect to land solidified the position of chiefs as rentiers to a degree that postcolonial regimes have been unable or unwilling to dislodge. Unlike private landowners, however, chiefs are officeholders: their authority over stool lands is contingent on their tenure in office, which, as we have seen, may be challenged if constituents grow dissatisfied with their conduct. In principle, then, chiefly rent-seeking is not unlike direct taxation:[6] the fact that chiefs are entitled to appropriate income through the allocation of stool land creates an incentive for citizens to demand that they account publicly for the way they use it.

Like officeholders in any society, chiefs in Asante may abuse their position or contrive to remain in office despite vociferous complaints from their constituents—patterns illustrated by some of the cases discussed in this volume. But, as we have seen, they are not oblivious to popular opinion, and some work hard to bring resources and amenities to their communities, as well as to profit personally from the prerogatives of office. When a stool falls vacant, rival candidates for the succession campaign for support among "youngmen" as well as stool elders, and the choice of a new chief often turns on people's assessment of how effectively s/he will represent local interests vis-à-vis the state. Yorubas also look to chiefs to represent their interests to the state,[7] but the stakes are not as high and the issue of chiefly accountability is less central to disputes over chiefly succession.

The resilience of chieftaincy in modern Asante is both a symptom and a source of the dense interpenetration of "public" and "private" wealth and influence. Like the colonial government's decision to bring Edward Prempeh back from the Seychelles in 1924 as a "private citizen"—a situation that proved untenable once he had returned to Kumase—the statutory abolition of chiefs' administrative and judicial powers after independence has served to rechannel their influence rather than undermine or eliminate it. Neither wholly public nor entirely private figures, many chiefs maintain extensive networks both within and outside state institutions, straddling public and private spheres in a way that calls the conceptual boundary between them into question and contributes to the proliferation of channels through which resources and influence are mobilized and deployed at all levels of Ghanaian society.

Like multiple, overlapping claims on land, the proliferation of political networks has complicated the history of accumulation, dispossession, and concentration of wealth and power in colonial and postcolonial Asante. In his forceful critique of the legacy of late colonialism, Mamdani divides postcolonial African states into two groups—conservative nationalist regimes whose willingness to work with the local divisions created by indirect rule has relegated the majority of citizens to "participation without representation," and radical nationalist states whose efforts at sweeping social transformation directed from above have often excluded the majority of citizens from meaningful participation in the institutions of representative government.[8] Both types, he concludes, are more despotic than democratic. The case histories presented in this volume suggest that Ghana does not fit comfortably into either category. Since independence, national regimes in Ghana have swung between programs of radical restructuring and accommodation to the status quo, while the dispersion of economic activities (among sectors as well as agents)[9] has been accompanied by a proliferation of formal and informal officeholders, whose pursuit of opportunity and influence tends to multiply the channels that link local communities to regional and national centers of power and wealth. Like the proliferation of claims and precedents brought to bear on acquiring land, the proliferation of claims on office contributes to a dynamic of participatory inequality that both links Ghana to the wider history of colonial and postcolonial Africa and sets it apart.[10]

The stories of land claims presented in these chapters also raise questions about the meaning of property in Asante and its relationship to the creation and distribution of wealth. If Asante points to the importance of understanding property as a social process, in which negotiations over ownership and use of resources inform and are influenced by relations of authority and obligation, how has "negotiable property" affected the course of economic development? If negotiations are inconclusive—acting to proliferate claims and precedents, rather than converging towards a single set of unique, exclusive rights and boundaries—does this mean that property rights are "incomplete" and thus an impediment to investment and sustained economic development? If negotiations over property are enmeshed in negotiations over authority, obligation, and belonging in multiple spheres of social engagement, does it follow that people are likely to squander scarce resources or use them in unproductive ways?

Such questions have attracted increasing attention in recent literature on development and governance. Going beyond the neoclassical revival of the 1970s and 1980s, in which social factors were largely dismissed or deplored as market "imperfections," a number of scholars and policymakers have taken up the idea of "social capital"—arguing that social arrangements sometimes facilitate rather than impede investment and increased production and should be systematically incorporated into analyses of economic and political performance. Some analysts approach these questions within the framework of methodological individualism, equating social capital with norms and attitudes that affect the way individual decision makers evaluate alternative courses of action.[11] Others have sought to identify structural variables—family, neighborhood, occupational or religious organizations, and so on—that channel both individual choices and collective action in more or less productive directions. If the former approach largely ignores social interactions, the latter underplays their historical contingency. If, as we have seen in the case of Asante, patterns of social interaction and the boundaries of social groups are subject to multiple, shifting interpretations, then typologies of attitudes and structures are not likely to take us very far towards understanding the place of social relations in the creation and distribution of wealth.

In a seminal contribution to the literature on social capital, Bourdieu suggested that social networks are not only differentiated but also dynamic—"the product of an endless effort at institution."[12] The essays in this volume suggest that we take Bourdieu's point a step further, to suggest that wealth itself—like relations of property or association, which shape the way people come together to add value to goods and productive resources—is continually in the making. Once produced, material objects may remain stable for long periods of time, but the values people place on them do not. Like the "quantity" of intangible goods, such as knowledge or credit, the values of all goods are subject to multiple interpretation. They are also continually reestablished and reworked, through countless acts of market exchange and through the myriad shifts in opportunity, obligation, and understanding that underlie and inform market transactions. Conventions of documentation—expressing values in terms of market prices, for example, to facilitate comparison and aggregation—are just that, conventions, convenient but ephemeral markers of complex, multidimensional, and ongoing social processes. To appreciate the significance of social relations for the creation of wealth, and vice versa, we need to study both of them in motion.

Students of African economies have sometimes argued that people and social relationships play a larger role in constituting wealth and value in Africa than in other parts of the world. Developed by historians to clarify the meaning of "slavery" in precolonial African societies, the concept of "wealth-in-people" has also been used to draw attention to some of the distinctive ways that human capacities in general have been mobilized and valued in particular African contexts.[13] As with all comparative analysis, these discussions sometimes walk a fine line between specificity and essentialism. The point is not that social relations are generically more important to the creation of wealth in Africa than in other parts of the world. Economic trajectories and transformations in all societies are shaped by the way people come together—to produce, consume, create, evaluate, and/or struggle over resources and commodities. What varies from one context to another is not the multidimensionality or the historical contingency of economic and social life; it is the specific conjuncture of activities, interests, relationships, and understandings that make up history at a particular time and place.

Relations of property and power, like those of kinship and community, are central to the way people mobilize and use resources, not as parameters that define individuals' options or channel their interactions into structured patterns of cooperation or command but as sources and subjects of ongoing debate, negotiation, and practice. Wealth is not contingent on achieving consensus concerning the rules that govern ownership and allocation, or the historical precedents on which they are based. Instead wealth, like property and history, is continually in the making—generated through the creative interplay of knowledge, skill, authority, and interpretation. What distinguishes Asante, and perhaps other African societies, from the exclusivist ethos of liberal political economy is not Asantes' indifference to self-interest or wealth (far from it!), but their frank acknowledgment that individual accomplishment is inseparable from interaction with others, and that there is no time limit to either. As a friend in Kumawu explained one day, during a long discussion of social values and responsibilities, if people "exempt themselves" from attending funerals, "no one will come to theirs."

NOTES

1. Austin, "No elders," 29.

2. Beckett, *Akokoaso*; P. Hill, *The Gold Coast cocoa farmer* (Oxford: Oxford University Press, 1956), 87–88; Ghana, Office of the Government Statistician, *Survey of cocoa producing families in Ashanti, 1956–57* (Accra: Government Statistician, 1960); C. Okali and S. Mabey, "Women in agriculture in southern Ghana," *Manpower and Unemployment Research* 8, no. 2 (1975): 13–40; G. S. Dei, "The changing land use and allocation patterns of a West African community," *Africa Development* 15, no. 1 (1990): 25–44.

3. Guyer, "Representation without taxation."

4. Berry, *Cocoa, custom*; P. Francis, "Power and order: A study of litigation in a Yoruba community," (Ph.D. diss., University of Liverpool, 1981); G. Myers, "This is not your land: An analysis of the impact of the Land Use Act in southwest Nigeria," (Ph.D. diss., University of Wisconsin, 1990).

5. Compare Grier, "Contradictions"; C. Boone, "The making of a rentier class: Wealth accumulation and political control in Senegal," *Journal of Development Studies* 26, no. 3 (1990): 425–49.

6. However earnestly colonial officials insisted on the difference. See ch. 2, 52.

7. Guyer, "Representation without taxation"; Berry, *Fathers work for their sons*, ch. 7; S. Barnes, *Patrons and power: Creating a political community in metropolitan Lagos* (Bloomington: Indiana University Press, 1986).

8. Mamdani, *Citizen and subject*.

9. During the economic recovery of the 1980s, export earnings from gold and timber rivaled or surpassed those from cocoa. While the threat of long-term depletion of the resource base is a real one, the diversification of export commodities and the relative ease of entry to cocoa, timber, and, to some extent, gold has helped to preserve a relatively dispersed pattern of export income distribution—as compared, say, to an oil exporting economy such as Nigeria.

10. Compare Berry, *No condition is permanent*.

11. For a useful review of the literature, which spells out the differences between individualist and structuralist approaches to social capital, see M. Foley and B. Edwards, "Is it time to disinvest in social capital?" *Journal of Public Policy* 19, no. 2 (1999): 141–74.

12. P. Bourdieu, "The forms of capital," in J. Richardson, ed., *Handbook of theory and research for the sociology of education* (New York: Greenwood, 1986), 249.

13. This term was developed, in part, through debate over the meaning of "slavery" in precolonial African societies. Miers and Kopytoff, eds., *Slavery in Africa*. Using ethnographic evidence from equatorial Africa, Guyer argues that people were valued not simply as interchangeable providers of labor, progeny, or political allegiance but also for specialized skills, knowledge, creativity, and even idiosyncracy. Although she does not emphasize the point, her evidence is also consistent with the argument being made here—that individualized, incommensurable values are realized through social interaction. Guyer and Belinga, "Wealth in people." Compare Barber, *I could speak until tomorrow*; Bledsoe, *Women and marriage in Kpelle society*; B. Cooper, *Marriage in Maradi: Gender and culture in a Hausa society in Niger* (Portsmouth, NH: Heinemann, 1997); S. Berry, "Negotiable property: Making claims on land and history in Asante, 1896–1996," in G. Bond and N. Gibson, eds., *Contested terrains: Contemporary Africa in focus* (Boulder, CO: Westview, forthcoming).

Appendix: Interviews

Much of the information presented and discussed in this study was provided by men and women in Asante, who told me about their personal experiences of acquiring, allocating, inheriting, and disputing claims to land and who shared their knowledge of land matters, history, and contemporary life in Ghana. All interviews were conducted in open-ended, conversational form, rather than through the use of structured questionnaires, and ranged in length from from brief conversations of half an hour to lengthy discussions lasting over several hours or taking place on more than one occasion. The following list gives the names of all those whom I interviewed, together with the dates and places where our conversations took place. As explained in the acknowledgments, I also learned a great deal through informal conversations with colleagues who advised or assisted with my research in various ways. All those listed here and at the beginning of the book were my teachers, and I thank them wholeheartedly.

ASOKORE-MAMPONG

Nana Boakye Ansah Debrah, Asokore-Mamponghene	8/24/93, 9/1/93, 9/7/93, 9/19/93, 9/29/93
Nana Akwesi Ampong II, Nifahene	8/28/93
Beatrice Bonsu	8/28/93
Nana Adua Fodwo	8/28/93
Akosua	8/28/93
Madam Bena Serwaa	8/28/93
Margaret Boakye	8/28/93

George Manuh	8/28/93, 11/7/93
Mr. Forkuor, Assemblyman	8/29/93
Patrick Oppong Bukure	8/29/93
Rev. Solomon Asante	9/4/93
Madam Ama Abraa	9/4/93
Nana Kwame Wireko, Benkumhene	9/4/93
Grace Adu	9/4/93
Kodwo Yeboah	9/4/93
Nana Kweku Tabi Dwomasa	9/4/93
Komfo Abenamin	9/18/93
Comfort Yaa Serwaa Buama	9/18/93
Ama Nkrumah	9/18/93
Peter Asare Bediako	9/18/93
S. S. Oduro	9/18/93, 9/25/93
Dr. Akyeampong	9/18/93
Adwoa Donkor	9/19/93
Ɔkyeame Kweku Marfo	9/25/93, 11/7/93
Ɔkyeame Akwesi Amoako	9/26/93
Madam Akua	11/7/93
Fosuhemaa	11/7/93
Agnes Mim	11/7/93

KENYASE KWABRE

Barima Owusu Agyeman, Kenyasehene	9/29/93, 11/2/93
Isaac Anokye	10/3/93
Kofi Anane	10/3/93
Mary Asantewaa	10/3/93
Adwoa Ode	10/3/93
Kaka Serwaa	10/3/93
Ben Adumako	10/6/93
Samuel Konadu	10/6/93
Akwesi Agye, Kwesi Koyee, Kwame Dapaah, Kwasi Amenanuh, Kwaku Freduah, and Kofi Adu	10/9/93
Abiraa Pokuwaa	10/9/93

Musa Kwadwo	10/9/93
Kodwo Owusu	10/9/93
Akosua Kyerewa	10/9/93
Kofi Poku	10/16/93
John K. Manuh	10/16/93
Janet Owusu	10/16/93
Kosi Adufi	10/16/93
Yaa Aduma	10/16/93
Akosua Wose	10/16/93
Georgina Mensah	10/16/93
Opanin Kwame Oti Kenyase	10/16/93
Thomas Boakye	10/23/93
Atta Koku	10/23/93
Kwabena Kwakye	10/23/93
Lawrence Ben Asare Bediako	11/14/93

AMAKOM

Nana Akusa Yiadom II, Amakomhene	10/8/93, 11/2/93
Nana Abenaa Akya, Obaapanin	9/29/93
Nana Kwesi Bronya Kwesi	10/5/93
B. A. Sarpong	10/5/93
Maame Yaa Fatima	10/5/93
Kweku Abu	10/8/93
Theresa Ansah	10/8/93
Adwoa Dwera	10/8/93
Kodwo Dura	10/10/93
Osei Akwasi	10/10/93
Nana Danso Abibio	10/10/93
Ama Maa	10/10/93
Nana Opoku Ahenkan	10/12/93
Akwesi Boakye	10/12/93
Francis Donkor	10/17/93
Kwame Oforibeng	10/17/93
Nana Asafo Nyamekye	10/19/93

Kofi Okyere	10/19/93
Abenaa Duku	10/19/93
Nana Obeng Asare	10/24/93
P. K. Darko Poku	10/24/93
O. A. Smith, Managing Director, Kumasi Breweries, Ltd.	11/1/93
Nana Boakye Agyeman, Essasohene	11/24/93

KUMAWU

Michael Adu Gyamfi	12/4/93
Isaac Owusu	12/4/93
Afua Kobi	12/4/93
Nana Kwabena Agyei, Kyidomhene	12/4/93, 7/9/94
Afram Joseph	12/4/93
Yao Ampong	12/4/93
Mohammed Ibrahim	12/11/93
Mohammed Salis	12/11/93
Samuel Yeboah	12/11/93
Yao Frimpong	12/11/93
John Adikum	12/11/93
Alice Aduana Norris	12/29/93
Agnes Akua Akyaa	12/29/93
Nana Kwesi Okyere Daako Forduor, Nsumankwahene	12/29/93
Abena Mfoum	12/29/93
B. A. Mensah	1/10/94, 6/6/94, 7/1/94
Opoku Mensah, Chairman, Gyedifoɔ kurom	6/14/94
Nana Anantahene	6/15/94
Mr. Akyeampong, Mr. Alhassan, Forestry Dept.	6/16/94
Oheneba Okyere Agyei-Diatuo, Tufohene	6/16/94
Charles Agyei Aye, Manager, Kumawuman Rural Bank	6/17/94
Nana Dua Awere II, Yaaduasehene and Amaniehene	6/18/94
Nana Serwah Amponsah II, Kumawuhemaa	6/22/94
Mohammed Sani Abubakr, Serikin Zongo	6/22/94
Nana Okyere Agyei, Gyaasehene	6/23/94, 7/13/94
Aduanahemaa Afua Komaa and Yaa Komfo Badu Marfuor	6/24/94, 7/3/94

Kwame Effah	6/27/94
Yao Wadu	6/27/94
Thomas Abaku	6/27/94
Charles Asiedu	6/27/94
Elijah Mensah	6/27/94
Mensah Albert	6/27/94
Abena Gyewa	6/27/94
Adwoa Pokuwaa	6/27/94
Nana D. C. Boadae, Ankase Abusuapanin	6/28/94
Nana Obiri Yeboa II	6/30/94
Barima Tweneboa Kodua IV	7/1/94
Ama Pokuwaa	7/2/94
Akua Afram	7/3/94
Panin Kwame Afram	7/4/94
Ofori Adwe	7/4/94
Kwesi Krapa	7/4/94
Akosua Serwaa	7/4/94
Yao Nkrumah	7/4/94
Nana Okyere Krapa Yiadom	7/5/94
Nana Osei Kodua IV, Krontihene	7/6/94
Nana Boadi Anim, Adontenhene	7/9/93
Panin Yao Mensah	7/11/94, 7/14/94, 7/16/94
Samuel Kwakye	7/12/94
Abraham Kodua	7/12/94
Kwame Bamfo Kesse	7/13/94
Joshua Adu	7/13/94
Kofi Minta	7/13/94
Nana Boagye II, Ankobiahene	7/20/94
Barima Asumadu Sakyi II, Kumawuhene	7/24/94

DRABONSO

Nana Mamadu al Hassan	7/15/94, 7/18/94
Buraimah, Abdullai Fuseni, Moro Abdullai, and others	7/18/94
Nana Emmanuel Bugri Sugri	7/15/94, 7/18/94

Yaw Manu, Nana Baffour Gyina, Nana Kofi Adomako,
    David Kuru, and Kingsley Obiri Yeboah   7/15/94, 7/18/94
K. O. Yeboah   7/19/94
Sister of Kwamanhene and other Kwamanfoɔ   7/19/94

OTHER LOCATIONS

Mr. Sarpong, Senior Lands Officer, Kumase	9/23/93, 12/2/93
Mr. Agyen, Asantehene's Lands Secretary, Manhyia	9/8/93
Nana Osei Amoako-Mensah II, Kwamohene, Kumase	12/8/93
Nana Gyambibi Owusu Afriyie, Aberadehene, Duase	11/20/93
Kwabena Poku, Duase	12/4/93
Nana Owusu Bempah, Buokromhene, Buokrom	12/5/93
Kweku Anane, Kumase	1/3/94
W.A.N. Adumua Bossman, Accra	7/28/94
Nana Owusu Yaw Abibio, Accra	7/28–29/94
Nana Agyeman Nkwantabisa III, Adontenhene, Kumase	7/24–26/96
E. Anaglate, Kumase	7/25/96, 7/26/96
Obeng Manu, Kumase	7/24/96
Kwame Koduah, Kumase	7/24/96
Emmanuel A. Frimpong, Kumase	7/11/94
Yao Amponsah, Kumase	7/11/94, 7/25/94

BIBLIOGRAPHY

SECONDARY SOURCES

Abankroh, K. 1977. "Aboabo: A study of an immigrant residential area in Kumasi." B.Sc. thesis, Department of Planning, University of Science and Technology, Kumase.

Adams, A., and J. So. 1996. *A claim to land by the river: A household in Senegal, 1720–1994*. Oxford: Oxford University Press.

Addo, N. O. 1972. "Employment and labour supply on Ghana's cocoa farms in the pre- and post-Aliens Compliance Order era." *Economic Bulletin of Ghana* 2nd series, 2, 4: 3–50.

Adomako-Sarfoh, J. 1974. "Migrant cocoa farmers and their families." In C. Oppong, ed., *Domestic rights and duties in southern Ghana*. Legon: Institute for African Studies.

Akyeampong, E., and P. Obeng. 1995. "Spirituality, gender, and power in Asante history." *International Journal of African Historical Studies* 28, 3: 481–508.

Allman, J. 1990. "The youngmen and the porcupine: Class, nationalism and Asante's struggle for self-determination, 1954–57." *Journal of African History* 31: 263–79.

————. 1993. *Quills of the porcupine: Asante nationalism in an emergent Ghana, 1954–1957*. Madison: University of Wisconsin Press.

Amanor, K. S. 1999. *Global restructuring and land rights in Ghana: Forest food chains, timber and rural livelihoods*. Research Report No. 108. Uppsala: Nordiska Afrikainstitutet.

Anyang Nyong'o, P. ed. 1987. *Popular struggles for democracy in Africa*. London: Zed.

Anyang Nyong'o, P. and E. Hansen, eds. 1989. *The African state in crisis*. Dakar: CODESRIA.

Arens, W., and I. Karp, eds., 1989. *Creativity of power: Cosmology and action in African societies*. Washington, DC: Smithsonian Institution.

Arhin, K. 1974. "Some Asante views on colonial rule: As seen in the controversy relating to death duties." *Transactions of the Historical Society of Ghana*, 15, 1: 63–84.

———. 1983. "Peasants in 19th-century Asante." *Current Anthropology* 24, 4: 471–81.

———. 1983. "Rank and class among the Asante and Fante." *Africa* 53, 1: 2–22.

———. 1986. "The Asante praise poems: The ideology of patrimonialism." *Paideuma* 32: 163–97.

———. 1986. "A note on the Asante *akonkofo*: A non-literate sub-elite, 1900–1930." *Africa* 56, 1: 25–31.

———. 1990. "Trade, accumulation and the state in Asante in the nineteenth century." *Africa* 60: 524–37.

———. 1992. *The city of Kumasi handbook: Past, present and future.* Legon: Institute of African Studies, University of Ghana.

———. 1994. "The economic implications of transformations in Akan funeral rites." *Africa* 64, 3: 307–22.

———. 1995. "Monetization and the Asante state." In J. I. Guyer, ed., *Money Matters: Instability, value and social payments in the modern history of West Africa.* Portsmouth, NH: Heinemann.

Asamoah, P.K.B. 1991. "The effect of city growth on land uses: Amakom Braponso and Atonsu-Kumasi." B.Sc. thesis, Department of Planning, University of Science and Technology, Kumase.

Asante, S.K.B. 1975. *Property law and social goals in Ghana, 1844–1966.* Accra: Ghana Universities Press.

Austin, G. 1987. "The emergence of capitalist relations in south Asante cocoa-farming, c.1916–1933." *Journal of African History* 28: 259–79.

———. 1988. "Capitalists and chiefs in the cocoa hold-ups in south Asante, 1927–1938." *International Journal of African Historical Studies*, 21, 1: 63–95.

———. 1995. "Human pawning in Asante, 1800–1850: Markets and coercion, gender and cocoa." In T. Falola and P. Lovejoy, eds., *Pawnship in Africa: Debt bondage in historical perspective.* Boulder, CO: Westview.

———. 1996. "'No elders were present': Commoners and private ownership in Asante, 1807–1896," *Journal of African History* 37: 1–30.

Awua-Peseah, K. 1982. "Kumasi—origin, growth and development of the city." B.Sc. thesis, Department of Planning, University of Science and Technology, Kumase.

Barber, K. 1981. "How man makes god in West Africa: Yoruba attitudes towards the *orisa*." *Africa* 51, 5: 217–37.

———. 1991. *I could speak until tomorrow: Oriki, women and the past in a Yoruba town.* Washington, DC: Smithsonian Institution.

———. 1995. "Money, self-realization and the person in Yoruba texts." In J. Guyer, ed., *Money Matters: Instability, value and social payments in the modern history of West African communities.* Portsmouth, NH: Heinemann.

Barnes, S. 1986. *Patrons and power: Creating a political community in metropolitan Lagos.* Bloomington: Indiana University Press.

Bassett, T. 1993. "Cartography, ideology and power: The World Bank in northern Côte d'Ivoire." *Passages*, 5: 8–9.

————. 1993. "Land use conflicts in pastoral development in northern Côte d'Ivoire." In T. Bassett and D. Crummey, eds. 1993. *Land in African agrarian systems.* Madison: University of Wisconsin Press.

Bassett, T., and D. Crummey, eds. 1993. *Land in African agrarian systems.* Madison: University of Wisconsin Press.

Bates, R. 1981. *Markets and states in tropical Africa.* Berkeley and Los Angeles: University of California Press.

————. 1989. *Beyond the miracle of the market: The political economy of agrarian development in Kenya.* Cambridge: Cambridge University Press.

Beckett, W. H. 1944. *Akokoaso.* London: Percy, Lund Humphries.

Bediako, J. 1991. "Impact of migration on low income housing in Kumasi." B.Sc. thesis, Department of Planning, University of Science and Technology, Kumase.

Berry, S. 1975. *Cocoa, custom and socio-economic change in rural western Nigeria.* Oxford: Clarendon Press.

————. 1985. *Fathers work for their sons: Accumulation, mobility and class in an extended Yoruba community.* Berkeley and Los Angeles: University of California Press.

————. 1992. "Hegemony on a shoestring: Indirect rule and access to agricultural land." *Africa* 62, 3: 327–55.

————. 1993. *No condition is permanent: The social dynamics of agrarian change in sub- Saharan Africa.* Madison: University of Wisconsin Press.

————. 1997. "Tomatoes, land and hearsay: Property and history in Asante in the time of structural adjustment." *World Development* 25, 8: 1225–41.

————. Forthcoming. "Negotiable property: Making claims on land and history in Asante, 1896–1996." In G. Bond and N. Gibson, eds., *Contested terrains: Contemporary Africa in focus.* Boulder, CO: Westview.

Biebuyck, D. ed. 1963. *African agrarian systems.* London: Oxford University Press.

Bledsoe, C. 1980. *Women and marriage in Kpelle society.* Stanford, CA: Stanford University Press.

————. 1990. "'No success without struggle': Social mobility and hardship for foster children in Sierra Leone." *Man* (NS) 25, 1: 70–88.

Bohannon, L. 1952. "A geneaological charter?" *Africa* 22, 4: 301–15.

Bond, G., and N. Gibson, eds. Forthcoming. *Contested terrains: Contemporary Africa in focus.* Boulder, CO: Westview.

Boone, C. 1990. "The making of a rentier class: Wealth accumulation and political control in Senegal." *Journal of Development Studies* 26, 3: 425–49.

Bourdieu, P. 1986. "The forms of capital." In J. Richardson, ed., *Handbook of theory and research for the sociology of education.* New York: Greenwood.

Bratton, M., and N. van der Walle. 1994. "Neopatrimonial regimes and political transitions in Africa." *World Politics* 46, 4: 453–89.

Bromley, D. 1989. "Property relations and economic development: The other land reform." *World Development* 17, 6: 867–77.

Brown, J. 1972. "Kumasi, 1896–1923: Urban Africa during the colonial period." Ph.D. diss., University of Wisconsin.

Bruce, J., and S. Migot-Adholla, eds. 1994. *Searching for land tenure security in Africa.* Dubuque, IA: Kendall/Hunt.

Buaduoh, J. 1978. "A study of large-scale acquisition of land by government and its impact on the urban fringes. A case study of UST and Ayeduase/Ayija." B.Sc. thesis, Department of Planning, University of Science and Technology, Kumase.

Burnham, P. 1996. *The politics of difference in northern Cameroon.* Edinburgh: Edinburgh University Press.

Busia, K. A. 1968. *The position of the chief in the modern political system of Ashanti.* London: Frank Cass.

Callaghy, T., and J. Ravenhill, eds. 1993. *Hemmed in: Responses to Africa's economic decline.* New York: Columbia University Press.

Chanock, M. 1985. *Law, custom and social order: The colonial experience in Malawi and Zambia.* Cambridge: Cambridge University Press.

————. 1991. "Paradigms, policies and property: A review of the customary law of land tenure." In K. Mann and R. Roberts, eds., *Laws in colonial Africa.* Portsmouth, NH: Heinemann.

Chazan, N. 1983. *Anatomy of Ghanaian politics: Managing political recession, 1968–1982.* Boulder, CO: Westview.

Clark, G. 1985. "Price control of local food stuffs in Kumasi, Ghana, 1979." In G. Clark, ed. *Traders versus the state.* Boulder, CO: Westview.

————. 1994. *Onions are my husband: Survival and accumulation by West African market women.* Chicago: University of Chicago Press.

Clark, G. ed., 1985. *Traders versus the state: Anthropological approaches to unofficial economies.* Boulder, CO: Westview.

Cleaver, K., and G. Schreiber. 1994. *Reversing the spiral: The population, agriculture, and environment nexus in sub-Saharan Africa.* Washington, DC: World Bank.

Comaroff, J., and J. eds. 1993. *Modernity and its malcontents: Ritual and power in postcolonial Africa.* Chicago: University of Chicago Press.

Cooper, B. 1995. "Women's worth and wedding gift exchange in 19th and 20th century Maradi, Niger." *Journal of African History* 36, 1: 121–40.

————. 1997. *Marriage in Maradi: Gender and culture in a Hausa society in Niger.* Portsmouth, NH: Heinemann.

Cooper, F. 1996. *Decolonization and African society: The labor question in French and British Africa.* Cambridge: Cambridge University Press.

Coplan, D. 1993. "History is eaten whole: Consuming tropes in Sesotho auriture." *History and Theory,* 32: 80–104.

Crehan, K. 1997. *The fractured community: Landscapes of power and gender in rural Zambia.* Berkeley and Los Angeles: University of California Press.

Crook, R. 1986. "Decolonization, the colonial state and chieftaincy in the Gold Coast." *African Affairs* 85, 1: 75–105.

Darko, S. A. 1971. "Changing settlement patterns in Ashanti, 1873–1966." Ph.D. diss., University of London.

Dei, G. S. 1989. "The economics of death and funeral celebration in a Ghanaian Akan community." *Culture* 9, 1: 49–62.

————. 1990. "The changing land use and allocation patterns of a West African community." *Africa Development* 15, 1:25–44.

Dilley, R. ed. 1992. *Contesting markets: Analyses of ideology, discourse and practice.* Edinburgh: Edinburgh University Press.

Donkor, K. 1997. *Structural adjustment and mass poverty in Ghana*. Aldershot, England: Ashgate.

Downs, R. E., and S. P. Reyna, eds. 1988. *Land and society in contemporary Africa*. Durham, NH: University Press of New England.

Drah, F. 1993. "Civil society and the transition to pluralist democracy." In K. Ninsin and F. Drah, eds., *Political parties and democracy in Ghana's Fourth Republic*. Accra: Woeli.

Dunn, J., and A. F. Robertson. 1973. *Dependence and opportunity in Ahafo*. Cambridge: Cambridge University Press.

Edmundson, A. R. 1975. *Land ownership and acquisition in Kumase*. Kumase: Land Administration Research Centre, University of Science and Technology.

Elliott, C. 1975. *Patterns of poverty in the Third World*. New York, Praeger.

Falola, T., 1995. "Money and informal credit institutions in colonial western Nigeria." In J. I. Guyer, ed., *Money matters: Instability, value and social payments in the modern history of West Africa*. Portsmouth, NH: Heinemann.

Falola, T., and P. Lovejoy, eds., 1995. *Pawnship in Africa: Debt bondage in historical perspective*. Boulder, CO: Westview.

Firmin-Sellers, K. 1996. *Transformations of property rights in the Gold Coast*. Cambridge: Cambridge University Press.

Foley, M., and B. Edwards, 1999. "Is it time to disinvest in social capital?" *Journal of Public Policy* 19, 2: 141–74.

Forde, C. D., and A. R. Radcliffe-Brown, eds. 1950. *African systems of kinship and marriage*. London: Oxford University Press.

Fortes, M. 1948, "The Ashanti social survey: A preliminary report." *Rhodes-Livingstone Journal: Human problems in British Central Africa* 6: 1–36.

———. 1950. "Kinship and marriage among the Ashanti." In C .D. Forde and A. R. Radcliffe-Brown, *African systems of kinship and marriage*. London: Oxford University Press.

Francis, P. 1981. "Power and order: A study of litigation in a Yoruba community." Ph.D. diss., University of Liverpool.

Fred-Mensah, B. K. 1996. "Changes, ambiguities and conflicts in Buem, eastern Ghana." Ph.D. diss., Johns Hopkins University.

Fuller, F. 1921. *A vanished dynasty: Ashanti*. London: John Murray.

Galaty, J. 1993. "Rangeland tenure and pastoralism in Africa." Session on policy, politics, and the crisis of pastoral property. Proceedings of the International Congress on Anthropological and Ethnological Science, Mexico City.

Geschiere, P. 1992. "Kinship, witchcraft and the market: Hybrid patterns in Cameroonian societies." In R. Dilley, ed. *Contesting markets: Analyses of ideology, discourse and practice*. Edinburgh: Edinburgh University Press.

Geschiere, P., with C. Fisiy. 1994. "Domesticating personal violence: Witchcraft, courts and confessions in Cameroon." *Africa* 64, 3: 323–41.

Ghana. 1984. *Population Census of Ghana. Special report on localities by local authorities, Ashanti Region*. Accra: Statistical Service.

———. 1992. *Constitution of the Republic of Ghana*. Tema: Ghana Publishing Corp.

Ghana Law Reports.

Ghana Law Reports Digest.

Ghana, Office of the Government Statistician. 1960. *Survey of cocoa producing families in Ashanti, 1956–57.* Accra: Government Statistician.

Gilbert, M. 1988. "The sudden death of a millionaire: Conversion and consensus in a Ghanaian kingdom." *Africa* 58, 3: 281–305.

Gocking, R. 1990. "Competing systems of inheritance before the British courts of the Gold Coast Colony." *International Journal of African Historical Studies* 23, 4: 601–18.

———. 1993. "British justice and the native tribunals of the southern Gold Coast Colony." *Journal of African History* 34, 1: 93–113.

———. 1994. "Indirect rule in the Gold Coast: Competition for office and the invention of tradition." *Canadian Journal of African Studies* 28, 3: 421–46.

Gold Coast Colony. 1945. *Report of the Commission of Inquiry (Havers) on expenditures connected with litigation.* Accra: Government Printer.

Goody, E. 1982. *Parenthood and social reproduction: Fostering and occupational roles in West Africa.* Cambridge: Cambridge University Press.

Grier, B. 1987. "Contradictions, crises, and class conflict: The state and capitalist development in Ghana prior to 1948." In I. Markovitz, ed., *Studies in class and power in Africa.* New York: Oxford University Press.

Guyer, J. I. 1992. "Representation without taxation: An essay on rural democracy in Nigeria." *African Studies Review* 35: 41–79.

———. 1993. "Wealth-in-people and self-realization in equatorial Africa." *Man* (NS) 28: 243–65.

———, ed. 1995. *Money matters: Instability, value and social payments in the modern history of West Africa.* Portsmouth, NH: Heinemann.

Guyer, J. I., and S. Eno Belinga, 1995. "Wealth-in-people as wealth-in-knowledge: Accumulation and composition in equatorial Africa." *Journal of African History.* 36: 91–120.

Gyekye, K. 1987. *An essay on African philosophical thought: The Akan conceptual scheme.* Cambridge: Cambridge University Press.

———. 1997. *Tradition and modernity: Philosophical reflections on the African experience.* New York and Oxford: Oxford University Press.

Gyimah-Boadi, E. ed. 1993. *Ghana under PNDC rule.* Dakar: CODESRIA.

Hailey, W. H. (Lord). 1951. *Native administration in the British African territories.* Part III. *West Africa.* London: Oxford University Press.

Hann, C. M. ed. 1998. *Property relations: Reviewing the anthropological tradition.* Cambridge: Cambridge University Press.

Harvey, W. B. 1966. *Law and social change in Ghana.* Princeton, NJ: Princeton University Press.

Herbst, J. 1993. *The politics of reform in Ghana, 1982–1991.* Berkeley and Los Angeles: University of California Press.

Hill, P. 1956. *The Gold Coast cocoa farmer.* Oxford: Oxford University Press.

———. 1963. *Migrant cocoa farmers of southern Ghana.* Cambridge: Cambridge University Press.

Hoebel, E. 1966. *Anthropology: The study of man.* New York: McGraw Hill.

Howard, R. 1978. *Colonialism and underdevelopment in Ghana.* London: Croom Helm.

Hughes, D. 1999. "Frontier dynamics: Struggles for land and clients on the Zimbabwe-Mozambique border." Ph.D. diss., University of California, Berkeley.

Hutchful, E. 1997. "Ghana." In P. Engeborg-Pedersen et al., *The limits of structural adjustment in Africa: The effects of economic liberalization, 1986–1994.* Copenhagen: Centre for Development Research.

Institute of African Studies, 1976. *Ashanti stool histories.* Legon: Institute of African Studies, University of Ghana.

Izumi, K. 1998. "Economic liberalisation and land question in Tanzania." Ph.D. diss., Roskilde University, Denmark.

Jackson M., and I. Karp, eds. 1990. *Personhood and agency: The experience of self and other in African cultures.* Uppsala: Almqvist and Wicksell.

Katinga, K. 1998. "The land question in Kenya: Struggles, accumulation and changing politics." Ph.D. diss., Roskilde University, Denmark.

Kay, G. B. 1972. *The political economy of colonialism in Ghana.* Cambridge: Cambridge University Press.

Klein, A. N. 1981. "Inequality in Asante: A study of the forms and meanings of slavery and social servitude in pre- and early colonial Akan-Asante society and culture." Ph.D. diss., University of Michigan.

———. 1994. "Slavery and Akan origins." *Ethnohistory* 41, 4: 627–56.

Konings, P. 1986. *The state and rural class formation in Ghana: A comparative analysis.* London: Kegan Paul.

Kyerematen, A.A.Y. 1971. *Inter-state boundary litigation in Ashanti.* African Social Research Documents No. 4. Cambridge: African Studies Centre, University of Cambridge.

Levin, R. 1997. *When the sleeping grass awakens.* Johannesburg: University of Witwatersrand Press.

Lewin, T. J. 1978. *Asante before the British: The Prempean years, 1875–1900.* Lawrence: Regents Press of Kansas.

Lewin, T. J., and D. Fitzsimons. 1976. "The political organization of space in Asante, Parts I–III." *Asante Seminar* 4–6.

London, J. C. 1993. "Investigation into the present state of production performance and the role of the Djallonke-sheep in small-farm-holdings in the Asante Region of Ghana." Ph.D. diss., Technical University of Berlin.

Loxley, J. 1988. *Ghana: Economic crisis and the long road to recovery.* Ottawa: North-South Institute.

Lund, C. 1998. *Law, power and politics in Niger: Land struggles and the Rural Code.* Hamburg: LIT Verlag.

Mabogunje, A. L. 1990. "Urban planning and the post-colonial state: a research overview." *African Studies Review* 33, 2: 137ff.

Mackenzie, F. 1998. *Land, ecology and resistance in Kenya, 1880–1952.* Edinburgh: Edinburgh University Press.

Mamdani, M. 1996. *Citizen and subject: Contemporary Africa and the legacy of late colonialism.* Princeton, NJ: Princeton University Press.

Mann, K., and R. Roberts, eds. 1991. *Law in colonial Africa.* London and Portsmouth, NH: James Currey & Heinemann.

Markovitz, I., ed. 1987. *Studies in class and power in Africa.* New York: Oxford University Press.

McCaskie, T. C. 1976. "The history of the Manwere *nkoa* at Drobonso." *Asante Seminar* 6: 33–38.

————. 1980. "Office, land and subjects in the history of the Manwere *fekuo* of Kumase: An essay in the political economy of the Asante state." *Journal of African History* 21, 2: 189–208.

————. 1981. "State and society, marriage and adultery: Some considerations towards a social history of pre-colonial Asante." *Journal of African History* 22: 477–94.

————. 1983. "R. S. Rattray and the construction of Asante history: An appraisal." *History in Africa* 10: 187–206.

————. 1984, "*Ahyiamu*—a 'place of meeting': An essay on process and event in the history of the Asante state." *Journal of African History* 25, 2: 169–88.

————. 1986. "Accumulation, wealth and belief in Asante history. II. The twentieth century." *Africa* 56, 1: 3–23.

————. 1986. "Komfo Anokye of Asante: Meaning, history and philosophy in an African society." *Journal of African History* 27: 317–39.

————. 1989. "Death and the Asantehene: A historical meditation." *Journal of African History* 30: 417–44.

————. 1995. *State and society in precolonial Asante.* Cambridge: Cambridge University Press.

McCay, B., and J. M. Acheson. 1987. T*he question of the commons: The culture and ecology of common resources.* Tuscon: University of Arizona Press.

Miers, S., and I. Kopytoff, eds. 1977. *Slavery in Africa.* Madison: University of Wisconsin Press.

Miescher, S. 1997. "Of documents and litigants: Disputes on inheritance in Abetifi—a town of colonial Ghana." *Journal of Legal Pluralism* 39: 81–118.

Migot-Adholla, S., et al. 1991. "Indigenous land rights systems in sub-Saharan Africa." *World Bank Economic Review* 5, 1: 155–75.

Mikell, G. 1986. "Ghanaian females, rural economy and national stability." *African Studies Review* 29, 3: 67–88.

————. 1995. *Cocoa and chaos in Ghana.* New York: Paragon Press.

————. 1995. "The state, the courts and 'value': Caught between matrilineages in Ghana." In J. I. Guyer, ed., *Money matters: Instability, value and social payments in the modern history of West Africa.* Portsmouth, NH: Heinemann.

Moore, S. F. 1986. *Social facts and fabrications: Customary law on Mt. Kilimanjaro, 1890–1980.* Cambridge: Cambridge University Press.

Murphy, W. 1980. "Secret knowledge as property and power in Kpelle society: Elders versus youth." *Africa* 50, 2: 193–207.

Myers, G. 1990. "This is not your land: An analysis of the impact of the Land Use Act in southwest Nigeria." Ph.D. diss., University of Wisconsin.

Ninsin, K., and F. Drah, eds. 1993. *Political parties and democracy in Ghana's Fourth Republic.* Accra: Woeli.

Nkansah, L. 1979. "Unauthorized development in residential areas in Kumasi." B.Sc. thesis, Department of Planning, University of Science and Technology, Kumase.

Nugent, P. 1995. *Big men, small boys and politics in Ghana: Power, ideology and the burden of history, 1982–1994.* London and New York: Pinter.

Nyambara, P. 1999. "A history of land acquisition in Gokwe, northwestern Zimbabwe, 1945–1990s." Ph.D. diss., Northwestern University.

Ocquaye, M. 1980. *Politics in Ghana, 1972–1979.* Accra: Tornado.

Okali, C. 1983. *Cocoa and kinship in Ghana: The matrilineal Akan.* London: Routledge.

Okali, C., and S. Mabey 1975. "Women in agriculture in southern Ghana." *Manpower and Unemployment Research* 8, 2: 13–40.

Okoth-Ogendo, H.W.O. 1981. "Land ownership and land distribution in Kenya's large-farm areas." In T. Killick, ed., *Papers on the Kenyan economy: Performance, problems and policies.* Nairobi: Heinemann.

Ollenu, N. A. 1962. *Principles of customary land law in Ghana.* London: Sweet & Maxwell.

Ollenu, N. A., and G. R. Woodman, eds. 1985. *Ollenu's principles of customary law.* 2nd ed. Birmingham, England: CAL Press.

Opoku, K. A. 1978. *West African traditional religion.* Accra: FEP International.

Oppong, C. ed. 1974. *Domestic rights and duties in southern Ghana.* Legon: Institute for African Studies.

Ostrom, E. 1990. *Governing the commons: The evolution of institutions for collective action.* Cambridge: Cambridge University Press.

Owusu, M. 1970. *Uses and abuses of political power: A case study of continuity and change in the politics of Ghana.* Chicago: University of Chicago Press.

Perbi, A. n.d. "The legacy of slavery in contemporary Ghana."

Peters, P. 1994. *Dividing the commons: Politics and culture in Botswana.* Charlottesville: University of Virginia Press.

Phillips, A. 1989. *The enigma of colonialism: British policy in West Africa.* London: James Currey.

Priestley, M. 1969. *West African trade and coast society, a family study.* London: Oxford University Press.

Ranger, T. O. 1983. "The invention of tradition in colonial Africa." In E. Hobsbawm and T. O. Ranger, eds.

Ranger, T. O., and E. Hobsbawm, eds. 1983. *The invention of tradition.* Cambridge: Cambridge University Press.

Rathbone, R. 1983. "Parties' socio-economic bases and regional differentiation in the rate of change in Ghana." In P. Lyon and J. Manor, *Transfer and transformation: Political institutions in the new Commonwealth.* Leicester, England: Leicester University Press.

———. 1993. *Murder and politics in colonial Ghana.* New Haven, CT: Yale University Press.

———. 1996. "Defining Akyemfo: The construction of citizenship in Akyem Abuakwa, Ghana, 1700–1939." *Africa* 66, 4: 506–25.

Rathbone, R., and J. Allman. 1991. "Discussion: The youngmen and the porcupine." *Journal of African History* 32: 333–38.

Rattray, R. S. 1923. *Ashanti.* Oxford: Clarendon Press.

———. 1927. *Religion and art in Ashanti.* Oxford: Oxford University Press.

———. 1969. *Ashanti law and constitution.* London: Oxford University Press. First published in 1929.

Reindorf, C. C. 1895. *History of the Gold Coast and Asante.* Basel: Missionsbuchshandlung.

Richardson, J. ed. 1986. *Handbook of theory and research for the sociology of education.* New York: Greenwood.

Riesman, P. 1986. "The person and the life cycle in African social life and thought." *African Studies Review* 29, 2: 71–198.

Rose, L. 1992. *The politics of harmony: Land dispute strategies in Swaziland*. Cambridge: Cambridge University Press.

Rothchild, D., ed. 1991. *Ghana: The political economy of recovery*. Boulder, CO: Lynne Rienner.

Sandbrook, R. 1985. *The politics of Africa's economic stagnation*. Cambridge: Cambridge University Press.

———. 1986. "State and economic stagnation in tropical Africa." *World Development* 14, 3: 319–32.

Sarbah, J. M. 1968. *Fanti customary laws*. 3rd ed. London: Frank Cass.

Sarpong, P. 1971. *The sacred stools of the Akan*. Accra-Tema: Ghana Publishing Corp.

Schildkrout, E. 1978. *People of the zongo*. Cambridge: Cambridge University Press.

Shivji, I. G. 1975. *Class struggle in Tanzania*. Dar es Salaam: Tanzania Publishing House.

Simensen, J. 1975. "The Asafo of Kwahu, Ghana: A mass movement for local reform under colonial rule." *International Journal of African Historical Studies* 8, 3: 383–406.

———. 1975. "Commoners, chiefs and colonial government." Ph.D. diss., University of Trondheim.

Soyinka, W. 1983. *Aké: The years of childhood*. New York: Random House.

Sutton, I. 1984. "Law, chieftaincy and conflict in colonial Ghana: The Ada case." *African Affairs* 83, 330: 41–62.

Swanson, M. 1977. "The sanitation syndrome: Bubonic plague and urban native policy in the Cape Colony, 1900–1909." *Journal of African History* 18: 387–410.

Tabatabai, H. 1987. "Agricultural decline and access to food in Ghana." *International Labor Review* 127, 6: 717.

Tipple, B. 1987. "Development of housing policy in Kumasi, Ghana, 1901–1981." Centre for Architectural Research and Development Overseas, University of Newcastle upon Tyne.

Tordoff, W. 1965. *Ashanti under the Prempehs, 1888–1935*. London: Oxford University Press.

Trouillot, M.-R. 1995. *Silencing the past*. Boston: Little, Brown.

Vail, L., and L. White. 1991. *Power and the praise poem: Southern African voices in history*. Charlottesville: University of Virginia Press.

Widner, J., with A. Mundt. 1998. "Researching social capital in Africa." *Africa* 68, 1: 1–24.

Wilks, I. 1975. *Asante in the nineteenth century: The structure and evolution of a political order*. Cambridge: Cambridge University Press.

———. 1993. *Forests of gold: Essays on the Akan and the kingdom of Asante*. Athens, OH: University of Ohio Press.

———. 1994. "Slavery and Akan origins? A reply." *Ethnohistory* 41, 4: 657–65.

———. 1995. *A portrait of Otumfuo Opoku Ware II as a young man*. Accra: Anansesem Publications.

———. 1999. "On which foot was the boot?" In C. Lentz and P. Nugent, eds., *Ethnicity in Ghana*. New York: St. Martins.

Wiredu, K. 1996. *Cultural universals and particulars: An African perspective*. Bloomington: Indiana University Press.

Woodman, G. R. 1966. *The development of customary land law in Ghana.* Cambridge: Cambridge University Press.

World Bank. 1996. *Towards environmentally sustainable development in sub-Saharan Africa. A World Bank agenda.* Washington, DC: World Bank.

Yankah, K. 1995. *Speaking for the chief: Ɔkyeame and the politics of Akan royal oratory.* Bloomington: Indiana University Press.

———. 1990. *Woes of a Kwatriot: No big English.* Accra: Anansesem Publications.

PRIMARY SOURCES

Council on Law Reporting, Accra

Unpublished High Court and Supreme Court judgments

Herskovits Library, Northwestern University

R. S. Rattray Collection, Royal Anthropological Institute

Manhyia Record Office, Kumase

Clan Court Records, 1924–1964
Kumasihene's Native Tribunal, 1926–1935
Asantehene's Native Court B, 1935–1960
Asantehene's Divisional Court B, 1935–1964
Kumase Traditional Council Record Books, 1967–1986

National Archives of Ghana, Accra

ADM 4 series: Ashanti files
ADM 5 series: Miscellaneous colonial reports
ADM 11/1 series: Secretary for Native Affairs files
ADM 12 series: Chief Commissioner, Ashanti, files

National Archives of Ghana, Kumase

Chief Commissioner, Ashanti, files
SCT 24 series: Divisional High Court, Civil Record Books
SCT 30 series: Boundary Record Books
SCT 211 series: Asantehene's A Court Record Books

Rhodes House, Oxford

Mss Afr S 593. Duncan Johnstone Papers

Selected Court Cases

Circuit Court, Kumase
High Court, Kumase
Stool Lands Boundaries Settlement Commission, Accra
Supreme Court, Accra

Newspapers

Daily Graphic
Palaver Tribune
The Pioneer (Asante)
The Statesman

INDEX

About the Author

SARA S. BERRY is Professor of History and Anthropology at Johns Hopkins University and the author of several books, including *Fathers Work for Their Sons*, winner of the 1985 Herskovits Award. Her most recent book is *No Condition Is Permanent: The Social Dynamics of Agrarian Change in Sub-Saharan Africa.*